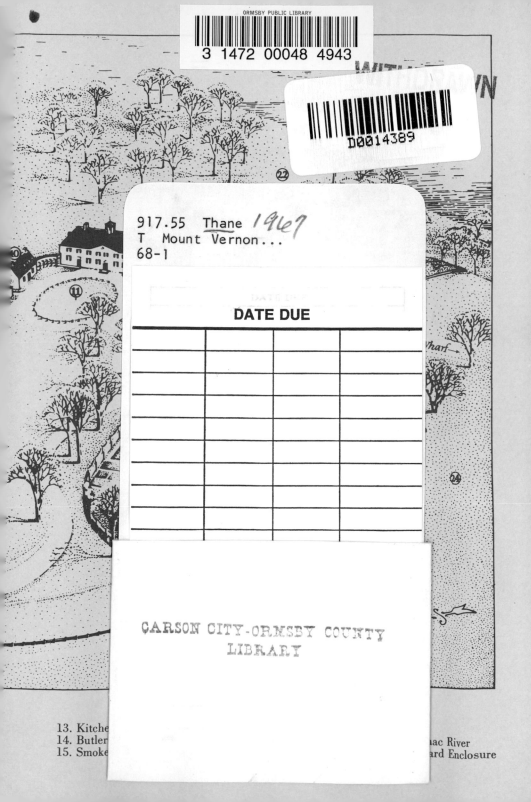

ORMSBY PUBLIC LIBRARY

3 1472 00048 4943

D0014389

917.55   Thane 1967
T   Mount Vernon...
68-1

DATE DUE

CARSON CITY-ORMSBY COUNTY
LIBRARY

13. Kitche
14. Butler
15. Smoke

ac River
ard Enclosure

MOUNT VERNON:
THE LEGACY

Books *by* ELSWYTH THANE

FICTION

Riders of the Wind
Echo Answers
Cloth of Gold
His Elizabeth
Bound to Happen
Queen's Folly

Tryst
Remember Today
From This Day Forward
Melody
The Lost General
Letter to a Stranger

THE WILLIAMSBURG NOVELS

Dawn's Early Light
Yankee Stranger
Ever After

The Light Heart
Kissing Kin
This Was Tomorrow

Homing

NONFICTION

The Tudor Wench
Young Mr. Disraeli
England Was an Island Once
The Bird Who Made Good
Reluctant Farmer

The Family Quarrel
Washington's Lady
Potomac Squire
Mount Vernon Is Ours
Mount Vernon: The Legacy

In preparation: The Children at Mount Vernon

PLAYS

The Tudor Wench

Young Mr. Disraeli

MOUNT VERNON: THE LEGACY

*The Story of Its
Preservation and Care
Since 1885*

By

ELSWYTH THANE

Author of MOUNT VERNON IS OURS

J. B. LIPPINCOTT COMPANY

Philadelphia *&* New York

Copyright © 1967 by Elswyth Thane

All rights reserved

FIRST EDITION

Printed in the United States of America
Library of Congress Catalog Card No. 67–25900

All illustrations are used by the courtesy of
the Mount Vernon Ladies' Association.

To Frank Morse

Foreword

Before this book was undertaken, the writer was advised that the present working Staff and membership of the Mount Vernon Ladies' Association should not be named in its pages. Too lightly, consumed by the subject, I agreed. But it has proved impossible to write an anonymous book about Mount Vernon, which is neither a corporation nor a museum. Since the death in 1937 of the third Superintendent, Harrison Howell Dodge, Mount Vernon has progressed vitally, intrinsically, along the road whose sign-posts were set by him. Not to refer to anyone by name since 1937 is out of the question, because everyone who works at Mount Vernon for any length of time, who leaves a room, a building, a flower-bed, different from what it was before he came is, whether he likes it or not, already history.

Mr. Wall, as Resident Director and Dodge's direct heir in authority, is of necessity a visible and accessible representative, and he accepts his position in the public eye gracefully and effectively, if reluctantly. The Regent, moving inconspicuously about the place between Councils, passes unrecognized except by the employees. But the Staff, who inhabit the Administration Building and other obscure offices tucked away above the Quarters and the Museum, leave the daily imprint of their hands and minds and knowledge on the exhibits, on the available literature, and most of all on the intangible, indefinable, and unique thing called "atmosphere"—the essence, pith, core, and kernel of the Association effort in the last three decades. This "feel" of serenity and integrity and fidelity has not maintained itself automatically, for nearly forty years. Dodge's successors, foremost among them Mr. Wall himself, and the men and women working under his daily supervision who have had the perception and the zeal to absorb from him and from the air around them the essential idea of Mount Vernon as it was conceived by Miss Cunningham and comprehended by Dodge are responsible for its survival now in a callous world. They have created there as it were a beleaguered bubble of endeavor, inside which they remain faithful against the march of time and the pressure of events. And it has not, therefore, been possible, despite the stubborn self-effacement which still animates Mount Vernon's guardians, to pretend that it is all done with mirrors.

This line of reasoning, adhered to with corresponding stubbornness by the writer, to the peril of cherished privileges already granted, has at length prevailed to some degree, with the permission to mention a few people who are, praise God, still alive, and to allow a few glimpses behind the scenes to catch the shy and furtive stage-managers at work. It is not just a matter of rendering unwanted credit for work well done—or of bringing undesirable publicity on private people doing private jobs—or of marring the steadfast good taste with which Mount Vernon is imbued. It is to answer the inevitable questions which must arise in the most casual visitor—How? And therefore—Who? Obviously there has been thought, research, authority, and toil. Not every one of the more than a million visitors a year can be personally conducted, or allowed after hours to see the silent wheels go round. But nearly every one wonders about the invisible mechanism and its attendant specialists. It is therefore to enlarge the appreciation and understanding of the people for whom Mount Vernon has been preserved that a few of its hidden personalities have with difficulty been persuaded to relinquish anonymity.

E. T.

Contents

Illustrations

Line Drawings:

"Let one spot in this grand country of ours be saved from 'change!' Upon you rests this duty."

—ANN PAMELA CUNNINGHAM in 1874.

The Guardians

1

In May, 1886, the Grand Council of the Mount Vernon Ladies' Association of the Union convened around a long table in the Banquet Room of George Washington's old home on the Potomac to inspect the new Superintendent, the third in its thirty years of eventful history. The Association was the oldest organization of its kind, its membership composed of Vice-Regents selected to represent each State in the Union—though the roster was never full—presided over by a Regent elected in Council. The Superintendent, the Treasurer, and an Advisory Board were masculine—but the Association was female, founded in 1853 by Ann Pamela Cunningham of South Carolina, and consisting of women who journeyed annually from Michigan, the Carolinas, and New England to meet at the pillared mansion above the river which they had rescued from dilapidation and preserved by their united efforts throughout civil war and financial depression, until now, a decade after the Philadelphia Centennial of 1876, it had turned the corner into relative security, and its daily management had come into the hands of a capable and dedicated man named Harrison Howell Dodge.

There were then twenty-six Vice-Regents on the roster, eighteen of whom were present when Dodge made his first appearance before Council to read to them the Superintendent's Report which was to become an annual delight to his listeners —its necessarily dull facts and figures graced by his slanting humor and old-fashioned deference to the formidable group of middle-aged women whom he always addressed individually as "My dear lady." It is safe to say that he was considerably younger than any one of the Vice-Regents. And while they beheld in the new Superintendent a youthful, immaculately dressed, self-possessed and cordial man, in place of the burly,

bearded Colonel Hollingsworth, his predecessor, who in later
years had come to resent inspection of his accounts, or queries
which seemed to him to cast a reflection on his good judgment,
Dodge was to confess in the fortieth year of his service that the
annual ceremony of reading aloud to the assembled Vice-
Regents his carefully compiled Report of the accomplishments
and frustrations of the past twelve months was always an ordeal,
which his good manners and somewhat stately jokes never
allowed them to suspect. His final paragraphs were always mas-
terpieces of urbanity and a certain obsolete playfulness which
charmed his hearers but would hardly do today—"Thanking
you ladies for your patient attention to my lengthy and prosaic
narrative and for your kind consideration of my earnest en-
deavors to serve you faithfully, I am, with great respect, Your
faithful and humble servant . . . ."

Heretofore he had worked obscurely in a bank, which happened to be in Washington, D.C.—and it happened to bear the
name of George Washington Riggs, who was the first Treasurer
of the Mount Vernon Ladies' Association. It is probable that
from childhood Harrison Dodge had heard about Mount Vernon and the Association, and had paid many anonymous visits
to that gracious, hallowed house which throughout its history
has acted as a magnet to a wide assortment of pilgrims.

Born in Washington City in 1852, the year before Miss Cunningham, the first Regent of the Association, began her long
and stormy crusade to save Mount Vernon from neglect and
desolation, he had as a boy spent the years of the Civil War at
his uncle's plantation in Maryland, where he was visiting his
cousins when hostilities began. Associated from early manhood
with the Riggs family, who were so intimately involved with
the Mount Vernon story, he could hardly have escaped the
mysterious attraction which the home of Washington always
exerted, even during the General's lifetime, until even his Virginian hospitality wore thin and in exasperation he likened it
to a sort of tavern.

By the end of the War Between the States, when Dodge was
able to pay frequent visits to the house, travelling by the little
steamer which ran daily from a pier in Washington to the wharf
at Mount Vernon—for the road was always bad—he found

evidence of the Association's loving care. The ancient wharf had been mended again, after a fashion, the garden walks were kept swept and cleared, the windows were washed and shining, the pillars of the piazza had been renewed, and there were odd bits of donated furniture in the rooms which were open to the public. An attempt was already being made by the Vice-Regents to furnish the house as a home again, and to re-capture something of its appearance as Washington had seen it last. Dodge may have encountered before 1868, with well-informed respect, the redoubtable secretary Miss Sarah Tracy, who with a woman companion and the first Superintendent had resided there throughout the conflict, doggedly defending by her mere feminine presence the neutrality of Washington's home and tomb, which were held to be above all sectional and politi-cal feeling, though the guns at Manassas were audible on the front lawn, and the dust of Burnside's march to Fredericksburg could be seen above the treetops to the west. Dodge may even have arrived there by accident on a day in the 1870's when Council was in session, and so glimpsed the Regent herself, and the Vice-Regents, grouped around the table in the Banquet Room, solemnly pursuing their amateur Parliamentary pro-cedure of chaired meetings and resolutions put to the vote, and Minutes kept, while they strove with their scanty, uncertain funds to provide for the future preservation of the house they had adopted against tremendous odds as their common endeavor and perpetual care.

In those post-War days the second Superintendent, James McHenry Hollingsworth, a Mexican War veteran, was in in-creasingly poor health, and his management of the place left much to be desired. Young Dodge's affectionate scrutiny of the estate must have revealed to him a need, apparent also to the Vice-Regents, of a younger and more vigorous hand at the helm. It was obvious that Hollingsworth could not go on for-ever. And Dodge told his wife, after wandering about the over-grown grounds and the bare, echoing rooms, that of all the jobs in the world he would like best, it would be to have charge of Mount Vernon. . . .

When in 1885 Hollingsworth retired and left Mount Vernon, Dodge sent in his application.

There is a legend that he was summoned for inspection, among five other candidates, to the Philadelphia home of the second Regent, Mrs. J. Scott Laughton, and that his resemblance to her young husband, who had died some ten years before, tipped the scales in his favor. Doubtless his courtly manners, which distinguished him all his life, and his notable charm, which wrought many miracles for Mount Vernon during his long tenure, had more to do with his selection for the post.

> "Diary Kept by Harrison H. Dodge
> Resident Secretary and Superintendent at
> Mount Vernon
>
> ———
>
> Appointed June 29, 1885—
> Entered upon duties July 15, 1885
>
> ———
>
> May God bless my efforts—"
>
> ———

These are the words, in a handwriting exquisitely readable, on the flyleaf of a pocket-size notebook, the first of many, in which would be recorded the daily realization of his great dream. Still a young man, he was old enough to be aware that most men go all their lives without once knowing the profound satisfaction, the sense of fulfillment he had now attained at thirty-three. The man who when he died at a very ripe old age would be known as "Dodge of Mount Vernon" was now embarking on a career unique in its single-minded devotion to an idea.

The Mount Vernon which came into his charge in that summer of 1885 was not the serene, well-groomed estate which crowns its grassy eminence above the broad Potomac today. The main approach was still from the river, where the wharf and the road leading from it up the steep incline past the Tomb to the lawn in front of the piazza were as always in need of repair. It took three weeks to get the riverfront cleared to his satisfaction. The outbuildings were shabby and wanted painting, their roofs leaked, and they had served for years as storage areas for miscellaneous oddments of little value, or as housing for the help. The rather ugly Greenhouse, built in 1869 on the remains of the burnt-out buildings which had suffered several fires since the one which destroyed the original in 1837, disfigured the Flower Garden. The south colonnade had blown down in a storm during the spring of 1861, and was not rebuilt until after the War, when the Vice-Regent for New Jersey raised the funds by contribution in her State; but to an educated eye the restoration did not quite match the one on the north, which would also require reconstruction in 1903. The rickety little porch which Washington's first heir, his nephew Judge Bushrod Washington, had tacked onto the south end of the house outside the Library, with new sash windows opening into the room, was still an eyesore. The Summer House, likewise added by Bushrod at the bottom of the lawn above the river, was now falling down.

Inside the Mansion, which was in dire need of paint, the west window of the stately room known as the Banquet Hall was eclipsed by Rembrandt Peale's colossal canvas depicting Washington and his horse before Yorktown, which Peale's daughters had presented to the Association in 1873 and which had been a white elephant ever since. In the same room stood for a time the expensive harpsichord which Washington had ordered sent from London as a present to Martha's granddaughter Nelly Custis in 1793—the first of the scattered original furnishings to return to its one-time home.

The rest of the rooms were inhabited by odds and ends of furniture left over from the first Regent's tenancy, which ended in 1873, during which time she had used the Family Dining-room as a sittingroom and the room behind it as a bedroom, while the library served as a dining-room, as it had done in Bushrod's time. Colonel Hollingsworth, with the approval of the Vice-Regents, had appropriated the more useful pieces for his own rooms in the little house at the end of the north colonnade, where he had established his office, with the two upstairs rooms as living quarters. This little building, known to Washington as the Servants' Hall or Guest House, would be reconditioned to serve Hollingsworth's successor in the same capacity, and it is still the office of the Resident Director, though it is no longer lived in.

It is difficult to say what remained in the Mansion when Hollingsworth and the Regent had finished, but the Vice-Regents were attempting to dress the rooms with an approximation of what they had once contained, soliciting the gift or loan of a table here and a chair there, a mirror, bedstead, or bureau from somewhere else—for during the annual Council some of them lived in the house, doubling up with cots and trundle-beds in the second- and third-floor rooms, and bundling out of sight the evidences of their occupancy before the visitors arrived each day.

The entries in Dodge's Diary reflect those in Washington's own daily record, and were kept in little books which were much the same size, the entries set down with the same loving fidelity. Like Washington, he never scribbled, and his Letter-books are models of penmanship and the gracious turn of phrase. The typewriter and the telephone have robbed posterity of valuable documentation for today's outstanding characters. It is doubtful if Dodge, at least in the beginning, had ever seen one of Washington's Diaries, and it must have been sheer coincidence, or some uncanny psychological echo, which resulted in the thought-provoking similarity of the two records. One wonders if this was apparent to Dodge himself, when in 1926 the four volumes of Washington's published Diaries came into his hands.

"Began my wheat harvest in the Neck," wrote Washington in July, 1771. "Worked ten cradles, 8 of which were my own Negroes."

"Put all male hands to work securing the oat crop," wrote Dodge, in July, 1885. And the next day, "Started men at cutting lawn early morning. On oats again after breakfast."

In less than a week, he had caught the true pitch.

For highlights on the early days of Dodge's Mount Vernon experience we are indebted to the lively recollections of his daughter Anna, now Mrs. Elvin Heiberg of Washington, D.C., who was eight years old when the family began to spend its summers there. It was of course an enchanting environment for an imaginative child, and she and her three sisters actually lived at Mount Vernon, inside the gates, for many consecutive summers, having the run of the whole place when the visitors had gone for the day, and on Sundays when Mount Vernon was not open to the public and the boat did not call at the wharf. The youngest sister, Molly, had been born in February of 1887, and she was christened in the Banquet Room at Mount Vernon, by two clergymen from Georgetown and Pohick churches. During the family's summer residence Anna's parents and the baby had the stuffy rooms above the Office, and the older girls and their nurse probably used the upper rooms in the Spinning House, which were later converted into dormitories for the Vice-Regents during Council.

Each day when the boat arrived the little girls would ride down to meet it in the horse-drawn bus which carried eighteen passengers and was driven by the old Negro coachman, Richard Broadus, with a young colored lad on the back steps to assist visitors who by reason of the weather or their infirmities felt unequal to the uphill approach on foot. Sometimes the children were allowed to postpone their afternoon naps long enough to rejoin the visitors as they emerged from the Mansion on to the west front courtyard while the conductor of the group, either their father or his assistant Mr. Young, pointed out the various dependencies or outbuildings which have now been gradually reclaimed, one by one, to a faithful simulation of their original functions as Laundry, Smoke House, Kitchen, etc.

In Mrs. Heiberg's childhood the Dodge family's dinner was served on the lower floor of the Office building on the north colonnade, with only a screen-door between them and the inquisitive public, when they heard themselves described to the visiting children as the "keeper-uppers" of the estate. In the summer evenings the family sat on the piazza until the night air and the mosquitoes from the swamp which Washington called Hell Hole drove them indoors. No one, says Mrs. Heiberg, had yet connected the swarms of these insects with the deadly malaria of Mount Vernon and the surrounding neighborhood, though a friend of Dodge's who was physician to the National Guard encampment between Alexandria and Mount Vernon discovered that by "filtering the night air" through fly-netting he reduced his malaria cases by three quarters.

It must have been a perfect playground for the sisters, surrounded by smiling good will and gentle indulgence from the devoted colored servants. They were free to play in the Mansion itself, entering the rooms as they pleased, and to gather fruit from the garden for Sarah the cook, who could tell them stories of the anxious days during the Civil War, then only twenty years in the past, when little Miss Tracy had stuck it out at her post, often hungry, often cold, often frightened, preserving the perilous neutrality of the place by insisting upon its recognition by both armies. They fished for perch off the wharf, where Miss Tracy's companion, Mary McMakin, had once fallen into the river and was only saved by catching hold of a corner of the apron Miss Tracy threw to her, while retaining tight hold of the other end. There were hunting dogs to accompany the children on their rambles in the woods within the boundaries, and there were excursions to the Accotink blacksmith shop when a horse had to be shod. They assisted at the evening milking, along with the black-and-white cat, and ran out each morning to watch the progress of the construction work on the wharf and the reclamation of the brick walls and paths through the gardens. Sometimes they accompanied their father when he rowed across the river to post a letter at Marshall Hall, the old Maryland homestead owned and operated as a picnic resort by the steamship company, and Colonel McKibbin, who ran it, allowed them to use the piano there for their practicing.

The rest of the year the family remained in Georgetown and Dodge returned there by the boat on Wednesdays and Saturdays, whatever the weather. The first winter of his tenure was unusually severe, and he once went by horse-car from his home to the Washington pier as usual, to find that the little steamer was frozen in solid. So he took a train to Alexandria and *walked* the nine miles to Mount Vernon, arriving at 2:30 P.M., having left home at 9:30 in the morning. Except for these conscientious bi-weekly family interludes, he lived at and for Mount Vernon, which soon became his very life, as it had been Washington's in his later years, so that Dodge seemed "always to know what to do," as by a sort of sixth sense. He was appointed postmaster, like the other Superintendents, and "conservator of the peace," or constable, and he was proud to be the first Mount Vernon vestryman since Washington of the at

one time derelict Pohick Church. As he gradually became
saturated with the inevitable Mount Vernon malaria, before
the drainage of Hell Hole in 1912, he was compelled to take
a month's vacation annually in the north to restore his system.
After 1910 he was given the privilege of staying at home in
town overnight whenever he chose, which when weighed
against the ensuing inconvenience of the daily trip to Mount
Vernon was of less value than might appear, and he continued
to make use of his bachelor quarters there. In order to simplify
the journey he did move his family from Georgetown to Washington City in 1901.

Just as his training as a teller in the Riggs Bank prepared him
for the complicated accounts and detailed reports which were
required of him when the Council of Vice-Regents met in
May of each year, so his boyhood spent on his uncle's Maryland plantation during the War qualified him to act as overseer,
farmer, and even vet, for as a youngster he had helped save the
horses from seizure by both armies by hiding and tending them
in nearby woods, and when the slaves ran away he had milked
the cows and fed the chickens. So when the favorite Mount
Vernon mare, Pet, behind which the Dodge family rode to
Pohick Church on Sundays, somehow became lacerated by
barbed wire Dodge himself dressed her wounds and sat up with
her at night till she recovered. The long Sunday drive meant a
late afternoon dinner, and the children came home to ice-cream
for dessert, under skies which in this idyllic childhood Mrs.
Heiberg remembers as always blue— and as Dodge took up the
reins for the homeward journey he would sing out, "Corn for
dinner, Pet!" to encourage the willing little horse.

Mrs. Heiberg's childish recollections of the second Regent,
Mrs. Laughton, remain vivid—a small, erect woman of great
dignity and charm, "with red-gold hair in a cascade of ringlets
which had been brushed over a curling-stick," who wore on
one occasion a frock to match the color of her hair. Mrs. Laughton was then in the fifteenth year of her regency, and under her
shrewd management the Association was slowly recovering
from the unsystematic though none the less devoted reign of
the first Regent and savior of Mount Vernon.

Of the eighteen Vice-Regents who were present on May 28th

in 1886, when Dodge made his first appearance before Council, the dean was Mrs. Philoclea Edgeworth Casey Eve of Georgia —in those days they signed their Christian and maiden names before their married titles (for it was a ladies' organization) just as the name of the State has traditionally supplanted the name of the Vice-Regent herself—so that the record reads that Michigan moved and Maine seconded, etc., that South Carolina had suffered a grievous loss in her family, that Massachusetts had gone abroad, that poor Kentucky had broken her hip in a fall, and that Pennsylvania's surgeon dentist had detained her but she hoped to arrive on Friday. Mrs. Eve was a schoolmate and lifelong friend of Miss Cunningham's, and had been the first to receive an appointment in the earliest days of the Association before the War began.

It is unnecessary to follow all the Vice-Regents—long known affectionately as "the Vices"—or even all the Regents, of which there have been only nine, through their remarkable careers in Mount Vernon's service. The roll-call on that May afternoon in 1886 therefore follows, in the order of seniority of appointment:

Mrs. Lily Macalester Berghmans Laughton, Regent
Mrs. Philoclea Edgeworth Casey Eve, Georgia
Mrs. Margaret Douglas Comegys, Delaware
Mrs. Letitia Harper Walker, North Carolina
Mrs. Margaret Mussey Sweat, Maine
Mrs. Lucy Holcombe Pickens, South Carolina
Miss Emily Harper, Maryland
Mrs. Nancy Wade Halsted, New Jersey
Mrs. Ella Bassett Washington, West Virginia
Mrs. Mary T. Barnes, District of Columbia
Mrs. Emma Reed Ball, Virginia
Mrs. Elizabeth Lytle Broadwell, Ohio
Mrs. Justine Van Rensselaer Townsend, New York
Miss Alice Longfellow, Massachusetts
Mrs. Ida Richardson, Louisiana
Mrs. Eliza Bland Woodward, Kentucky
Mrs. Mary Carver Leiter, Illinois

Mrs. Elizabeth Bacon Adams Rathbone, Michigan
Mrs. Janet deKay King, Vermont

Only two of the surviving seniors were absent that day, and both of them would return in subsequent years to command Dodge's respect and devotion—Mrs. Martha Reed Mitchell of Wisconsin, and Mrs. Susan E. Johnson Hudson of Connecticut.

Some of the early Vice-Regents, like Mrs. Magdalen Blanding of California, took no visible part in the proceedings. Mrs. Blanding resigned in 1882 after having served over twenty years without once attending Council, to be succeeded a few years later by Mrs. Phoebe Apperson Hearst, who generously continued to finance the improvements to the wharf and riverfront already contributed to by her State through the efforts of Mrs. Blanding—which indicates at least an acquaintance between them.

Others, like Mrs. Rebecca Willing Pepper of Pennsylvania, will live forever on a single line in the Minutes—in 1946 the Regent read aloud to Council purely as a matter of general interest the qualifications for Vice-Regents as prepared and enumerated by Miss Cunningham. Whereupon Mrs. Pepper, overcome by a sudden grand despair, promptly moved that they all resign and go home.

Dodge's early Reports are fascinating to read. The record of recent years tends to become more straight-faced and discreet, though his successor has caught something of the Dodge style and incidental humor—as when he recently remarked on the death of an old guard who had become eccentric, "His idiosyncrasies were unobjectionable"—surely the last word in tolerance and compassion. The establishment in 1948 of a Director's Monthly Report which is mailed to the Regent and Vice-Regents has dispensed with the more lengthy ceremonial at Council time. The Director's commission is still on a yearly basis and must be signed by the Regent in the presence of Council and with their consent, always with expressions of mutual esteem, which sometimes took the form of spontaneous applause from the ladies. Dodge never failed to acknowledge his debt to "the employees who so faithfully assist me," and the Regent always paid gracious tribute to "the judgment and faithfulness of our

Superintendent." As late in Dodge's service as 1933 the annual comedy went like this, as recorded in the Minutes:

"The Regent then summoned Mr. Dodge the Superintendent to the Council Room. Mr. Dodge brought his book, and upon his entrance laid it before the Regent. The Regent then addressed the members of the Council as follows: 'Ladies, is it your wish that I sign this commission, authorizing Mr. Dodge to continue as our Superintendent?'

"There was at once a responsive outburst in the affirmative, and the Regent signed the commission for another year; this being the forty-eighth time for this act on the part of the Regent for the Mount Vernon Ladies' Association. [Four Regents, one Superintendent, in that time.]

"Mr. Dodge accepted this commission, saying it was with great pleasure and appreciation that he received his commission and that he would continue to do everything in his power to serve the ladies of the Association to the very best of his ability. Mr. Dodge then withdrew from the Council Room . . . ," etc.

But however cordial relations may be—and to this day the little formality is often followed by warm applause for the re-appointed Superintendent—it seems just possible that the procedure might have the same general effect as that awkward moment in a wedding when the clergyman pauses to say, "If any man can show just cause why they may not be lawfully joined together . . ." The Superintendent could have an annual nightmare of standing there with his book on the table, the Regent puts the routine question and it is met with an ominous SILENCE . . . .

The nomination and choice of the Vice-Regents used to lie entirely in the hands of the Regent, and was a responsibility much lamented by Miss Cunningham. Nowadays the nominations are made in Council and a discreet year elapses for consideration before a general vote is taken, during which time the name of the nominee is not to be discussed except among the membership. Most of Miss Cunningham's stringent requirements still prevail, and most of her anxiety and liability still weigh on the current Regent, as the posts fall vacant. Vice-regencies for the far western States, remote from Virginia acquaintance, are naturally the most difficult to fill, though along with Mrs. Hearst,

Miss Mary Failing, the first for Oregon, Mrs. Alice Hale Hill, for Colorado, and Mrs. Frances C. Maxey, Texas, have been outstanding. The membership hangs around in the thirties, and sometimes there is a bad year when three or four chairs are suddenly emptied by death or resignation on account of ill-health.

Some years, as in 1886, the Regent's opening words could announce the largest attendance ever, a welcome to new members, and a thankfulness that there had been no losses among the old. There is no way to volunteer, and some embarrassment was felt in 1881 when the Regent read to Council a letter from "a Mrs. S——," offering to become Vice-Regent for Louisiana. Fortunately the appointment was already made—Mrs. Ida Richardson—"and it was decided not to act in the matter." Apparently the misguided lady was simply consigned to the waste-paper basket unanswered. On the other hand, Mrs. Lew Wallace (Susan Arnold Elston, herself a writer) was nominated in 1891 for Indiana, and seems to have declined. The vacant Indiana vice-regency was not filled until 1903, by Mrs. Martha Fitch Denby, who may have been the delightful first Vice-Regent's daughter.

The appointment is for life, and in a hundred years only one Vice-Regent has had to be expelled—Louisiana again—when Mrs. Margaretta Smith Wederstrandt Morse developed an unreasoning hostility to Miss Cunningham and was read out of meeting in 1870. The Regent's term, which used also to be for life, in 1947 was made for a period of five years with one possible re-election, which has never failed to take place except that in 1948 Mrs. Mary Esther Vilas Hanks preferred on the grounds of ill-health to resume her less arduous vice-regency for Wisconsin, and Mrs. Hope Knight Hodgman Powel of Rhode Island became Regent. The responsibilities of office are heavy, and require frequent visits to Mount Vernon for consultation with the resident Staff.

There are touching little ceremonies and traditions in the Association, their origins lost in the mists of the early Minutes— a sort of innocent etiquette which preserves as in amber the grave and formal atmosphere of the hoop-skirted era when it all began. For it is their own traditions they preserve now, as well as Washington's.

Each year as Council opens it is the duty of the Regent to take notice of the losses among their ranks during the interim, and one of those present is delegated, or volunteers, to prepare a brief memorial which is read at an evening session by candlelight in the Banquet Room. "We tread softly, for surely we seem to walk among graves, and our most honored and fondly loved ones are passing beyond the veil," said the articulate Mrs. Ball in 1892 during her eulogy on Miss Harper's twenty-six years' service. At the end of the last century the relentless march of time was such that a year in which their circle had remained unbroken was always a matter of prayerful thankfulness—and in fact it still is. And yet, in a self-perpetuating organization like this, the inevitable sorrow for the end of a long association in a common effort, which breeds so many affectionate friendships, is compensated by the arrival of new blood, fresh enthusiasm, and a younger energy—daughter sometimes following mother, or niece succeeding aunt, in the service of their purpose. Attendance at Council was once likely to be erratic, especially for those who had far to come, and whose family responsibilities and emergencies detained them—until in 1910 a motion by Rhode Island (Mrs. Anne Cranford Allen Brown) was passed that three consecutive years' absence would constitute resignation. This caused some hardship and grief, and was occasionally modified to honorary membership with the privilege of attending as a guest when possible. With the improvement in transportation in recent years this rule has been more or less allowed to lapse, as attendance becomes more regular.

The Regent, whatever her name may be, leaves it at the gate, just as the Vice-Regents shed their names to become States, and in casual lunch-table conversation as well as in official correspondence she is addressed unselfconsciously as Madam Regent. When in 1933 the Vice-Regents, standing in the order of their seniority, were presented to the President's wife, the Minutes recorded that: "The Regent received Mrs. Roosevelt and her guests at the door of the Council Room, where the Vice-Regents were presented to Mrs. Roosevelt, in each case by the name of the State she represented—as is the custom at Mount Vernon." In a paper written for the guidance of new members a few years ago Mrs. Elizabeth Throckmorton Cooke (New

Jersey) referred to this custom: "While some of the Vice-Regents may have known each other intimately for years before coming to Mount Vernon, others will arrive as total strangers. The custom of calling each other by State names, a tradition of value, places us all on an equal basis, and while in the Exhibition Area it is more dignified than to greet someone by a first name."

Even in these very flexible times, when the Resident Director, unlike poor Hollingsworth, is a vigorous, knowledgeable man of wide experience and great personal charm, with the advantage of having served for several years as assistant to Dodge, and being therefore capable of assuming many of the cares and decisions which Miss Cunningham was compelled to bear alone—the Regent remains the ultimate authority. An outside inquiry which touches on any subject which might be called classified, such as finance or protocol, is not immediately answered off-hand, but is first referred to her, and the reply comes from her. She is surrounded and upheld by a circle of trained male advisors and experts, but she is the law, and after her the Council.

"The only Vice-Regents permitted to give orders and directions to the professional staff or employees are the Chairmen of Committees during Council," wrote Mrs. Cooke in her latter-day book of rules. "In the interim she must deal directly with the Regent, who *alone* gives orders to the staff. Much confusion would result if thirty-five or forty women were all giving directions, some of which might be contrary to or contradict others. Any Vice-Regent having criticisms or suggestions in any department should bring them either to the Chairman of that Committee or to the Regent."

By a resolution presented by Mrs. Eve in 1885, each session of Council opens with a reading of Scripture by the Regent and recital of the Lord's Prayer by the Ladies. Roll-call is by seniority (of office not of age) as is the reception line at formal occasions and the church procession. The freshman Vice-Regent is not expected to take part in discussion during her first Council, but it is her fearsome duty at the end of it to express her gratification, which was gracefully dealt with in 1939 by Ohio (Mrs. Frances Payne Bingham Bolton) who rose and said: "Madam Regent—In accordance with a most happy traditional courtesy, may the newest member of the Council table express her keen interest in and appreciation of the manner in which the Regent has led the deliberations of Council, as well as her deep sense of privilege in having been elected to serve Mount Vernon as Vice-Regent for Ohio; and may she thank the Regent and Vice-Regents for their friendly welcome and the courtesy meted out by each and all."

One's first appearance at Council was not always so happy. Mrs. Edwine Blake Danforth, New York State, appointed in 1922 and resigning in 1948 "because of age" (though she was described some fifteen years later as "erect and beautiful" at ninety-seven) gave in her recollections an amusing account of her school-girl panic (at fifty-eight) under Miss Harriet Comegys's regency, when she described life among the old-timers of that period as "sometimes wearing but never dull. My last few years on the Board," she continued, "I used to wonder if the older group of Vice-Regents, of which I was one, looked as individual as those I found there. I wouldn't have missed for anything Miss Evarts for Vermont, exactly like a narrow slab of New England granite; Miss Longfellow for Massachusetts, redundant [sic] and silent except for her suit of white and scarlet two-inch wide stripes; and voluminous Mrs. Johnston for Alabama, completely deaf, a genuine orator and the only person I've known who veritably walked hand in hand with God and had a gay time doing it." At the same time she quoted the confession of Mrs. Eliza Ferry Leary (Washington State) whose experience went back to 1907, that she had been so intimidated by her reception in Council that as darkness fell on the first day she had actually climbed the fence and set out on foot for Alexandria— until her native spunk revived in a vow that "they had elected me—and I'll stay!" And before long she had been accepted into the innermost group.

Mrs. Danforth, who except for her husband's years in Congress lived in Rochester, was a woman of great charm and beauty, and was sufficiently well known before her arrival at Mount Vernon that her appointment as Vice-Regent was received in Council with applause. Her home was in the "old" part of town in Rochester, where she gave famous New Year's parties for all ages, her spacious high rooms lit only by gas-jets and candles. Ethelbert Nevin was said to have dedicated his

"Rosary" to her. She was a militant believer in women's rights, and worked for the Red Cross in both German wars. In Washington City she was noted for her dry humor and wit, and she never hesitated to express her opinion in Council. In 1946 she took part in a lively discussion on the manner of informing the new Vice-Regents of their election, recommending a letter instead of the customary telegram. Years later in her recollections she gave an account of her own reaction to the somewhat arbitrary summons: "Before the first World War," she recalled, "we lived most of the time in Washington, and as we had a house naturally we had guests, and quite as much as a matter of course the guests were taken down the river to visit Mount Vernon. I remember once asking somebody there 'Who is running this place?' and the answer—'Some women's organization.' So Mount Vernon was handed over, as far as I was then concerned, to the DAR's or Colonial Dames without even a thank-you to them, and there it stayed until May, 1922, when a telegram reached me in Rochester saying: 'You were today elected as Vice-Regent for the State of New York as a member of the Mount Vernon Ladies' Association of the Union. It is hoped you can attend the present meeting which will continue for a week.' I had no recollection of ever having heard or seen the name, so I committed what I also learned later to be the most inconceivable solecism, of replying that having already taken on some important work it was not possible for me to answer the kind message without knowing what duties were implied. The letter that followed tactfully ignored errors in procedure and made acceptance a joyful leap into the unknown, which proved to be one of the high privileges of my many years."

Mrs. Leary too reported on another occasion that hardly a week went by that she did not have to explain to somebody that Mount Vernon was not owned and operated by the DAR or the Federal Government. Mrs. Hill (Colorado) wrote in 1895: "A generation having grown up since the purchase of Mount Vernon, complete ignorance prevails among most of our people as to the patriotic work so long carried on by the Association." In 1908 the sale of President McKinley's home in Canton, Ohio, caused some editorials on the preservation of former presidents' homes, and mention was made of Mount

Vernon as the only one to be maintained as such. The *Omaha Bee* commented that neither Congress nor the men of America were entitled to any credit for Mount Vernon's survival, and William Jennings Bryan's *Commoner*, published at Lincoln, Nebraska, with a circulation of several hundred thousand, printed in full a paper read at the Omaha Ladies' Club by the Nebraska Vice-Regent, Mrs. Rebekah Manderson, and remarked that "the ignorance in regard to Mount Vernon is deplorable, and information concerning it should be given to grown folks as well as children." The following year Mrs. Manderson reported many requests for material for children's essays and women's club talks and librarians' data.

As late as 1915 Miss Failing (Oregon) found "much ignorance as to the way in which Mount Vernon was first rescued from decay, and also as to the present guardianship and care, so I am giving information in season and out of season." Mrs. Pringle astonished a South Carolina Chapter of the DAR when in an address she said that the Association was the first such women's organization in the country. Relations with the younger sisterhoods have now become cordial, however. In April, 1933, the DAR "came in a body as our guests," and in the same year the Colonial Dames Council was entertained at Mount Vernon by the Association. Many of the Vice-Regents are also members of either or both of the other two organizations.

In 1907 the subject of a badge or insignia to indicate membership in the Mount Vernon Ladies' Association was raised in Council, and despite some "adverse sentiment" the vote was 12 to 7 to have badges made. The year 1908 passed with no decision, but in 1909 designs from Tiffany and from Bailey, Banks & Biddle were submitted. The choice fell on Tiffany's blue enamel oval, "with a miniature painting of Mount Vernon in the center under glass, surrounded by a wreath of small pearls, the whole suspended from a ribbon, blue with white edges." The badges were to be the property of the Association, and must be returned to Mount Vernon on the death or resignation of the Vice-Regent, for the use of her successor.

Texas (Mrs. Maxey), always thinking big, moved that a special badge be made for the Regent, to be absolutely her property and not returnable. Seconded and carried. In at least

one instance, the Regent's badge was worn into the grave. A
resolution by Michigan (Mrs. Rathbone) for the addition of a
gold bar at the top and a red ribbon, was withdrawn after discussion, and the order was given to Tiffany to proceed, with for
obvious reasons a buff-and-blue ribbon. There was some later
discussion as to the appropriate time to wear the badge, one
suggestion being that it should be worn only when representing
the Association, and not as personal jewelry, but this was finally
left to the discretion of each Vice-Regent. The badges now
repose the year round, except during Council, in the safe in the
business office at Mount Vernon. The Regent's badge is no different from all the rest, except that it is worn on the ribbon
around the neck and not pinned on.

In 1949 Mrs. Powel, as Regent, felt that the new Vice-Regents
were too casually received into Council, and henceforth the
newcomer was obliged to come forward while the badge was
bestowed by the Regent herself, with a few words of welcome.
Mrs. Susan Rutledge Moore, at that time newly elected for
South Carolina, was the first to receive her badge thus from
the Regent's hands. If the Regent dies suddenly in office, as
happened with Mrs. Laughton and later with Mrs. Richards
and Mrs. Towner, an emergency meeting is called and an Acting Regent is appointed until an election can be duly held at
the next Council. But if the Regent voluntarily retires and
chooses to step back into the vice-regency for her State or
honorary status, while retaining the privilege of attending Council, as did Mrs. Townsend in 1909, Mrs. Hanks in 1948, and
Mrs. Harkness at the end of her two terms in 1958, then the
succeeding Regent must sometimes take over the chair in the
presence of her experienced predecessor, which must indeed
be a nerve-wracking contingency.

Since 1903, on a motion by Mrs. Maxey, Miss Cunningham's
Farewell Address has been printed in each number of the Annual
Report and the Minutes, and since 1916 it has been read aloud
at the opening of Council, after the prayer, originally by the
Vice-Regent for South Carolina, more recently by the senior
Vice-Regent or the Secretary, and its bracing admonition—
*"See to it that you keep it the home of Washington. Let no ir-
reverent hand change it; no vandal hands desecrate it with the*

fingers of—progress! Those who go to see the Home in which he lived and died wish to see in what he lived and died. Let one spot in this grand country of ours be saved from 'change!' Upon you rests this duty."—is the watchword of the Association. Since 1914, by a resolution adopted the year before, the Council then repairs as a group to the Tomb, in the old days on foot, and the Regent places a wreath of Mount Vernon boxwood on the sarcophagus of Washington. The senior Vice-Regent lays another on that of Mrs. Washington. Footnote: "The Regent announced that she would postpone the usual visit to the Tomb of Washington until five o'clock that afternoon, owing to the rainy weather." *Minutes, 1929.*

In 1938, when Mrs. Harriet Cole Towner of Iowa was Regent, an annual birthday ceremony was by her suggestion established, during which the employees gather as a family at the Tomb, before the gates are opened on the morning of February 22d. The iron grill at the entrance to the Tomb is opened, and two identical boxwood wreaths made by the gardener, one for Martha, one for George, are placed at the foot of each sarcophagus by a woman and a man employee, chosen in rotation by seniority of service. It was the writer's privilege to be present in 1965, and it was not the sharp winter wind which made the eyes water that morning. The eighty-odd men and women who form the present Mount Vernon family, indoors and out, were gathered before the Tomb. The Regent had driven over from her Maryland home and stood bareheaded in the cold, to say a few simple words. It was the turn of the waitress from the Staff dining-room, with a white silk scarf tied over her head and wearing a black coat, and the driver of the Mount Vernon cars in his fitted top-coat and peaked cap, to place the wreaths. Their faces were serious and proud, and the silence as they stepped forward to perform the graceful act was as solemn and reverent as though death had occurred only the day before.

Then everyone drifted away to the day's work, and the public poured through the gate at the end of the long gravelled drive which leads from the north entrance. February 22d is not a holiday at Mount Vernon, and everyone is on duty to cope with the attendance. Therefore each employee has his own birthday off, to compensate, no matter what the date may be. He will not, however, find the banks closed in his honor, and there are no Birthday Sales.

Since 1942, admission on February 22d is free. Following a local tradition, the first people through the gates that morning composed an endless stream of silent, awed little Boy Scouts who arrive by busses to form an uneven double line which passes slowly in front of the Tomb. On its fringes are parents, usually carrying a smaller child. It was bitterly cold in 1965, with a wind off the river, and reddened, unmittened hands were often raised in an uncertain salute as the children caught sight of the sarcophagi. There was nothing planned, they had not been rehearsed or instructed. The gesture, like their unbroken solemnity, was instinctive and genuine. It was said at Mount Vernon that they were "neighborhood people"—paying tribute as to a beloved relative or friend.

Too much cannot be made of the spirit of courtesy, deference, and self-effacement which reigns in the Administration Building where the business of the Association is now carried on. There was once, it appears, a man who came down from Massachusetts, by invitation, of course, and along with the job he had been engaged to do, and doing it very well, he expanded, and tried to run things. It was not long before it was borne in upon him, no doubt to his righteous astonishment, that this was not done at Mount Vernon. And not long after that, despite the partisanship of one or two mistaken Vice-Regents, he was encouraged to depart whence he had come, and everyone settled back with a strictly inaudible sigh of relief, and there was peace again, on the Potomac.

Weight is not thrown about, rank is not pulled, though a certain protocol is tacitly observed. There is a general sunniness, and the traditional appearance of leisure where no leisure exists, as established by Dodge, who was said to be "never in a hurry, always on time, and seeming to have endless leisure to extend hospitality to visitors to Mount Vernon"; a cheerful dedication, untheatrical and sincere, from top to bottom.

In her 1901 Regent's Report, Mrs. Townsend, after taking note of a new century and finding the Association's finances secure, the fire-fighting equipment established, and the riverfront wall progressing against the tidal erosion, added, "All the employees do good and conscientious work; all is harmony upon the place, peace, and good will." And in 1912 Miss Comegys as Regent commented on the fact that "when our employees are off guard duty they may be found at work somewhere on the place, after our gates are closed, with their tools and brushes."

From Dodge's time on, there has been no exclusive specialization. A man is hired to do what comes up. In the old days, Mrs. Heiberg recalls, when a task was finished the employee appeared at the Superintendent's door with the willing query, "Mr. Dodge, what'll I git at now?" And the ready reply, whether it was "Clean the harness—sort over the potatoes in the cellar—paint the woodwork in the kitchen—" was happily obeyed.

ii

Much of the help is now of the second or third generation at Mount Vernon, and a fourth is growing up into its teens. The Neitzey family perhaps holds the record for versatility. There was a Neitzey—Joseph—at Mount Vernon in 1893, as a night watchman, at $40 a month, and Chris was head night watchman in 1927. Joseph became a guard in the Mansion, which was his post for twenty-nine years till he died in 1923. He was succeeded by his son Wilfred, always one of the most capable men on the payroll, who was first a guard and then in the 1940's an engineer. Attached to the fire and security department, he also had the time and the skill to re-upholster the chairs in the West Parlor when they needed repair, made new H-L hinges in his shop, and did over all the picture-frames in the Mansion. During repairs to the cupola in 1947 the original bearing of the weather-vane was found to be badly worn and its wooden base revealed internal decay from water seepage, so he fashioned a new base made of a poplar plank like the first one, which can now be seen in the Museum. When "Bill" Neitzey's service reached the traditional forty years, he was presented with the traditional gold watch by the present Regent (Mrs. Rosamond Randall Beirne) in a ceremony held in the west front courtyard. After that he went on to the tedious job of repairing the delicate plaster-work of the ceiling in the Family Dining-room, working many days all day on a ladder. In 1962 he retired, with the rather vague title of cabinet-maker and handy-man, to take up farming. Before long he was back at Mount Vernon, farming having palled, to continue into his forty-fifth year of service to the Association, and he is now one of the senior men at the "Shop" by the Service Entrance. Albert Neitzey served on a destroyer in the South Pacific in 1945, and returned to a warm welcome when the war ended. Randolph survived Korea and came home safe to Mount Vernon.

The Rouse family has always been mechanically minded. W. L. arrived at Mount Vernon in 1902, when his son James was four years old. In 1942 he received his gold watch for "forty years of loyalty and devotion," and was dean of all the employees when he died in 1945. James grew up on the place and in 1923 after some special training at Thomas Edison's shop in New Jersey he did the electric wiring for the new generator and the following year took charge of the fire-crew's daily drills with the mechanized equipment. His daughters served in the Sales Room. On a mid-afternoon in 1928 the precious Washington mirror, which bore the Washington crest in reverse and had been acquired at a sale of Washington relics and presented by Mrs. Laughton in 1891, and which hung in the West Parlor, fell without warning and shattered itself on the old French clock beneath it. Dodge on his hands and knees retrieved all the pieces, and "our wizard Jimmie Rouse" reconstructed it like a jig-saw puzzle, backed it with silver paper as the old quicksilver was lost forever, and it was pronounced "better than before." The cracks can still be seen.

Equal to any assignment or emergency, Rouse's technical knowledge made Mount Vernon as self-contained in this complicated modern age as it had been in Washington's time, and as chief engineer during the second German war, when new equipment was impossible to secure even with a priority, Rouse nursed the old machines along and kept things running. When he died in 1947 his son Harry—born at Mount Vernon and named for Dodge—succeeded him, after a brief interval away, and is now in charge of everything from the wiring of new buildings to the repair of unhappy tape recorders and typewriters in the office. In his spare time he cures clocks and electric ranges, and installed the dishwasher in the Administration household department.

Other names—Miller, Embrey, Thomas, Taylor, Permar, Duvall, Rogers—run like a bright thread of loyalty and competence and good nature through the years. Sons grow up inside the gates—there are three cottages on the grounds for the families of the always on duty security men, and there were once as many as fifteen—and their off-spring plan their lives to follow their fathers in what has always been to them home.

Nowadays, in the long summer evenings, when the gate is supposed to close at 5 o'clock, the uniformed guards stand about patiently for an hour or more longer, while stragglers are slowly cleared from the Kitchen Garden and the outbuildings—it is against the custom of the place to shoo people out, lock up, and go home. The doors of the Mansion close on time, or as soon after 5 as it can be emptied tactfully—but it is conceded that people may have come a long way to see Mount Vernon, and should not be hurried, it would not be polite. However, the complicated watering system cannot be turned on—and off— and suppers cannot be eaten, until the grounds are emptied and the gates are locked for the night. The men are sometimes on duty, resigned and pleasant, until nearly dark.

Most of the thousands who come to Mount Vernon yearly appear to have some idea of why they are there, and what the place stands for, and admonitory signs have been largely dispensed with. There is nothing that says KEEP OFF THE GRASS, though in 1880 there were signs imposing fines on people who took the flowers, and signs prohibiting picnics in the grounds or the Mansion. In 1902 the Minutes took notice of the necessity for large NO SMOKING signs. Now there is one at the gate, more politely put, and a personable young guard is posted in the path a few yards from the outer door of the Mansion. He has an eagle eye for the presence of an unlawful cigarette concealed in the palm of a cupped hand, and it is his duty to remind the possessor in a low voice that one does not smoke in the Mansion. The nearest they come to a KEEP OUT is a low green-painted board stuck in the lawn at the turning into the Administration

Building parking space which says in discreet white letters: NOT AN EXHIBITION AREA. DO NOT ENTER. No one does.

During the summer months, when the attendance is heaviest, 10,000 people may pass through the gate and up the shady gravel path to the Mansion in a single day. As the number which can be conveniently contained in the Mansion at one time is limited to approximately 150 by the space in the roped-off walkways which appear when attendance is at its peak, this necessitates a long queue outside, which is patiently endured by the public on even the hottest days, the line moving forward in groups with a guard at the door to regulate the flow. The Association policy is never to shut anything in anybody's face, and therefore all who are waiting in line at closing time are admitted to the Mansion. Even the entrance gate is held open for belated arrivals hurrying in from the parking lots, who merely receive a courteous warning that time is limited. But visitors owe Mount Vernon the equal courtesy of allowing themselves at least a half hour's leeway.

In 1941, commenting on the extension of visiting hours during the long summer afternoons, and the steady rise in attendance since the 1934 Depression low, the present Director said: "This liberalization of hours has long been desirable. Many travellers were disappointed, especially during the summer months when the days are long. We are not in the position of an institution serving a local community which can be informed of visiting hours; if this were so we might properly consider closing one day a week. Our visitors come from forty-eight states and points more distant; many, if disappointed, do not have an opportunity to return. For this reason our visiting hours should be as liberal as possible. By comparison with the hours of all the principal points of interest in the Washington area they are now quite generous."

The guards report in uniform at 8:45 A.M. The janitor work has by then been done by the Housekeeping Department, which has the use of part-time assistants from the day labor force for two hours each morning. The Mansion always shines and sparkles, and there is very little visible gardening done during hours. The Director's 1941 Report concludes: "It would be impossible to live and work here without feeling the inspiring challenge to preserve, restore, and present Mount Vernon as effectively as possible. Within the limits of our abilities we strive toward this goal and we hope that our efforts will meet with your approval."

The question of the Sunday opening was for years a vexed one. When George Washington Parke Custis, who was Martha's grandson and the last surviving member of Washington's household, came to write his *Recollections,* published just after his death in 1857, he was assisted by his daughter, who was Mrs. Robert E. Lee, and by the journalist-historian Benson Lossing. Somehow amongst the three of them they seem to have superimposed upon Washington's robust and God-fearing 18th-century Episcopal faith, as expressed almost unconsciously in his writings, a sentimentalized Victorian sanctimoniousness which does not go with the rest of him. Certainly he played his part as a country squire of his time, attending Pohick Church with his family when the weather and the state of the roads permitted, and bringing home guests for an informal dinner party at Mount Vernon after the service. His early Diaries often skip over the day, indicating a general inactivity, and there was never a detailed work schedule as on other days, though he used the leisure to catch up on his correspondence.

In September of 1784, accompanied by his friend Dr. Craik, he made a strenuous trip on horseback up country to view his extensive properties around Chartier's Creek, and there occurs in his Diary then a Sunday entry which is alight with his characteristic irony, always aroused by hypocrisy in any form: "19th. Being Sunday, and the people living on my land *apparently* very religious, it was thought best to postpone going among them till tomorrow—but rode to Doctr. Johnson's who had the keeping of Colo. Crawford's (surveying) records—but not finding him at home was disappointed in the business which carried me there."

The record of his travels was as faithfully kept as when he was at home, and in 1789, during his New England tour, he wrote on November 8th: "It being contrary to law and disagreeable to the People of this State (Connecticut) to travel on the Sabbath Day—and my horses, after passing through such intolerable roads, wanting rest, I stayed at Perkins' tavern (which, bye the bye, is not a good one) all day—and a meeting-house being within a few rods of the door, I attended morning and evening service, and heard very lame discourses from a Mr. Pond."

Other entries written at Mount Vernon list a stream of unexpected guests arriving on a Sunday as on any other day, often to spend the night. "At home all day alone," seems to indicate disappointment at too much peace and quiet. It was the era of fox-hunting parsons, and he numbered several clergymen among his Fairfax County cronies. During the presidency, city-bound and setting a good example, he was quite regular in his church-going. But when George Washington Parke Custis seventy years later wrote that no one was admitted to the house on Sunday because of its master's strict observance of the day of rest, he was way wide of the mark, and left a false impression which had much to do with the reluctance of the Association to open the gates on a Sunday.

"To keep this, the home of Washington, which is a pledge exacted by our Charter, and the same which our Founder gave for us to the Nation 61 years ago, we must conserve the spirit of his day, the customs he established in the home he so dearly loved, 'as if he were looking on, and do everything as if he could see it,' and by this means strive not only to teach the rising generation patriotism but to emulate the example set in his home by Washington," Miss Comegys struggled to explain, in 1914.

Moreover, the Vice-Regents prized their Sundays at Mount Vernon during Council. The ride to Pohick Church in the comfortless horse-drawn vehicle which on week-days carried visitors up the steep incline from the wharf to the house—the 7-mile drive each way, sometimes in 90-degree heat, obliging them to take along their luncheons, which must have resulted in a decorous picnic before returning to Mount Vernon in the afternoon. The advent of the motor-car changed that, and they were home in time for a late luncheon, which left them the rest of the day to stroll in the gardens, sit on the piazza, and get acquainted with each other.

But the public began to complain. Many people had no other day but Sunday to make so long a pilgrimage. The first relaxation of the Sunday closing came during the 1914–1918 War, when soldiers from nearby camps were admitted to the grounds on Sunday afternoons, but as the Mansion remained closed few of them were sufficiently interested to make the concession seem worth while, and the old rule clamped down again in 1919. In 1922 a New Orleans paper fostered an Anti-Blue Law campaign to compel a Sunday opening, and was silenced by the Vice-Regent for Louisiana, Miss Annie Ragan King. Then the Washington and Alexandria Chambers of Commerce both tried, and were refused. At the Council of 1931, with the Bicentennial Year expectations of a record attendance ahead, the Regent (Mrs. Alice Haliburton Richards of Maine) acknowledged the seriousness of the situation with regard to public opinion, and asked for comment. The Vice-Regents said they had tried to keep an open mind on the subject, with the implication that they had not succeeded very well, and a fear was expressed that Mount Vernon would become "an amusement park," whereas the Association wished to treat its visitors as pilgrims rather than sight-seers. Mrs. Violetta Lansdale Berry, the new Vice-Regent for Maine, spoke "clearly and at some length," to the effect that as an experiment the Sunday opening might be advisable. Mrs. Elsie de Cou Troup of Nebraska said, also at some length, that it was only an opening wedge by people financially interested in bus and railroad lines, etc. In 1933 the question was still open, and Mrs. Richards quoted George Washington Parke Custis's shaky recollections in support of the Association policy.

Later that year the step was taken which the Regent said "marked for us the end of an era." Notice was sent to the Press that Mount Vernon's gate would be open on Sunday afternoons from 2 to 4 o'clock. The Easter Sunday crowd was so early and so large that they had to be admitted before 2, but the Sunday hours thereafter remained at 2 to 5 P.M. The Minutes' account of the momentous decision should be taken into consideration: "The Regent gave some interesting incidents which had happened in connection with the decision to open Mount Vernon on Sundays. She spoke of the great pressure she had been under all these years, and said she had come to this decision the past winter, feeling it was necessary; the Association was antagonizing the public by not responding to an often expressed wish and of course could not afford to do that, so she advised the change, but with regret that she felt obliged to do so. She stated that she had received many expressions of appreciation in favor of this action and was happy to say there had been no indication of any vandalism, only the greatest respect had been shown by tourists and visitors in general."

It is difficult to see why it was anticipated that Sunday visitors would be any less desirable than those that came on week-days.

The first all-day Sunday opening, which has since been maintained to everyone's advantage, came about late in 1936, and again the Minutes can best tell the story, in the words of the Regent's Report to Council, the Regent being then Mrs. Towner of Iowa. "An important matter decided at the October meeting was the desirability and feasibility of opening the gates to the public on Sunday mornings as well as Sunday afternoons. The question was precipitated by a letter to President Roosevelt from a small boy voicing his keen disappointment at not being able to visit Mount Vernon on a certain Sunday morning when in Washington with his father, it being his only opportunity to do so. This incident was only one of many determining factors which led the Regent to lay the matter before the Committee. She explained that it had become the custom for people to crowd about the gates on Sunday morning awaiting the time for opening in the afternoon until it had become embarrassing. The Vice-Regents present agreed that it would be wise to extend the time of opening, and the gates have been open all day Sunday since November 1st. Permanent action should be taken at this Council."

A letter from a small boy.

And surely the simple statement that "Mount Vernon is open every day in the year from 9 o'clock" makes nonsense of the involved schedules of lesser historic sites which charge more, to the effect that the said house will be "open weekdays, except Mondays, from 10 A.M. to noon, and from 1 P.M. to 5 P.M., and on Sundays from 2 to 5 P.M."

The year 1937 was anyway one of change and strangeness at Mount Vernon. The fifth Regent, Mrs. Richards, had died suddenly in the previous autumn at her home in Washington, after conducting a meeting of Committee Chairmen at Mount

Vernon only a few days earlier, when she appeared to be in her usual health. Like all the Regents before and after her, she was a woman of unusual ability, and what her successor called "that unbought grace of life which is one of Nature's rarest gifts," and she was greatly beloved. Her loss brought grief and consternation to all. The situation was supposedly covered by the By-laws, but nevertheless the change-over had not before been made with so little warning. Miss Annie Burr Jennings (Connecticut) as Recording Secretary went at once to Washington where all other available Vice-Regents gathered with their legal advisor, Mr. Gardner Boothe.

The indicated successor and senior Vice-Regent, Mrs. Maxey, was gravely ill at her home in Austin, and quite unable to advise or serve. The next ranking Vice-Regent was Miss Failing, who replied by wire from Portland that she did not feel "competent or willing" to serve as Regent, and recommended Mrs. Towner, who was third in seniority and who reluctantly took the chair as Acting Regent. She still held that temporary position when the annual Council met the following May. They then assembled in the shadow of a new disaster, Mr. Dodge having collapsed at his desk a few days previously and being critically ill in hospital. Poor Mrs. Towner, confronted with the enormous double emergency, read a moving report as Acting Regent, covering the final months of Mrs. Richards' administration and her own brief office.

"I have become impressed this year as never before with the solemn obligation which is ours as the custodians of the home and tomb which has become a Mecca not only for the people of our own country but for all the world," she said. "George Washington has come to be regarded not only as the founder of this republic but as the greatest symbol of democratic institutions and the most important link between our own day and that far off time when America was new. Upon this Association rests the privilege and responsibility of restoring, preserving and protecting this home which speaks so eloquently of the character and ideals of Washington, and of keeping his burial place inviolate. The fidelity with which we fulfill this trust is the test of our realization of the opportunity which is ours to have a part in keeping alive those spiritual qualities which are the soul of America.

"To achieve truly the feeling of the home which Washington knew requires that all the many incidentals be faithfully re-established. To do this requires research, for human memory can no longer help. Even when the exactions of war were great-est, Washington kept in close touch with the development of his estate; and in revealing his intimate environment there is made possible an understanding of a side of his personality about which too little is known. From his homely relations with tradesmen and servants we obtain a picture of his principles, his philosophy, and his superb ethics.

"In making available at an unchanging Mout Vernon the broadest possible information of those early years, Mrs. Richards felt that there would be established a permanently stabilizing influence. She knew that during her membership on the Mount Vernon board she herself had grown—had felt that impalpable influence of Mount Vernon which touches all those who become associated with it. She had seen those influences affect others, and wished to evolve a means of making them widely and permanently felt. For the years that saw the evolution into the maturity of coherent nationhood of that hitherto loose group of murmuring colonies are probably the most significant this coun-try will ever see.

"It is the hope of those who follow that they may interpret her dream and execute her wish, that they may link her vision with that of her first predecessor through the broad application of the words of Miss Cunningham, 'Let them see that we know how to care for the home of our hero.'"

Mrs. Richards had inaugurated the custom of meeting with the Committee Chairmen and Staff annually in October at Mount Vernon, at the opposite end of the year from the May Council, to consult on such routine matters as the acquisition of relics, urgent repairs, and restoration plans, and in 1936 to discuss the imperative decision about the Sunday opening. So it was in effect the final act of the fifth Regent, and the first of the sixth, and in the unthinkable circumstance of Dodge's incapacity, that the momentous step was taken. No one present could re-

member a Council without Dodge, and his annual Report had
been in his typewriter when he was stricken. It was read to
Council by his assistant Mr. Wall, who after Dodge's death
during that same session was elected Superintendent for the
coming year—unanimously—and his first overwhelming task
was the rearrangement of work schedules and payroll adjust-
ments to meet the change in hours for all the employees. But
by May of the following year both he and Mrs. Towner had
grasped the reins and Mount Vernon was never seen to falter.

Although Washington's presidency had passed before the
White House was built, and he never lived there, its occupants
have often shown a neighborly interest in his home. It was Mrs.
Rutherford B. Hayes who in 1880 established the annual presidential custom of presenting flowers to Mount Vernon on Memorial Day. Mrs. Taft invited the whole Council to tea at the
White House in the inaugural year of 1909, when the March
attendance of crowds drawn to Washington reached 20,000 at
Mount Vernon. The first official motor-car to visit Mount Vernon was that which brought President Taft's sister and a party
of friends there in 1911. A telephone message after they were
on the way was the only warning received. Council was then in
session and adjourned at noon in something of a flutter, but
luncheon was provided for the uninvited guests, after which
Dodge showed them around the Mansion and grounds with his
customary aplomb. Relations with the Wilsons were cordial, and
the President's appreciation of the work done by the Association
was informed and sincere. He once said: "No stranger visits
America but thinks first of Mount Vernon in planning where
he shall go and what he shall see," and very few citizens of the
United States now visit the city of Washington without coming
to Mount Vernon.

The rule prohibiting automobiles from entering the gate was
suspended for Wilson's arrival with friends in two cars in 1913.
He had allowed only an hour, made a hurried trip through the
Mansion and grounds, declined lunch, wrote his name in the
visitors' book, and invited the Vice-Regents to the White House
Garden Party a few days hence. Six of them attended, and found
it delightful. On July 4th, 1918, the Wilsons, members of the
Cabinet and Diplomatic Corps, and some fifty delegates repre-

senting foreign-born citizens of the United States, made a pilgrimage to the tomb of Washington. The presidential party
came by the yacht *Mayflower* and walked up to the Tomb from
the wharf, each delegate bearing a wreath. Soldiers and sailors
lined the route, and a crowd quickly gathered at a respectful
distance. John McCormick sang *The Star-Spangled Banner*, and
Wilson made his famous address on "Liberty." Only the lower
floor of the Mansion could be opened because of the crowd, and
cameras and parcels were stopped at the gate by the President's
security men.

The Hardings apparently never came, sending regrets to the
customary invitation of Council, and the Coolidges declined in
1925 and '26. There is a story, however, that word was suddenly received at Mount Vernon that the *Mayflower* was on its
way, and Dodge rushed home to change into his "claw-hammer
coat" and striped trousers, and the white V in his waistcoat—
and then President Coolidge stepped off the yacht in a rather
rumpled grey business suit. Mrs. Hoover's motor was met at the
gate by Dodge, formally attired, in 1929, and she was served
tea in the Family Dining-room, while Mrs. Harrison (Virginia)
and Mrs. Denham (Florida) "poured." The Regent and Vice-
Regents accepted a return invitation to tea at the White House,
travelling by motor-cars, and after tea and a brief conversation
with their gracious hostess saw the old china "in the little room
at the foot of the stairs" where it was shown—a very pleasant
afternoon. Mrs. Hoover returned to Mount Vernon with two
house guests the following year, and the President accompanied
her, unannounced, to pay silent tribute at the Tomb on February
22d.

Dodge had made Theodore Roosevelt's acquaintance during
a western vacation, and the two men became spontaneous
friends. The Roosevelt children naturally had the freedom of
Mount Vernon during his administration, and in 1908 a Roosevelt party arrived on horseback and stayed for lunch with
Dodge. In 1933 Mrs. Franklin Delano Roosevelt came with
guests in an open car which she drove herself, and was given tea
in the Blue (West) Parlor and stayed till after 5, while photographs were taken on the piazza. She returned in 1934, remarking that she enjoyed Mount Vernon so much that she came

"perhaps oftener than they were aware of," and in 1936 tea was served to President Roosevelt in his wheel-chair on the piazza on a beautiful afternoon, the rest of his party gathering in the Family Dining-room for refreshments. In 1943 the Roosevelts brought the exiled Queen Wilhelmina of the Netherlands and Mme Chiang Kai-shek to Mount Vernon, on separate occasions.

In 1947 on a blustery February 22d after a nine-inch snowfall had blown into drifts, President Truman arrived with the Veterans of Foreign Wars to lay a wreath at the Tomb and give an address. "All hands were mustered out to clear the walks," which immediately filled in again, but 1,500 visitors took advantage of the birthday free admission. In 1953 President Eisenhower was prevented by out-of-town commitments from attending the Association's Centennial celebration, but he sent a letter of greeting to the Regent (Mrs. Powel) emphasizing that he had visited Mount Vernon "not once but frequently" before. It was Mr. Eisenhower's habit, while President, to send two wreaths for the Birthday—the second to be placed in Washington's chair beside the desk in the Library—a more personal tribute than the customary official offering displayed at the Tomb. Just before Council time in 1960 Mrs. Eisenhower came informally to tea, which was served to her on the piazza on a warm October day.

It remained, however, for the late President Kennedy to restore on a truly grand scale for one evening the traditional hospitality of Mount Vernon to a distinguished visitor from overseas, with the famous State Dinner for the President of Pakistan, which was staged on the lawn in 1961. The weather played up, the catering and service functioned perfectly under Mrs. Kennedy's supervision, without cost or inconvenience to the Association, and the Mansion, though open, was not made use of.

A list of distinguished visitors to Mount Vernon if tedious is nevertheless enlightening in proof of the high renown and drawing power of the white house on the Potomac. Beginning with the Prince of Wales who was to become Edward VII, and who travelled in this country in 1860 under the flimsy incognito of Baron Renfrew, down to the visit in 1920 of the slender, romantic figure of his grandson, that Prince of Wales who was to

become the exiled Duke of Windsor; Queen Liliuokalani of the
Sandwich Islands (Hawaii) who in 1887 deplored the "levity"
of the visitors, and desired to go alone into the room where
Washington died; Prince Henry of Prussia, 1902; Admiral Togo
of Japan, 1912; Albert of Belgium, 1920; Mme Curie, 1921;
Foch, Joffre, and Briand, 1922; the Queen of Rumania, 1927;
Prince Chichibu of Japan, 1927; General Allenby, 1929; Prime
Minister MacDonald, 1930; Lord Tweedsmuir, Governor-Gen-
eral of Canada, 1937; Anthony Eden, 1939, descendant of the
beloved 18th-century Governor Eden of Maryland, who was
Washington's host and friend; King George VI and Queen
Elizabeth of England, 1939, in a pitiless heat-wave; the exiled
Princess Juliana of the Netherlands, 1940; Winston Churchill,
1942; Prime Minister Nehru, 1949; Princess Elizabeth and
Prince Philip of England, 1951; Queen Frederika of Greece,
1958; Castro of Cuba, 1959, with a party of eighty, for whom
at great inconvenience the gates were closed to the public on
a sunny Sunday, after a warning from the Government Security
Service of possible violence, which did not materialize; Madame
Khrushcheva, who appeared never to have heard of the Bastille
or of Lafayette, or (possibly?) of George Washington, but
whose interest was awakened by the restored Family Kitchen
and its appurtenances; the President of Guinea, who made a
spectacular entrance by helicopter on the Bowling Green in
1959; and a parcel of East Indian journalists who were bewildered and disappointed to learn that their hostess, the Regent,
was Mrs. Francis Beirne and not Mrs. George Washington in
person.

If the present Regent is asked about the Endowment Fund,
which was so often mentioned in the '80's and '90's she laughs
ruefully. There was one once, there is invested capital now,
but it isn't called that any more. Each year when the Treasurer
makes his report to Council he repeats his inevitable admonition
that the reserve fund should be sufficiently built up to carry
the expenses for one year, and it never is. The present budget
would of course make Miss Cunningham's head swim. The payroll alone is in the neighborhood of $500,000, and the employees
number in the eighties, with some day-labor added. Yet there

was a time when the first Regent couldn't even afford a Superintendent's salary, which was then $1,500 a year.

The office Staff and the guards and maintenance people are
paid at the prevailing rate, which in the Washington vicinity is
high. The Regents and the Vice-Regents have always served
without compensation, and Miss Cunningham impoverished
herself by unrecorded sums poured out in the initial effort, as
long as she had anything to give. The Vice-Regents, usually
well-to-do, have contributed from their personal funds at critical
times, or for an imperative purpose like a vital repair job or the
purchase of a precious item at an auction or sale of Washington
memorabilia. As the basic financial position improved after the
Civil War and the 1876 Centennial-year prosperity, an offer
was voted in Council to pay the Vice-Regents' travelling expenses to and from Mount Vernon for the annual Council—an
outlay which amounted to hardship in some cases, especially in
the post-War South, where large fortunes had been lost. These
funds have often been returned, as not needed.

It is difficult in this hard-headed, iconoclastic modern world
for the general public to assimilate the idea that the people who
rescued Mount Vernon more than a hundred years ago, and
those who maintain it today, have not expended all that effort
and money because there was "something in it for them"—
something besides a slowly realized dream of perfection which
is still being refined and improved upon. To them George Washington has been a guiding spirit, a presiding genius, the highest
type of honest, modest, right-thinking man the world has seen.
He too served without profit to himself throughout the Revolutionary War, refusing at the time of his appointment the
salary he was entitled to as Commander-in-chief, and accepting
only minimum expense money for the arduous years of the
presidency, aware that his depleted personal fortune would be
inadequate to the discharge of the duties and the dignity
of the office as he felt it should be maintained. His election in
1789 had found him financially embarrassed even for ready
cash, and two terms left him no better off. He too was generally
supposed to have considerable wealth, but it was in land and
property not readily negotiable, and with a large family of rela-

tives and their dependents he was always pressed for plain
money.

The Association depends for its income on the paid admissions, which have risen perforce, like everything else, from the
original 25¢ for each adult, by unwilling stages to the present
modest fee of 75¢, children below junior high school grade and
people in uniform free. The ridiculous compulsion on the part
of some visitors to circumvent the entrance fee, even when it
stood at 25¢, can only arouse amusement mixed with contempt.
Large parties comprised of various club memberships, people
who could afford to arrive in their private yachts or were in a
position to command the service of government motor-boats, as
well as distant relatives of Miss Cunningham and the early Vice-
Regents, were insistent on the privilege of free entrance to the
grounds which had no other source of income. There was once
an organized "anti-fee" society which sought to deprive the
Association of the small charge which kept the place from falling apart. When in 1914 free admission for school children was
inaugurated Miss Comegys as Regent commented to Council:
"The fact that the opportunity has not been more widely availed
of would seem to disprove the assertion of our Anti-fee friends
that so many children were clamoring for a chance to see the
Home and Tomb of Washington and were only prevented from
doing so by the 'enormous fee' charged."

The attendance, which was once considered satisfactory at
84,000 in 1900, is now well over a million—300,000 over—each
year. There is an occasional small bequest, there is the interest
on their slowly accumulated capital investments, there are the
sales of their literature, plants and seeds, and post-cards. That is
all. The souvenir shop and lunch-room outside the north gate
has been an independent concession since before 1886, has no
connection with the Association, and pays no tribute to it for
occupying land which the Association does not own. But Mount
Vernon pays its own way. If ever there is a surplus it is at
once ploughed back into additional repairs and maintenance.
Or another outbuilding is equipped and opened for exhibition,
as the Store House in the North Lane has recently been readied.
Something is always waiting for money.

In Miss Cunningham's time an unfortunate situation existed

between Mount Vernon and the Press, which then unaccount-
ably lost no opportunity to criticise the Association and meddle
in its affairs and management. This helped to create among the
Vice-Regents a defensiveness against publicity, a passion for
privacy and anonymity, which was both awkward and harmful,
and has been gradually resolved to some degree by a sensible
recognition that credit should be rendered where it is due, and
not allowed to drift away to some better advertised organization
which had nothing to do with the original concept or its accomplishment.

"While the earlier Vice-Regents dreaded and avoided publicity," Mrs. Cooke wrote in 1962, "changing times have made it
desirable for the Mount Vernon Ladies' Association not to hide
its light under a bushel. The Public Information Committee
was formed as a means of spreading desirable publicity from
Mount Vernon, and the Vice-Regents can help to do this in
their own States." Meanwhile error persisted, to an almost amusing degree. In 1920 Mrs. Rathbone, still Vice-Regent for
Michigan on an honorary basis, had written a stinging letter to
the *Detroit Free Press* demolishing them for a printed statement
that Mount Vernon was bought and maintained by the DAR,
and reminding them that the Association was founded and
chartered more than thirty years before the DAR was born.

Mrs. Richards, while Vice-Regent for Maine, went abroad
in 1925, and reported that during the voyage and her travels
she was kept busy letting her fellow-countrymen know that
the honor of preserving Mount Vernon was due to the oldest
patriotic association of women in the country, and not to the
Colonial Dames or the DAR. "The old story always finds at
least one new listener."

This often embarrassing anonymity, which is not entirely
dissipated today, was the natural result of the Association's in-
grown aversion, individually and collectively, to publicity per
se, which was perhaps a hangover from the days when a lady's
name was only supposed to be seen in print three times—when
she was born, when she married, and when she died. Yet the
obstinate insistence on privacy was maintained. Permission to
photograph the interior of the Mansion and its separate treasures
was repeatedly refused, and participation in magazine articles or

the growing motion picture field was courteously declined with a reference to a ruling established by Council in 1900. A very distant photograph taken from the front lawn of the Regent and twenty-nine Vice-Regents grouped on the piazza was briefly noted in the 1925 Minutes—the only such group, except for one in 1883 which is never mentioned, since 1870 when the first Regent posed with the Houdon bust of Washington and the eleven members present at that Council. The 1925 picture shows, among others, Miss Longfellow, enormous in a white dress, Miss Comegys in black with ropes of pearls, Miss Evarts (Vermont) ramrod straight with a white stole around her shoulders, and Miss Jennings wearing the fashionable black velvet band around her throat. Nowadays the Council group photograph taken on the lawn in front of the piazza is an almost yearly custom, with Mr. Wall and Walter Densmore, the Assistant Director, like masculine book-ends at the outer edges.

There were a few exceptions to the short-sighted ban on publicity. *House & Garden* was the first periodical to receive co-operation from the Association, when in 1902 it was permitted to take photographs in the gardens and grounds, and forty years later, in the middle of a war, the same magazine produced a striking cover design showing the American flag's protective folds unfurled above the Mansion. But the *Delineator* put its foot in it with an article "significant of the prevailing belief that Mount Vernon is taken care of by the DAR," not having troubled to consult anyone at Mount Vernon before publication, and although the *Ladies' Home Journal* and *Country Life* were granted pictures and basic information in 1904, the *Journal* in 1922 was required to submit its manuscript for approval. The *National Geographic* in 1928 printed an illustrated article, and another at the time of the 1953 Centennial. Mr. E. V. Lucas, that delightful if almost forgotten British essayist, after visiting Mount Vernon in 1921 expressed his appreciation in the London *Times*, and his piece was sufficiently gratifying to be reprinted in the Minutes, and it also appeared in a volume of his collected writings called *Roving East and Roving West*. Mr. Lucas had obviously "caught on," and needed no instruction or editing: He said, in part:

"We have no place of national pilgrimage in England that is so perfect a model as Washington's home at Mount Vernon. It is perhaps through a lack of a figure of the Washington type that we have nothing to compare with it; for any parallel one must rather go to Fontainebleau; but certain shrines are ours and none of them discloses quite such pious thoroughness as this. When I think of the completeness of the preservation and reconstruction of Mount Vernon, where largely through the piety of individuals a thousand personal relics have been reassembled, so that save for the sightseers this serene and simple mansion is almost exactly as it was, I am filled with admiration. For a young people largely in a hurry to find time to be so proud and so reverent is a significant thing. The orderliness of the place is not its least noticeable feature. There is no mingling of trade with sentiment, as at Stratford-on-Avon, for example. Within the borders of the estate everything is quiet. I have never seen Americans in church (not, I hasten to add, because they abstain, but because I did) but I am sure that they could not, even there, behave more as if the environment were sacred."

Lossing, of course, was the first outsider to write about Mount Vernon, and he had the full co-operation of George Washington Parke Custis. A desire for a dignified, accurate history of the Association was often expressed in Council and some abortive attempts were made by various Vice-Regents from time to time. Nevertheless, with a few exceptions like Thomas Nelson Page and James Penniman, whose small authorized books were placed on sale and kept in print by the Association, the aloof attitude towards the Press and professional writers persisted. The unfortunate result of this policy became apparent when Miss Longfellow discovered that the list of President Coolidge's appointments to the Commission for preparing the celebration in 1932 of the 200th anniversary of Washington's birth included the President of the DAR but not the Regent of the unsung Mount Vernon Ladies' Association. The oversight was of course speedily rectified. An article submitted by *Good Housekeeping Magazine* was passed at this time, and Dodge's rambling book recounting with his characteristic charm his own forty-seven years at Mount Vernon was published that year.

Thomas Nelson Page, lawyer and amateur author, whose name alone was a passport in the South, in 1908 had been on the strength of several previous publications invited to prepare a short history of Mount Vernon's rescue and administration. He obliged with a manuscript delivered to Council the following year. The ladies, after lengthy deliberation, deleted all mention of specific gifts and restorations made by separate States as "inappropriate"—the old female anonymity complex again—and accepted the work with thanks. Mrs. Manderson (Kansas) Chairman of the Committee which had chosen Mr. Page, undertook the expense of publication, and the little volume went through many printings. At the time of its acceptance a resolution was passed in Council that all future requests for photographs and data to enable "others" to prepare books about Mount Vernon must be submitted to Council with a copy of the proposed article.

They did, however, co-operate with James Penniman, who in the 1920's wrote and presented to the Association several scholarly pamphlets on Washington and Mount Vernon which were accepted for sale, the expense of their continued publication being met by Mrs. Rathbone. Owen Wister, acquainted with the Vice-Regent for Pennsylvania (Mrs. Ella Waln Harrison), presented an inscribed copy of his *Seven Ages of Washington*, for which he had apparently asked no favors, in 1908. When Paul Wilstach, with his name spelled wrong in the Minutes in 1915, requested permission to have photographs taken to illustrate his projected book on Mount Vernon, the vote went against him and he was coolly referred to the official Guidebook. His volume appeared the following year, with illustrations, and was dedicated to Dodge, who may have smoothed his way somewhere. An autographed copy presented by him to the Association was duly acknowledged in Council without praise or censure. The vote on Eugene Prussing's request to make use of journals and letters in the Association's files was negative. He too brought out a book, which was refused a place in the Association Sales Room, where only their sponsored literature was permitted.

Mrs. Marian Ramsay Furness (Minnesota) had moved in 1917 that a printed leaflet with the essential facts about Mount

Vernon should be prepared for free distribution to visitors, supplementing the modestly priced Guide-book—and she was promptly commissioned to write it, which she accomplished with the assistance of the Vice-Regent for Vermont (Miss Evarts) and the leaflets were placed in convenient receptacles labelled "Take One." An up-to-date folder is similarly available today, and at a small cost there are also handsome booklets prepared by the Staff and illustrated in color, on the Silver, the China, the Military Equipment, and the Mansion Furnishings.

But considering the many attempts at free exploitation of Mount Vernon the caginess of the Association is understandable, especially as an occasional relaxation of their rule against the use of their files by even accredited writers usually cost them money for small return. However, the publication in 1926 by Houghton Mifflin of the four-volume edition of Washington's *Diaries*, edited by Dr. J. C. Fitzpatrick and underwritten by the Association, was a success, and repaid a considerable investment, as well as supplying invaluable source material to an understanding of Washington.

Resistance to motion picture and radio coverage was equally resolute, though as the Association Centennial approached (1953) considerable thought was given to the need of a history in depth and material was released, even to a one-reel documentary film distributed through McGraw-Hill, with a running narrative and interpretive music—undertaken with the close supervision of Mr. Wall and the Regent. A small sponsored volume by Gerald Johnson, illustrated, and containing as an appendix extracts from the Diary and letters of Washington selected and annotated by Mr. Wall, was published by Random House in the Centennial year. Another small volume compiled by Dorothy Troth Muir and devoted mainly to Miss Tracy's experiences during the Civil War was authorized in 1946.

Innumerable suggestions, from both cranks and well-wishers, have always poured in. Once a Colonel Berry had a "cherished idea" that the Association should petition the Federal Government for funds with which to erect a fabric of iron and glass, like a large railway station, that would entirely cover the Mansion from the weather and thus retard decay. A few years later the Institute of Archaeology seriously proposed to build a "temple" over the Tomb—which was "declined with courtesy." In 1941 an advertisement showed a bedspread claimed to be a reproduction of George Washington's choice for a wedding gift to his wife, and the manufacturer's agent requested that it might be so mentioned in the Mount Vernon literature. The Minutes were curt: "The statement is not correct, nor was the request granted."

The District Audubon Society was welcomed in 1941 to make an early morning walk in the grounds before the gates opened— now an annual occurrence—and reported 73 species of spring migrants in this natural sanctuary. To the northern visitor, bird-watcher or not, the sight of half a dozen cardinals in full plumage pecking around in the official parking lot like chickens in a barnyard quickens the heart.

Captious criticism and wilful doubt cast on the carefully authenticated memorabilia, extending even to the bed and swords, which can certainly show a continuous history, required a firm reply in the Washington papers in 1909. Even now, querulous letters and articles are written by the small lunatic fringe which always exist in the mistaken belief that they have been sent by heaven to put things right in a mismanaged world, and who remain impervious to anything not explained with a club. These tiresome manifestations arrive inevitably on the tidy desk of the current Director, and are dealt with by him with sublime tact and courtesy.

It has apparently always been the fashion to hate the man in the White House, for people who have no conception of the load that man carries or of his superior opportunities to learn and act upon facts which are unavailable to the man in the street. But surely the last word in futile character assassination was the recent fabrication that Washington had himself sold stone to the Government from his own quarries during the erection of the new Capitol Building in the Federal City—thereby profiteering, the implication was, from the Government he had devoted most of his mature life to protect and establish. The story gained sufficient credence among those always ready, willing, and able to believe the worst of everybody to reach both newsprint and television, and the obvious rebuttal promptly made by the Association that Washington owned no quarries of

useful stone and had himself habitually purchased stone for use
at Mount Vernon never achieved an equal amount of attention.
Apart from any question of Washington's character and personal probity, the unquestioning acceptance of such a slander is
a disheartening commentary on the cynical disillusion of the self-
appointed opinion-makers today.

More than a million people a year, nevertheless, come to see
where and how George Washington lived. They vary infinitely
in culture, capacity, and origin. They include irreverent wise-
crackers and inaccurate sentimentalists, but for some reason, perhaps hardly realized by themselves, they come. Mount Vernon
recognizes impartially the uninformed, the misinformed, and
partially informed, and—the informed. Some are there merely to
boast that they have been there, the kind of tourists who visit
places as if stringing beads. Some arrive in busses which allow
them only half an hour, and some have half a day to spend. There
are eager children, too young to disguise their awe and enthusiasm, and there are raucous would-be-sophisticated teen-agers
with a desperate desire to know and an equally desperate desire
to hide their ignorance. And there are serious-minded students,
who are prepared to identify and appreciate what they see.
There are old people, making the trip of a lifetime, for which
they may have saved dimes for years; and there are young people doing their duty by their families and worried that they may
have spent too much on the expedition. It is safe to say that no
one leaves Mount Vernon without having gained something of
which they may be still unaware, found something, perhaps in
themselves, which was not there before. But they have not been
spoon-fed with culture. They have been allowed, even compelled, by what they see, to deduce more, to imagine further, to
try to think. And that is thanks to the Association's wisely determined policy of preserving and restoring, without attempting
resurrection.

A particularly dense recent complaint has been that Mount
Vernon does not sufficiently exert itself to entertain and divert
its visitors with discursive devices which are employed at other
more aggressively promoted show-places such as Williamsburg
and Boscobel-on-the-Hudson. There are no costumed guides
with memorized recitals at Mount Vernon, it is true—no indoc-

trination movies at the gate, no wall-maps with little colored lights that click on and off, nobody with pointers, no little boxes with mechanized lectures on tape. The dissatisfaction of the unimaginative minority is therefore summed up in the peevish allegation that "Mount Vernon is just *there!*"

It is, indeed. It is there, in a tranquil, enchanted silence of its own, where alien voices are automatically lowered, and children are not inclined to romp and run. There are labels to read—always provided that one can read. There are the give-away folders and the handsome illustrated hand-books at a small fee. There are soft-voiced, friendly guards who have been carefully briefed to attend to the most idiotic and ignorant questions and come up with courteous answers while keeping their faces straight. Otherwise—the silence, reflecting the dignity and reticence of Mount Vernon's 18th-century master.

The roses in the Regent's bouquet—and only the Regent's—were always yellow.

And now, Mr. Dodge, it's all yours.

iii

May, 1886. Dodge stands before the attentive Council, many of whom are inspecting him for the first time.

"My first official act," runs his Report as he read it, "was to summon all the employees and state to them as clearly as possible my views as to certain rules and regulations which I should require in the governance of the estate, and I received from them severally and jointly their expressed willingness to cooperate with me in all measures having for their object the interest of your honored Association and the welfare of Mount Vernon."

The employees at that time numbered all of ten, including a colored lad, Harry Parker, added to the list as an afterthought at $10 a month.

Foremost among them was Franklin Whelan, the gardener, at $50 a month—Dodge started at $135, but his salary rose regularly year by year as their appreciation of him grew. Mrs. Heiberg recalls Whelan as "a tall Lincolnesque figure, quiet, efficient, and kindly, whom everyone liked." He proved to be a valuable and remarkable man, described as "faithful and com-

petent" by Mrs. Pickens, who was Chairman of the Greenhouse
and Gardens Committee, and he had the imagination and enterprise to plan a garden of old-time plants and flowers such as
would have grown there in Washington's time. Thanks to an increasing desire on the part of the public to possess plants, seeds,
and cuttings from Washington's garden, Whelan was soon
running a mail-order business (with a notice to that effect inserted in the Guide-book), keeping books, making a budget,
and rendering his own Report to Council. Under his management the Greenhouse and the Flower Garden were soon a modest
source of income to the Association—just as in the lean years
of the 1860's Miss Tracy supplemented the entrance fees on
which the wartime household depended for necessities by making and selling bouquets from seeds she had bought and tended
herself. Whelan had a wife and four children, and lived in a
cottage on the grounds—not to be confused with the building in
the North Lane known as the Gardener's House, which was
never used as such by the Association. To increase his income,
he made and sold little wooden souvenirs, until in 1911, on a
motion by New Jersey (Mrs. Helen Field Conover) it was
ruled *infra dig* for an employee of Mount Vernon to sell anything for his own benefit in the grounds, and he was given a
small raise instead. When in 1898 repairs to his cottage were
undertaken by Rhode Island (who signed herself A. I. C. D.
Ames—Anne Ives Corrington Dwight) she financed the project
by organizing in Providence a Patriotic Dance, where the tunes
ranged from *Yankee Doodle* "up and down," to which the company sang as they danced. "The favors for the cotillion were
medals of General Washington, suspended from red, white, and
blue ribbon held in an eagle's beak, and *Mount Vernon* in gold
letters across the ribbon." This charitable frolic yielded some
$260, of which $50 was saved for the Endowment Fund.

In 1912 Whelan's annual Report took note of his thirty-two
years of continuous service—"more than half my life—assuring
you of my unabated, increased love for Mount Vernon." The
Council voted him a gift of $100 and a vacation with pay. But
vacations were not much use to Whelan, though his health was
deteriorating. When he was finally induced to accept a year's
leave of absence with salary, he hung around until June instruct-

ing the man who was to fill in for him, rested all summer under a doctor's care, with his wife and daughters to attend him, pined for Mount Vernon and returned on part time in October, and by November was back at his full duties again, despite failing strength. His work was gradually lightened by tactful assistants, such as Monroe Thomas, until he died, after forty-five years in the place he loved best in the world he had seen.

Dodge was the first Superintendent to have a relatively free hand to inaugurate his own ideas and reforms, for Hollingsworth had taken office in the shadow of the first Regent's jealous sovereignty. He was a disciplinarian from the start, with initiative, decisiveness, and an orderly banker's mind, and he left no doubt as to where authority would henceforth reside. John Nicholls, the clerk he inherited from Hollingsworth, was "removed" in the autumn of 1886, "because of direct violation of my official wishes in several instances, and after he had been cautioned repeatedly," Dodge reported to Council with noticeable vexation the following year. The Regent had concurred. Nicholls was followed by two or three other young men who proved unacceptable or felt they could do better for themselves elsewhere, until the arrival of James Young of Georgetown, who was to become in all ways a treasure.

In those days a conducted tour was given, discontinued in 1910, and it was part of Mr. Young's job to release Mr. Dodge from this duty by meeting the boat and accompanying the visitors to the Tomb and through the Mansion. He had a prepared speech which never varied and which the Dodge children soon learned by heart, though Dodge's daughter Anna records that he himself always spoke the familiar story extemporaneously, and while the facts never altered he presented them each time in a different way. James Young was a fair, handsome man of proud Southern family, and his good manners were perhaps just a bit high and mighty, as was demonstrated one day when some unperceptive member of the little flock he had just shepherded through the Mansion and back to the boat was mistakenly moved to bestow on him a tip of a quarter, which Young then and there flipped contemptuously into the river. After ten years he was made Assistant Superintendent, and remained faithfully at Dodge's elbow till declining health forced his resignation in 1934 after forty-five years. He was followed as Assistant Superintendent by Charles Cecil Wall, the present Resident Director, who was to succeed Dodge when the latter died in harness in 1937.

The colored help in 1886 were nearly all old, experienced, and ready to welcome a strong new leadership. Nathan, the devoted major-domo who with his wife Sarah had loyally supported Miss Tracy all through the Civil War anxieties, weathered the gales of Miss Cunningham's tenancy during the post-War upheaval, and upheld Hollingsworth's incapacities with tact and efficiency, had died just too soon to see the place come into Dodge's safekeeping. Ever since Mount Vernon had belonged to the Association Nathan had been there, smiling, good-tempered, with meticulous manners and pride in his many responsibilities, waiting upon Council, receiving distinguished visitors with an air all his own, overseeing sales, and engaging extra help at his own discretion. His loss was keenly felt by all who had known and relied on him, and there was no one immediately to take his place.

Sarah claimed to be a descendant of Washington's own servants, born and raised at Mount Vernon. As cook and housekeeper to the Association, she too had served Miss Tracy with devotion, and was in charge of the Mansion, the Dairy, and the poultry. She was eventually supplied with an assistant named Eliza Colbert, and when she retired to her nearby farm in 1892, after thirty years' service, she left a void which was not filled satisfactorily for years.

"Aunt Millie" Mitchell tidied the rooms used by the Superintendent and clerk, and clad in bright calico and a turban, dispensed milk at the lunch-table as long as it was kept up. Her husband Thomas Mitchell had been for years a farm-hand and substitute coachman on the ancient vehicle which plied between the wharf and the Mansion, until superseded by Richard Broadus, who also lived to a great age as a pensioner of the Association. Warner May was a farm-hand, afflicted with a violent stammer, and there was still the aged West Ford, who boasted that his father and grandfather had worked at Mount Vernon before him. He must by then have reached his eighties, as he was not young when Benson Lossing drew his portrait in 1850, and was considered old and feeble by Miss Tracy when she brought him back to Mount Vernon for nursing during the War. There may have been more than one West Ford, and a son George was listed as herdsman, and later as a guard at the Tomb. The Fords were perennial.

At the Tomb in 1886 was Edmund Parker, following Nathan as dean of the colored men, having run away during the War and then returned to Miss Tracy for employment. His native superstitions warred with his pride at holding what was considered the post of honor at Mount Vernon, but he was the finest of his type, and was much indulged by Dodge. When he died in 1899 he was succeeded by "Uncle Tom" Bushrod, who had been the sexton at Pohick Church, and came of Judge Bushrod Washington's old slave stock.

The last of the old-timers among the colored guards at the Tomb, Will Holland, retired in 1965 at the age of seventy-nine, having held that proud post with inimitable dignity since 1936. He had received his gold watch in 1963, and a tape recording was made of his gentle, lilting voice reciting his account of the Tomb. With a brief interval Holland's employment at Mount Vernon dates back to 1903, when he arrived as a lad of sixteen, and acted as waiter at Dodge's table when meals were served to the Superintendent in the Office on the north colonnade. There is no one of his type to fill his place, and the position of Tomb Guard now goes by rotation among the younger men.

Dispensing with an insubordinate clerk was not the only show of authority which Dodge thought necessary at the time of his installation—always, of course, with the Regent's concurrence. He transferred the sale of photographs and canes from a stand in front of the Tomb to the Post Office, located then in that useful building called the Gardener's House, which for years has been the Watch Room and security headquarters. During repairs to the furnace he was startled to find the timbers above it actually charred, so that everyone marvelled that they had so long escaped ignition. He had the furnace taken down and re-set, in a pit twenty inches lower, and the rafters above it were covered with asbestos cloth—"a material it is impossible to burn"—and that in turn was overlaid with galvanized iron, with which the old chimney was also lined clear to the top, thus preserving the Mansion, he believed, from the perpetual menace of destruction by fire.

His inspection and inventory were thorough, and might well have been discouraging, but no hint of any such weakness shows through the forward march of this first Report, though in later years he described as "pitiable" the condition of the buildings as he had found them, with leaking roofs and crumbling foundations. There was dry rot in the Banquet Room floor, and the Sitting-room carpet had covered an even more serious condition of decay. The little stairway leading up to Washington's Bedroom was nearly worn away, and new planks were laid on top of the old. The interior of the Cupola had been so picked at by "relic-hunters" who had carried away bits of plaster and lath that it had to be entirely refinished. Except as a special dispensation, no one is now allowed to climb the twisting steps to this superb look-out where a small colored boy used to be posted to give warning of visitors' approach from the Alexandria road. Pencil-marks covered the woodwork of the third-floor rooms, which are not now shown. Dodge had them all cleaned and painted, and posted notices imposing a fine for further defacement, and in one instance actually collected, he does not say what sum. The main staircase was in critical condition and had to be bolted from the second-floor landing to the floor of the attic room above. The Baltimore firm of Emmart and Quartley had been engaged at her own expense by the Vice-Regent for New York State (Mrs. Townsend) to repair damage caused in the Banquet Room by the fall of the central part of the ceiling, which necessitated the re-tinting of the walls when the ceiling had been restored, and Dodge called on their workmen to refinish the doors of the ground-floor rooms as well. Even the lightning-rods received his attention, and being judged insufficient by an expert were at the Regent's desire economically re-tipped at a cost of $12. To install new hollow copper rods would have cost $60. Today as a precaution against the violent Potomac thunderstorms there are about a hundred lightning-rods on the buildings, and some thirty-five trees also carry rods and are grounded.

The old lunch-room, affixed to the Family Kitchen and long a contentious point between the Vice-Regents and Hollingsworth, was now removed entirely, and the Kitchen with a stove in its fireplace was to be kept warm in winter for the use of visitors who found the weather too much for them. Some of the lunch-room fittings were sold to a man named Gibbs, who continued to run an unsightly sort of stand outside the north, or landward, gate, which was a nuisance for some time to come. The old lunch-room's roof was utilized by Dodge on a wagon-shed and store-house for tools.

Some tiles in the floor of the portico, or piazza, were broken and had been replaced by a contractor who had made imitations of Portland cement. Washington had imported the originals from England a hundred years before, and replacements appeared impossible to secure, though they were eventually traced to their source in 1914, by one of Dodge's major miracles. A brick pavement was laid in front of the Tomb. $80.

The wharf was, as always and continually, a grave and expensive problem, and repairs were undertaken by Captain Blake, who ran the little daily steamer *W. W. Corcoran* from Washington City—an estimable man with an imposing white beard and a towering temper, whose habit it was to welcome the passengers at the gang-plank with a flourish and then retire to the cabin for a game of cribbage with Dodge during the voyage. Besides new cribbing and timbers, the pavilion waiting-room on the wharf was improved against the weather by replacing lattice-work with windows and doors, and the ugly black fence was done away with, the surface being then finished off with gravel and crushed oyster-shells. They were able to make do with this patchwork until the turn of the century when Mrs. (George) Hearst poured thousands of her own money into the riverfront repairs.

The walks and roads inside the grounds were in such need of attention that the Regent authorized Dodge to hire extra labor from the neighborhood at 90¢ for a 10-hour day, and he set them to cleaning the drains and ditches of leaves and rubbish, and cutting away the undergrowth from the sloping lawn above the river in front of the Mansion. The piping and draining of a pool of stagnant water was interrupted by a downpour of rain, illustrating the necessity of more extensive drainage measures, which were undertaken by James Archer a few years later.

The old Greenhouse boiler had collapsed during the winter of 1885, imperilling the plants there, some of which were believed to go back to Washington's time by direct descent, and the Regent had ordered a new one, the bill for which was awaiting the convenience of the Association. At the suggestion of the Vice-Regent for Georgia (Mrs. Eve) the old Kitchen Garden, long in disuse as too shady for growing vegetables, was now put into shape for the culture of small fruits, and currants, gooseberries, raspberries, and strawberries had been set out and were doing well, and might in time prove profitable—in 1869 they had sold fresh strawberries out of a big yellow bowl for 25¢ a saucer. The sod of the 8-acre lawn around the house was defective, and Dodge had limed it with oyster-shell, harrowed, sowed blue-grass, and purchased a horse-mower for $90 to economize labor.

"Farming for profit at Mount Vernon I should never advocate under the present circumstances," he reported, adding his belief that it would always grow sufficient provender for the livestock, and he went into some detail on the advantages of a forty-ton silo which he desired to build. Unhappily, his pessimistic view was justified, and except for hay and cover-crops farming at Mount Vernon was gradually abandoned. At this time he listed 5 horses, one very old and only good for light work about the grounds; 3 old cows, two of them milkers, the other of no account; 2 young cows, one of poor quality; 2 heifers; 2 calves; and 1 bull, "an inferior specimen." With the Regent's permission he had done a little trading, and acquired a fine new cow with a good calf. There were 30 old chickens and about 100 hatched that year, and the poultry department under Sarah had yielded some $30.61, presumably in eggs sold.

"To the fencing of the estate I must call your especial attention," he continued, while the Vice-Regents sat enthralled, for Hollingsworth was never like this. "That along the north line is in the worst condition. Built so long ago, it has stood the wear and tear of the succeeding years with more or less strength of character, but its ability longer to uphold the dignity and protection of Mount Vernon has departed. Every season the fox-hunters ride over it and break it down without difficulty, the neighbors' stock jump in, and ours jump out. You will readily understand, therefore, the necessity for an entirely new structure . . . .

"There is another matter the importance of which is so prominently before me as to cause the gravest consideration and watchfulness. It is the protection of the Mansion from accident by fire. I found upon my arrival that several modern appliances had been adopted from time to time for this purpose. An old-fashioned suction engine had been tried and finally put aside. Three chemical extinguishers were presented to the Association, but through disuse were rusted and found to be unserviceable . . . ."

Paragraph by paragraph the intelligent, painstaking summary went on, until he came to the last one.

"In conclusion, please allow me to state that while my interest in Mount Vernon is great, and my efforts untiring, I have not been able to accomplish all my plans by reason of the fact that in every direction I turn something important to be done looms up before me. My incessant communications to the Regent must have indeed wearied her, and I am more than grateful for the kindness and consideration with which my importunities have been treated.

"Trusting that my very earnest efforts, as shown by the foregoing report, may meet your entire approbation, I beg the honor to subscribe myself, Your very obedient servant, HARRISON H. DODGE. E. & O.E." [Errors and Omissions Excepted.]

There would come a time before long when the conclusion of his Reports would be answered by spontaneous applause, but it is probable that in 1886 he had given them too much to think about. His payroll was some $4,000, his expenditures were over $10,000, his gross receipts were only a little over $8,000. His commission as Superintendent for the coming year was still to be signed, with the approval of Council. Some of them must have wondered if he was going to be worth it, and he must have wondered if he was already fired. But the decision was unanimous. They wanted him to stay.

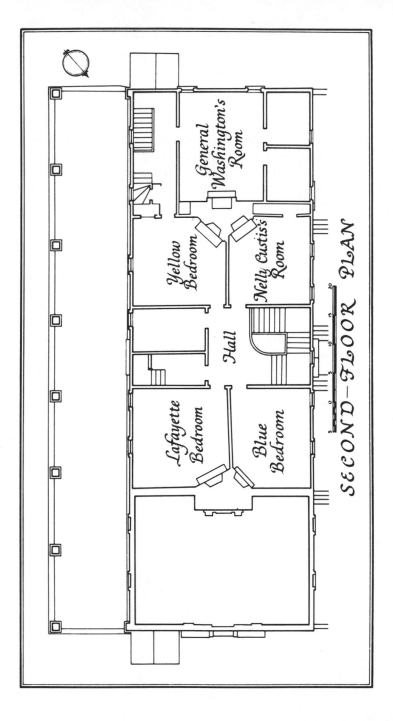

Lafayette
Bedroom

Yellow
Bedroom

General
Washington's
Room

Hall

Blue
Bedroom

Nelly Custis's
Room

SECOND-FLOOR PLAN

The Mansion

2

Nowadays the visitors enter the Mansion through the door into the Banquet Room from the west front, which is confusing, as it is probable that Washington's guests arriving by the Alexandria road must have entered the Central Hall by the middle door on the west front behind the staircase, from where they could pass into the parlors and the Family Dining-room. But Dodge's visitors until 1936 approached from the river side and the path from the wharf, and passed through the door from the piazza to the little stairway which leads abruptly to the second floor and Washington's Bedroom.

The room in which Washington died was remodelled by Judge Bushrod during his tenancy in the early 1800's. He introduced sash windows which when raised opened on to the upper story of the South Porch, also added by Bushrod, outside the Library beneath. As his wife was a chronic invalid it was doubtless a convenience to her to have access from the bedroom to the outer air without negotiating the staircase to the piazza which was so much used by Washington's household and guests.

In 1868, on the suggestion of the Vice-Regent for New Jersey (Mrs. Halsted) the rooms of the Mansion were assigned to any Vice-Regent who would undertake to repair and furnish one. The Association history of Washington's Bedroom began with Mrs. Emma Reed Ball, who immediately after her appointment as Vice-Regent for Virginia assumed its care. Mrs. Ball and Mrs. Ella Bassett Washington of West Virginia both had Washington connections, by marriage as well as by blood, Mrs. Ball having married the grandson of Washington's brother Charles, through his daughter Frances who married Burgess Ball. Judge Charles Burgess Ball of Leesburg served on the Advisory Committee until his death in 1884, and his widow would be an active member of Council for forty-four years, until 1919, and was dean of the whole Association when she died. The latter part of her life was singularly lonely, as she had lost all five of her sons and was without a living relative except for a devoted cousin. She was always eloquent in Council debates, especially when on the opposite side from Mrs. Washington, and their flashing wit provided many a sparkling interchange.

She was notably kind to timid new Vice-Regents, who had good reason to remember her warm Southern voice and ready handclasp with affection. Mrs. Mary N. Walcott (Indiana) speaking a brief memorial in 1919, left a delightful impression of this great lady: "It was my privilege to go with her from Council last May. She was happy almost to elation over the meeting; she spoke again and again of her love for and confidence in our Regent [Miss Comegys]; she related many anecdotes of the early days at Mount Vernon, and spoke of her own girlhood, of her family and friends, of her love of music—all in her own charming and eloquent manner. When we arrived at Washington, she saw two soldiers (privates) standing near the car. She asked one of them to carry her bag and the other to call a cab, and they did her bidding with evident pleasure, placing her as carefully in the cab as would her own sons. She thanked them graciously and, as she rode away, leaned far out and waved her hand to us as we three stood watching her out of sight."

In 1877 Mrs. Ball had reported to Council the return of the wide walnut bedstead with slender turned posts on which Washington had died, and which through Mrs. Ball was entrusted to the Association by General Custis Lee, great-great-grandson of Martha. There was no doubt of its authenticity, as it had been removed from Arlington by his mother when she left there in the tragic spring of 1861, just before the Federal Army took possession of the house. Writing in 1909, General Lee said that Mrs. Lee had conveyed the bedstead in a wagon to Ravensworth, which was her mother's home and later his, where it remained until at Mrs. Ball's request it was sent to be cleaned and renovated by an Alexandria furniture company, from where it went back to Mount Vernon. This disposes of the legend which somehow found its way into the early guide-books that the bedstead had passed through many ownerships since leaving Arlington until it was finally "discovered" by General Lee in a Negro cabin in Alexandria—one of many far-fetched myths which flourished during the 19th century concerning everything that Washington ever owned or touched.

Installed where it had stood at the time of his death, the bed was dressed as it was believed to have been, with the white dimity curtains mentioned in Martha's will. But when in the 1950's, after many replacements and a "war-time expedient" of unbleached material, new dimity was required, the word and the fabric were no longer in use and the curtains had to be reproduced, that is to say specially woven, from an ancient fragment as a sample. Dimity, which continued to engage the attention of the experts for years, was a fine, thin, corded cotton cloth, with self-stripes of varying width, heavier than would be used today for similar purposes, but in the 1951 Minutes the Regent recorded: "The dimity curtains for General Washington's room are in exact reproduction of the dimity of the slip-cover to the cushion which was on Martha's own chair in that room. This came to us in the Edmund Law Rogers Smith Collection. The tape and fringe are also duplicated, even to the point of 720 hand-made knots to the yard." The Regent added that they were "simple, dignified, and 'genteel,' as Mrs. Washington would have wished." What may now appear as tedious minutiae only illustrate the energy and careful research with which the Association has always striven to learn and to restore or reproduce the actual appearance of Mount Vernon as Washington knew it. The Smith Collection, which had come down through Martha's granddaughter, Eliza Parke Custis Law, was the most important accession of 1949, and was contained in an original trunk of Washington's—it consisted largely of articles of clothing, needlework, and the famous false teeth, which have gained such an unwarranted amount of notoriety and have never been exhibited.

In 1901 Mrs. Richardson (Louisiana) bought and presented to the Association a small lap-desk once owned by Martha, having traced it to a great-granddaughter of Nelly Custis Lewis. Its pedigree appeared in her State Report, and proved the meticulous care with which the "relics" were researched before being exhibited as genuine. "It was the property of Mrs. Washington, who gave it to her granddaughter, Eleanor Parke Custis (Mrs.

Lawrence Lewis) who bequeathed it to her daughter, Frances Parke Lewis, who married Edward G. W. Butler, who left it to her daughter, Isabel Butler, who became Mrs. George Williamson, whose daughter Isabel Butler Williamson is now Mrs. Arthur Hodges, from whom it was purchased."

Louisiana had been temporarily without a Vice-Regent at the time the rooms were first assigned, and therefore had none designated. Mrs. Richardson was, however, generous in contributing to other rooms when each was still known by the name of the State which had undertaken to provide for it, a tradition which was discontinued in 1910. Martha's desk was accordingly placed in the Virginia Room, as Washington's Bedroom was then known. However, the writing desk now in the room was purchased in the 1930's from descendants of Nelly's sister Martha Parke Custis Peter. They possessed an authentic collection of furniture known to have belonged to Martha Washington, which had been inherited by them from her great-granddaughter Mrs. Beverly Kennon of Tudor Place in Georgetown, who died in 1911 at the age of ninety-six. By renting the mansion to Union Army officers during the Civil War Mrs. Kennon had preserved it from the confiscation which was visited upon nearby Arlington after Mrs. Robert E. Lee had fled from it, in haste and in tears, taking with her what Washington treasures could be loaded into a wagon, along with the bedstead. Some of the Arlington memorabilia were also brought to Tudor Place and joined to those already there, but most of the furniture received by the Association from the Peter heirs had never moved in the one hundred and thirty-four years since it left Mount Vernon as the heritage of Martha Peter after Mrs. Washington's death in 1802. And it was in this writing-desk, with its tambour top and brass gallery, that the only two surviving letters from Washington to his wife were found—those written just before he left Philadelphia in 1775 to take command of the army outside Boston—those beginning "My dearest—" and signed "Yr. entire—G. WASHINGTON." All the rest she burned.

Mrs. Kennon's grandson, Freeland Peter, of Tudor Place, in an address on the annual Governor's Day ceremonial at Mount Vernon in 1922, gave some reminiscences which were preserved in the Minutes. He recalled coming as a child to Mount Vernon with Mrs. Kennon and hearing of her own childhood visits there with her mother, who was Martha Custis Peter—her baby sister Columbia trotting alongside the tall General up and down the piazza, a little hand clasped around one of his massive fingers. Freeland Peter had often sat at the desk himself to write his letters, had dwelt all his life among Washington memories and relics, and his favorite stories were those told by his grandmother who had had them from her own mother, who had known Washington from the days of her own childhood and early married life.

The Peter desk is French. When the eccentric French Minister, the Comte de Moustier, representing his country to the first administration, was about to return home in 1790, he sold the contents of his fine New York house, which then became briefly the presidential mansion until the seat of government was moved to Philadelphia. It is believed that this desk, which was a lady's and was probably used by de Moustier's equally eccentric sister-in-law, who acted as his hostess in America, remained in Washington's possession, having been purchased by him along with the larger "shaving-table" which was recovered in 1905 from the heirs of Dr. David Stuart. Stuart was the second husband of Jacky Custis's widow, and Washington willed the table to him. The money to purchase the Stuart table was contributed equally by five Vice-Regents.

Mrs. Richardson was for years relentless in her pursuit of items associated with the Washington family, many of which had migrated to Louisiana through the marriages of Nelly's daughters Frances Parke and Mary Angela Lewis to Edward Butler and Charles Conrad respectively. She rarely came to Council without bringing some gift which she had acquired by purchase or persuasion. In 1893 the Relic Committee took official note of her "generous energy" in collecting contributions which ranged from a miniature of Washington (with affidavit) and three pieces of lace worn by Martha and a needle-book, to Washington's spy-glass, which had somehow passed through the ownership of Senator Yancy of Alabama and Jefferson Davis to reach the Association via the friendship between Mrs. Davis and Mrs. Richardson. The exquisite carved ivory fan with a painted medallion now in the Museum was one of Martha's

possessions entrusted to Mrs. Richardson by the Conrads in
1894. And it was she who was responsible for the presentation
to the public schools of large framed photogravures of the Gilbert Stuart portrait, in her endeavor "to create a love and ven-
eration for the character of Washington." She also presented to
the Association an "original" of Stuart's many copies of the
painting, which he turned out for sale for years after the sitting,
and which she had secured, with certificates of its genuineness,
from her sister-in-law at Louisville. The whole Council rose
spontaneously to its feet to receive this valued gift in 1904, and
it hangs now above the mantel-piece in the Banquet Hall. This
widely circulated portrait, which has become the standard image of the first President, was painted late in his life (1798) by
an unlikable man for whom he felt no friendliness such as he
had had for Peale and Trumbull, and consequently it lacks
much, especially in the copies, of the good looks and benevo-
lence of the man as other painters saw him.

Unlike some of the Vice-Regents, who made the grand gesture
and then would collect by contribution and other expedients
from their State to reimburse themselves, Mrs. Richardson bore
all the expense herself. At the same time she was closely identified with Tulane University, where the medical building was a
memorial to her husband, who died in 1892. Described as a
"joyous, humorous spirit," she received from Miss Comegys the
finest tribute anyone could ask for, when the fourth Regent
wrote: "It always did you good to be with Mrs. Richardson."

Owing to the desire to have in the room only genuine Washington articles, it remained rather bare until in 1912 Mrs. Lizzie
Johnson Johnston (Alabama) spoke to the Council on the importance of making Washington's room "more homelike." Certain additions were therefore made, and the rug from the Yellow
Bedroom next door was offered by the Vice-Regent for West
Virginia and accepted, though the Bedroom carpet was to
remain a vexing problem for years.

In the general overhaul, repair, and refurbishing which was
undertaken in anticipation of the Association Centennial in 1953,
the brown Aubusson carpet which had been placed in the room
in 1912, "while dignified and quiet in feeling," was not favorably regarded, as there was no record of Washington's ever hav-

ing purchased an Aubusson, though his orders for Wiltons remain. The first investigation had dragged on through the 1920's, with committees and offers of donations, until Mrs. Hetty Cary Harrison, then Vice-Regent for Virginia, was authorized to buy "at any price it was necessary to pay" a suitable carpet for the Bedroom.

Mrs. Harrison, who married her first cousin Fairfax Harrison, was a descendant of Gouverneur Morris, and thus also a connection of Constance Cary (Mrs. Burton Harrison) whose lively reminiscences rival the famous Diary of Mrs. Mary Chesnut as a vivid account of life in the Confederacy during the Civil War. She was later associated with Mrs. Townsend (New York) in the amateur theatricals which raised such substantial amounts for the Mount Vernon Endowment Fund in the 1870's. The Vice-Regent was inoculated from girlhood with the ideals of the Association, and was an enthusiastic supporter of later restoration enterprises such as Williamsburg, Stratford, and Monticello. As Chairman of the Furnishings Committee she discovered many valuable pieces, including the table long displayed in the Family Dining-room, which found their way to Mount Vernon. She was less successful in the matter of the rug, and finally a rag carpeting sample, woven on a hand-loom, was copied under the auspices of the New Hampshire Arts and Crafts, and is now on the floor.

In 1928 Dodge accomplished in this room a feat of efficiency and overtime which must hold some kind of record. The white mortar finish of the ceiling was discovered to be "letting go," and on a Friday evening it was decided that repairs were imperative. Saturday night when the visitors had gone the room was completely cleared, and a scaffolding was erected. Mount Vernon employees—probably the Neitzey-Miller-Rouse team— worked that night to remove the loose plaster. On Sunday morning two skilled plasterers from Washington City arrived and pronounced the laths, especially above the bed, so defective that they too must be renewed. By sundown this had been accomplished, and the new base coat had been put on. The scaffold was taken down, the débris cleared away, and the floor cleaned and scrubbed. Early Monday morning before the gate opened, the furniture was replaced, and the room was opened to view.

By Wednesday the "rough coat" had dried ready for the white finish coat, and that evening the room was dismantled for the second time. The scaffold was again erected, and at 7:30 A.M. on Thursday the plasterers "white-coated" the entire ceiling in time for a thorough clean-up and the replacement of all the furniture and the rug before the first visitors came through the gate. Thus demonstrating the usefulness of the Sunday closing, of course.

In January, 1949, the room was again dismantled and this time closed briefly "for structural research" under the direction of Walter Macomber, who had become the Architect for Restoration at Mount Vernon after having done valuable work at Williamsburg. During this upheaval the bed was set up in the Yellow Bedroom, and the other furniture was distributed through the rest of the rooms. The plain white walls are now as they were when Washington finally returned from the War to occupy the chamber, and Bushrod's sash windows have been rebuilt to their original proportions.

The story of the Bedroom wall-paper, a fragment of which was found beside the mantel-piece during the 1928 repairs, occupied many pages of the Minutes and caused considerable correspondence and excitement during the 1930's. Enough of the pattern remained so that some hope of identification with existing blocks was aroused. Washington was believed to be the first person in America to order wall-paper for his house, and his invoices, one as early as 1757, still survive. Therefore the date 1775, when the room was completed in his absence at Cambridge, seemed a logical conclusion. The pattern of the paper was carefully reconstructed and reproduced by a New York firm, and the paper was hung in 1931. A photograph taken at that time shows a somewhat positive design of landscape lozenges enclosed by widely spaced vertical stripes, which was echoed by the slip-cover of a large wing-chair near the bed. Subsequent investigation dated the wall-paper design nearer 1840, during the tenancy of Bushrod's nephew John A. Washington, Sr., when a family letter mentioned that the room was then being papered for the first time. A letter from Lund Washington, who managed the estate while the General fought the War, established further that the room was not papered at the

time of its original finish. In November of 1775, when Martha
was already on her way to join Washington at the Cambridge
winter headquarters, Lund wrote to the General: "I have not
yet got rid of the plasterer. Perhaps my next letter will tell you
he is done. Mrs. Washington concluded to leave the room intended for her chamber done quite plain, no ornaments upon the
ceiling, the sides plain stucco." Obviously impatient at the endless
delays which afflicted the whole building operation, Martha had
elected to make do with the plaster "white coat" alone, so that
she could take possession of the room and arrange it for what
was hoped at that time would be Washington's imminent return.
Actually it was six years before he saw the room, on his way to
Yorktown.

The Windsor armchair now placed beside the bed was presented by Mrs. Hearst in 1892. Traditionally it stood there during the long night when Washington died, and had been given
to a faithful slave (probably the one called Christopher) who
was in constant attendance on him. The chair occupied by Mrs.
Washington was said by Tobias Lear in his eye-witness account
of the death chamber to have been at the foot of the bed. Mrs.
Hearst's report on her gift gives no inkling of how she traced
the servant's chair to his granddaughter, from whom she purchased it in Washington City, but she was somehow satisfied
of its authenticity. Her long residence in the capital as the wife
of the Senator from California doubtless established the contact.
In the seat is a handsome reproduction of the cockle-shell pattern needlework cushions worked by Martha, one of the originals having been presented for the room by Mrs. Ball in 1891.
Two more originals came later from Mrs. Eleanor Agnes Goldsborough, second Vice-Regent for Maryland. The same design
now occurs on the chair-cushions in the Music Room.

In 1910 money was raised by contribution to purchase a
leather-covered armchair supposed to have belonged to Washington's mother, Mary Ball Washington, "when he was an
infant." This piece was already on loan at Mount Vernon, and
had been placed in Washington's Bedroom, though its presence
there during his lifetime is very unlikely—there is no record of
her ever having visited the house after it came into his possession in 1752. The chair's elderly owner's decision to sell it was

a form of blackmail, and the Association paid. There was for years a sort of sentimental Mary Ball cult, fostered by Benson Lossing, for one, with his book called *Mary and Martha*, as well as by the Vice-Regent for Virginia who had married into the Ball family and devoted a great deal of research to its history. Even doubtful Mary Ball items were zealously sought out, regardless of the embarrassing fact that no very close attachment existed between that intransigent woman and her strong-willed son, who nevertheless rendered her always the unfailing courtesy and generosity he felt was due. Various imaginative claims were made from time to time by owners of traditional relics of Washington's mother—a bookcase with a Fielding Lewis pedigree, which also stood for a time in the Bedroom—her aunt's bedstead—her wedding ring (with history)—some earrings said to have been given by her to Martha as an engagement present (she lived at Fredericksburg and there is no evidence that she encountered either her son or his fiancée during the brief "engagement")—and at least four portraits, all "so-called." The last of these was banished from Mount Vernon's walls in 1939, with the reluctant conclusion that no authentic likeness would ever be found.

The arm-chair with the Mary Ball association, re-covered in chintz, has been moved to the Library, and the wing-chair now in the Bedroom is known to have been at Mount Vernon before it returned there on loan in 1951. The trunk at the foot of the bed is one used by Washington during the Revolution, and carries his name on a brass plate, with the simple address, "Virginia." It must have been brought home by him, and after being taken away by the heirs, was sent back in 1882 by Mrs. Goldsborough.

Meanwhile the room has acquired the small touches which make it look real, and lived in—Martha's darning-basket, with the needles still in a piece of knitting, bequeathed by Jacky Custis's widow; a medicine box-table which came back in 1875; a "cap table" presented in 1927 by Mrs. Hanks (Wisconsin); a lacquer dressing-mirror, oval, with drawers, presented in 1894 by Mrs. Conrad—again thanks to Mrs. Richardson—and the portraits by Pine of the Custis granddaughters, which had hung on the walls during Martha's lifetime.

ii

The Yellow Bedroom, through which visitors used to pass from Washington's Bedroom to the upper hall and the main staircase by a door which Bushrod had cut through to the little passage above the back stairs, was the last to be adopted and furnished. It was undertaken by Mrs. Ella More Bassett Washington (West Virginia) who described its forlorn appearance then as "an aching void." Her husband was Colonel Lewis Washington, great-great-grandson of George's elder half-brother Augustine, called "Austin." As aide to Governor Wise of Virginia in 1859 Lewis had the unique experience of being captured and held as hostage by John Brown at Harper's Ferry, before the hopeless fight there which ended in Brown's surrender. Colonel and Mrs. Washington were cousins, and their only son, D'Hertbern Washington, who died unmarried in 1914, was one of the last close blood-links to the General. The Lewis Washingtons' house, Beallair, from which he was taken in the middle of the night in his own carriage to Harper's Ferry, stands near his Uncle Charles's house called Happy Retreat, which was left unfinished at his death. Happy Retreat was given an imposing classic central section in the mid-1800's and renamed Mordington. It is still occupied and in good condition, with its original name restored.

Mrs. Ella Washington had been a beautiful and fortunate young woman, reared in luxury and happiness, but like so many Southern families hers survived the Civil War "rich only in misfortunes," and she bore her later sorrows and reverses with dignity and fortitude, a very great lady to the end.

Besides a small bureau and wash-stand, she placed in the Yellow Bedroom the bedstead which had been used by Washington during his visits to Eltham, the Bassett home near Williamsburg. It was to this house that Martha's son Jacky Custis was conveyed after contracting camp-fever during the siege at Yorktown, and there, possibly on the same bedstead, he had died in the autumn of 1781. It stands now in the Blue Bedroom, where it has more room for its size.

The Yellow Bedroom was believed to be the one which the Washingtons had occupied before the addition on the south was raised in 1775, providing a private wing with the Library on the ground floor and the master's bedroom above, reached by its own stairway. Some confusion resides in the fact that for a few years the Yellow Bedroom was done over in green, but by 1928 it had been restored to its original color, as discovered by Miss Cunningham in 1869 when she wrote to Mrs. Halsted: "I crawled up the staircase since I wrote you last and examined the papering in the room above me. There are seven layers. . . . You remember I sent you a copy of a paper in General Washington's handwriting about the bedrooms, in which two were spoken of as the Blue Room and the Yellow Room, and the others the River Room and the Lafayette Room. The inside paper is the yellow paper, solid color; that is a guide, I think, for the bedrooms, at least." As she was then occupying what is now furnished as a downstairs bedroom, this letter of hers leaves little doubt about the one above it.

Now that traffic moves in the opposite direction and arrives last of all at Washington's Bedroom through the Yellow Room, it is amusing to note that an antique bird-cage, with a stuffed cardinal therein, hung in this room until on the suggestion of the all-seeing guards it was removed to "a less provocative spot," as it "induced a spirit of levity" especially in the young, at odds with the reverence which the approach to the General's room should command.

iii

Emerging from the Yellow Bedroom into the upper hall, Dodge's flock would find on their right the little room sometimes known as the Guest Room, fronting on the center of the piazza, and supposed to have belonged to Jacky Custis, who arrived at Mount Vernon as a child of six after his widowed mother's marriage to Washington. It was appropriate that little Delaware should claim this smallest room, and Mrs. Comegys had begun to furnish it at the time of her death in 1888. It was finished by her daughter Harriet, who sent on the articles chosen for the room by her mother.

Next to Mrs. Eve in seniority, most admired and trusted by Miss Cunningham of all the early Vice-Regents who came together at the end of the Civil War, Mrs. Comegys was without doubt a powerful influence and support during the agonizing years when there was no money and it seemed sometimes as though there never would be enough—but she left very little correspondence to speak for her and remains something of an enigma. She had twice offered the warmth and comfort of her Dover home to the frail first Regent, who found there an enfolding family affection which soothed and strengthened her beleaguered soul. "Now, Lady fair," Mrs. Comegys would say reasonably, to a wilful colleague, before uttering her well-considered counsel. She was one of three close friends to whom Miss Cunningham, dying almost alone at her South Carolina plantation in 1875, left her private papers, and it was to her that Miss Cunningham's piteous last letter was written. She served as Vice-Regent for all of thirty years, and her daughter Harriet succeeded her and then became the fourth Regent.

At her death in 1927 at the age of eighty-four, Miss Harriet was the last person who had actually seen the then almost legendary founder of the Association, with the single exception of Miss Jane Riggs, daughter of the first Treasurer, who was born in the year Miss Cunningham launched her crusade for Mount Vernon and followed her own mother and Mrs. Barnes as Vice-Regent for "the District." Ten years younger than Miss Comegys, Miss Janie's recollections of Miss Cunningham would have been mainly those of a child.

Miss Comegys herself was to become a legend, holding the vice-regency for Delaware from 1888 to 1909, when the third Regent, Mrs. Townsend, resigned during Council because of failing health, after fifteen years as Vice-Regent for New York State and eighteen years as Regent—a woman "of exquisite courtesy and tact, charitable, with a keen sense of humor," and a commanding presence. At Mrs. Townsend's request her letter of resignation was read for her to Council by Mrs. Christine Blair Graham of Missouri—an affecting occasion for her colleagues, only relieved by Mrs. Maxey's gracious inspiration to propose an honorary Regency for life, which was instantly seconded by every Vice-Regent rising to her feet. An impulse to adjourn and compose themselves was interrupted by Mrs. Hudson's recollection of the necessity to nominate a successor. Mrs. Richardson named Miss Comegys, who was by no means next in seniority, but she was at once "elected by acclamation," passing over among others Mrs. Hudson, who at eighty-six was the dean, Mrs. Ball, who would have another ten years as Vice-Regent for Virginia, and Miss Longfellow, whose attendance at Council was rather irregular owing to her many trips abroad for her health.

When Council met the following day, Miss Comegys was in the chair, but Mrs. Townsend read the Psalm and the prayer. She was never again able to attend in her honorary capacity, but wrote a touching letter of thanks when her badge was sent on to her, to remain in her possession. Miss Comegys therefore took over in the fiftieth year since Mount Vernon came into the actual possession of the Association in 1860, and her long memory went back to the days when she had as a child accompanied her mother to Mount Vernon, and the Vice-Regents at Council time slept three in a bed in the upstairs Mansion rooms, and had to put up umbrellas over their pillows when it rained.

Her close friendship with Mrs. Frances Johnson Rogers of Maryland who was Corresponding Secretary resulted in an exchange of many intimate if rather formal letters between them —"My dear Maryland—" and "My dear Regent—"—which nevertheless revealed that behind the prickly spinster façade of the fourth Regent there existed a lonely, lovable, if acerbic character—a woman so desolate that when two young visiting cousins gave her the closer title of "aunt" she was grateful for the extra warmth it conveyed.

Her tart comments to Maryland spared not even Dodge himself, whom she accused of always getting his own way, notwithstanding his soothing "my dear lady" tone. Of the Treasurer, Mr. Brice, who seemed to her not to be satisfied with anything in 1918, she wrote in exasperation, "I *never* knew a more trying man!" She thought the very capable, if elusive, chief engineer Archer "an unnecessary addition to our Staff," and she was "not impressed" by a paper Miss Longfellow had written and submitted for her opinion. "I dont approve of *any* of the DAR business methods!" she announced with her Victorian imperiousness, resenting the general impression, which was hardly the fault of the DAR, that they owned Mount Vernon.

Miss Comegys suffered a painful fall in 1919, and Mrs. Rogers was named Acting Regent during her enforced absence from Council. She had thereafter a bad knee, but would not use crutches, preferring to lean on her maid. Taxes worried her, and she complained that her servants had become lax and not sufficiently respectful, and she was too much alone in her big house, called The Green at Dover—"It is a sad time for me—I am the last of my line, and am low in my mind," she confided to the Secretary. She could not get along with Mrs. Rathbone, who as one of the seniors became dictatorial. "Illinois [Mrs. Harriet Isham Carpenter] has charm, cleverness, and much else, but no hesitation about coming forward *at once* with upsetting propositions," she remarked, in 1919. Apparently Mrs. Carpenter had spoken up too soon, though a search of the Minutes fails to reveal anything upsetting in her continuance of the work on the Illinois Room, or West Parlor, for which she made a needlework chair-cover and provided funds raised in her State. But Miss Comegys, having formed her opinion, was once heard to mutter during Council, "I wish she would sit down. I don't like her."

"It was not given to all to see the human side," Mrs. Rogers confessed years later, conceding the spiny exterior. But when in 1927 Miss Comegys in her turn came to resign there was earnest protest in Council, and Mrs. Mary Simpkins Denham (Florida) rose to remind her that "the best work ever done for Mount Vernon was done by a woman who was almost a complete invalid, such an invalid as the present time scarcely ever sees," and proposed an assistant Regent to divide the work and responsibility if Miss Comegys would continue. Miss Comegys was touched, but firm in her determination, and Mrs. Maxey again proposed the honorary expedient, which was graciously accepted. Mrs. Leary (Washington State) then nominated Mrs. Richards of Maine to succeed, and she was unanimously elected by a rising vote of Council. Again the chosen Regent was well down the list in seniority. And while Miss Comegys might have preferred her dear friend Mrs. Rogers, whose age was becoming a factor, her demeanor was perfect: "Miss Comegys called Mrs. Richards to her," the Minutes read, "and with gentle dignity placed over her head the Regent's badge of office, placing in her hands the bouquet of yellow roses, which sentiment gives to the Regent alone the privilege of wearing. After this beautiful ceremony the newly elected Regent took the chair."

But the saying which Miss Comegys should be most remembered for occurred in one of her letters to Dodge during some minor crisis: "Nothing is ever as bad at Mount Vernon as we fear it is going to be," she wrote, out of long experience and many false alarms.

iv

It is probable that Nelly Custis had always been accustomed to consider as hers the bedroom on the east front now known by her name, which she was occupying with her husband, Lawrence Lewis, when her first child, Frances Parke Lewis, was born there during the winter when Washington died. Their new home, called Woodlawn, was still to be built on the Dogue Run Farm tract down the road beyond the Mill, which was bequeathed to them by Washington in his will. He had already made known to them his intention, but he of course never saw the beautiful and pretentious brick house they erected there in the classic "federal" style. There is a persistent legend that he had a hand in its design—now accredited to William Thornton —and if so, it may represent his idea of the residence he might himself have enjoyed if the smaller and more austere Mount Vernon had not already possessed his heart and symbolized his sole ambition. The young Lewises remained at Mount Vernon with Martha until her death in 1802, for Nelly's devotion to her grandmother was passionate, despite what many people had considered Martha's undue severity during Nelly's girlhood.

The room was furnished for Maryland in 1877 by Miss Emily Harper, descendant of the splendid Carrolls of Carrollton, who was once described by Miss Cunningham as her "tower of strength" and who made an annual gift of $50 from her own pocket towards maintenance. "Grace and elegance" were the words most often used by those who cherished her memory when she died, in the same year that the Association lost its second Regent, Mrs. Laughton. She had lived to a great age, with "silvery curls" replacing the smooth Victorian coiffure of Sully's portrait, and with her kinswoman Mrs. Walker of North Carolina had helped to bridge the perilous transition from civil war to chaotic peace, and from Miss Cunningham's tragic decline to the competent wisdom of her successor, during whose tenure the Association turned the corner into the comparative prosperity it has since, with occasional scares, enjoyed. She left a bequest of $1,000 to the Endowment Fund, establishing a precedent which has been followed by several Vice-Regents since then, though it is always a mystery why so many of them in comfortable circumstances allowed Mount Vernon to beg or borrow funds and furnishings for its various needs, rather than take the apparently simpler way of writing a check on their own substantial bank accounts. There was perhaps a sentiment that the thing should be done voluntarily, by a concerted effort and contribution, instead of by a more direct and business-like personal procedure.

A wash-stand and chair were donated to the Custis Room through Miss Harper, by the grandsons of the great Charles Carroll, one of whom was then Governor of the State. There was also a fine mahogany bedstead, "carved and fluted," hair-mattress, linen, and bed-steps, a mahogany bureau with gilt handles, carpet, mirror, pier-table, and a china toilette set.

In 1893 the room passed to the care of Mrs. Goldsborough, long before then a generous contributor to the Association, and she was warmly greeted on her first arrival at Council "by old friends and new." Mrs. Goldsborough was the granddaughter of Nelly's sister Eliza, whose daughter married a Rogers of Baltimore. Like Miss Harper, with whom she was undoubtedly acquainted, Mrs. Goldsborough was "one of the last representatives of the 18th century in dignity of manner and speech"— a lovely white-haired old lady who wore old-fashioned bonnets which tied under her chin. An accident which occurred soon after her appointment and left her permanently lame, so that she referred to herself cheerfully as "an invalid," failed to dim her spirits, but in 1904 she appeared at Council to tender her resignation in person and to nominate as her successor Miss Comegys's devoted friend-to-be, Mrs. Rogers of Baltimore— who may have been Mrs. Goldsborough's cousin.

Few of the Harper pieces now remain, except for the Hepplewhite chairs, from 1877. The crib, which with its charming white net canopy is the feature of the room, was presented in

1915 by Mrs. Marie Worthington Conrad Lehr, the last of the
Conrads. It was believed to have been given by Martha to Nelly
at Mount Vernon in the autumn of 1799, before the birth of
Frances Parke, who would marry Edward Butler and live in Louisiana. There was no apparent family connection, it is to be noted,
between the young veteran of the Mexican War and the notorious Federal General "Beast Butler," whose administration of
New Orleans in 1862 aroused such resentment even in the
North. The crib was probably borrowed for Nelly's Conrad
grandchildren, who were sent to her at her son Lorenzo's house
Audley after the early death of their mother in 1839.

Mrs. Lehr also presented a set of dentist's tools said to have
been used for the slaves by Washington in the rough home doc-
toring of the plantation. More attractive Conrad "relics" were
a piece of Nelly's needlework, framed, with the story that she
had embroidered one for each grandchild, "often working late
at night with only two candles"—one wonders if the implication
was economy; a cane which had belonged to Washington and
which Nelly had had cut down for her own use in her inva-
lided last years, and which she would never let out of her sight;
such personal trinkets as Martha's oval brooch set with pearls
and given by her to Nelly—the Washington women's jewelry
has a certain inexpensive pathos; and a beaded bag, or reticule.

The work-frame which stands on a cherry card-table belonged
also to Nelly, and is part of the magnificent Yale-Kountze
Collection which came to Mount Vernon in 1945. The unfinished needlework piece on the frame was set up by Mrs. Abigail
Parson Coolidge (Massachusetts) who was Chairman of the
Furniture Committee at that time, and it follows Martha's
cockle-shell pattern which is repeated elsewhere in the Mansion.
Mrs. Coolidge, "a gay and buoyant spirit," was the second wife
of John Templeman Coolidge, who had bought the Wentworth
mansion at Portsmouth, New Hampshire, to save it from destruction. It was her privilege to transform that beautiful old
house from an austere "restoration" to a delightful family home,
an accomplishment which was obviously an asset to Mount Vernon. Her Report for 1945 described the "exhilarating day" she
had spent at Mount Vernon rearranging furniture and pictures
to accommodate the priceless accessions in the Yale-Kountze

loan—"under the smiling acquiescence," she added, of the Regent, and with Mr. Wall's "cordial co-operation." It must have been a great day, indeed, when doubtful make-shift pieces could be moved out and replaced with genuine ones of unquestioned pedigree. "Never before," said the Regent's Report for that year, "have so many original Washington pieces and other memorabilia been acquired in one year."

In 1959 the Custis room was entirely done over and received the unique wall-paper which was reproduced from a chintz paper binding on an old domestic account book recording the sale of shad and herring from the local fishery in 1793. It had apparently been covered with a fragment of wall-paper left over from the finish of some undetermined room. Reproduced again as a cover for the 1960 Annual Report of the Association, the paper shows an attractive scrolled and floral pattern of chalk white and plum-to-pink, on a background of the familiar putty-grey so much used in the 18th century. At the same time new dimity window-curtains were added, new bed hangings, and the crib canopy.

v

Crossing the head of the stairs, Dodge's visitors came to the River Room, or Lafayette Room, known as the Pennsylvania Room in the years when the rooms were designated by the name of the State to which they were assigned. Writing to Mrs. Comegys in 1874, when she still considered herself only Acting Regent in Miss Cunningham's absence, Mrs. Laughton said: "I have furnished the Pennsylvania Room, the front chamber next to the Lafayette Room"—and in May she forwarded to Hollingsworth two double mattresses "for my room," indicating her intention to share it during Council. After Mrs. Laughton's death in 1891 Mrs. Hudson moved in Council "that inasmuch as the room known heretofore as the Pennsylvania Room has for 18 years been occupied by the late Regent, and was furnished by her and not by the State of Pennsylvania, that this room be hereafter reserved for the use of the Regent and be known as the Regent's Room." Seconded by Wisconsin (Mrs. Mitchell) and adopted.

It would sometimes seem as though the exceptional women

who formed the Association accumulated in their several lives
an unusual amount of grief for their limited numbers, and the
second Regent was beset by family misfortune from childhood,
when she lost her mother. She had been the close companion of
her financier father, Charles Macalester of Philadelphia, especially after the death of her only brother, and the business training she received from him in the management of her considerable
estate was of great value when after his death she succeeded to
the regency at Mount Vernon.

As a débutante heiress and social belle in Philadelphia and
Washington society before the Civil War, and a friend of President Buchanan's hostess-niece, Harriet Lane, she was on the first
list of appointments made by Miss Cunningham, as Vice-Regent
for Pennsylvania, and was always a tactful and tolerant influence in the stormy early days. She married, quite young, a
Belgian diplomat named Berghmans, who was suspected of being
a fortune-hunter. She spent some time abroad with him during the 1860's, returning to her suspended vice-regency before
Miss Cunningham's death, and was indicated by her as her chosen
successor. In the 1870's Mme Berghmans married again, an obscure Washington clerk much younger than herself, who was
said to be of Cuban origin, despite his conventional name of
Laughton. He must have been in poor health at the time of the
marriage, and after the fashion of the times, which so often
prescribed foreign travel as a remedy for invalids almost too ill
to be moved at all, they went to Algiers, in the hope that the
climate would be beneficial. Within a few months he died there,
and her grief was said to be almost suicidal. But she returned to
Washington, "swathed in crepe," and for the second time resumed her duties to Mount Vernon, attending Council regularly, and going to auctions and sales where Mount Vernon
items could be purchased, meanwhile launching her daughter
by Berghmans into society with a series of brilliant entertainments in her Washington home. Camilla Berghmans married a
Spanish nobleman from the Legation and went abroad to live.
The announcement of the birth of her second child arrived
dramatically by cable during Council in 1891, and was read out
to the Vice-Regents by the delighted grandmother, whereupon
her colleagues voted her "leave of absence" to visit the family

in Madrid. Mrs. Laughton made all possible arrangements to remain in close touch with the Superintendent and Treasurer during her absence, and the date for the next Council was set for June 2, 1892. Whether as a result of the visit to Spain or not, she died suddenly in December of 1891 in her Philadelphia home, and Mrs. Justine Van Rensselaer Townsend of New York became the third Regent by a unanimous election.

Mrs. Laughton had warmth, dignity, and a sparkling wit, besides the executive ability and financial sense which Miss Cunningham so sadly lacked in her later years. Without doubt and in spite of her many tragic preoccupations she brought Mount Vernon to a state of stability and prestige it had never enjoyed before. The Association was "the work of her life," and her unexpected death rocked them all, for they had by then lost twelve of the oldest and most valued members.

In 1912 the then Vice-Regent for Pennsylvania, Mrs. Ella Waln Harrison, reported that the Pennsylvania Room, "to be occupied in the future, as always in the past, by the Regent, has had the bed curtains replaced by new ones, and linen, etc., supplied." Mrs. Harrison's buoyant spirits made her a delightful companion, and it was said that "no situation was so dark that she could not see a way out." She was a descendant of Robert Morris, and had been a Philadelphia society belle in the Laughton tradition. In 1914 she reported wryly that "The Vice-Regent for Pennsylvania has made herself most unpopular by insisting on all of her friends reading and then passing on to their friends the Mount Vernon literature."

The Regent's Room was subsequently occupied by Mrs. Townsend, Miss Comegys, and Mrs. Richards. During the latter's regency the present Administration Building, or North Quarters, was erected, in 1929–1930, across the north lane from the old restored West Quarters—supplying accommodations therein for the Regent and a limited number of Vice-Regents during Council. This ended the occupancy of the Mansion at any time, and with the removal of the cooking operations from the Family Kitchen on the south colonnade to more modern arrangements in the new building the eternal spectre of fire was once more diminished.

There has been some confusion as to whether this room or the

one next to it on the west front was the one occupied by Lafayette on his visits to Mount Vernon, and it is possible that as
he was there more than once he or his son may have used two
different rooms. The tradition in Miss Cunningham's time was
strong that the Blue or New Jersey Room had that honor ex-
clusively. Some time before 1931 the River Room somehow
acquired Lafayette's name. In 1939 it was voted to restore the
original labels to each room "as formerly," but the following
year a memorandum of Washington's was found which seemed
to unsettle the decision again. It is certain that the first Superintendent, Mr. Herbert, who as a kinsman had been assigned
that room during his stay in the house as a guest of the last
Washington to own it, believed that Lafayette had slept in the
room on the west front, which Herbert continued to occupy
until he left Mount Vernon in 1869.

The bedstead, which Mrs. Laughton was convinced that
Washington had used "somewhere in Pennsylvania" on his way
to Valley Forge, the sword-chair beside it, and the Queen Anne
highboy and lowboy are all part of the original furnishing of
the room by the second Regent. The beautiful old red Toile de
Jouy hangings were renewed in 1955 and required a quieter
wall-paper thereafter. The rosy antique Turkish Ghiordes rug
replaced in 1950 an Aubusson judged to be of too late date.

vi

The first Vice-Regent to whom it had occurred that they
themselves might donate or cause to be donated suitable furniture of the right period to restore at least in some degree the
appearance of the house in Washington's time, and incidentally
to provide accommodations for themselves during Council, was
Mrs. Nancy Wade Halsted of New Jersey. Miss Cunningham
promptly turned over to her the bedroom on the west front
then known as Lafayette's, which had been recently emptied
by the departure of Mr. Herbert for his home in Fairfax County.
It was the first room to be completely furnished by the Association—even to a Bible—and by 1872. Mrs. Halsted stipulated
only that she should be allowed to do the room in blue, and
when it was repainted in 1940 scrapings revealed that it had

been blue ever since, though several times redecorated by succeeding Vice-Regents for New Jersey.

Mrs. Halsted was an almost daily correspondent of Miss Cunningham's during the latter's lifetime, and became an indefati-
gable collector of funds and gifts for Mount Vernon. In 1870
she had provided the first furnace for the Mansion, complete
with a plumber from Newark to install it gratis as his own
contribution to the cause. She sent as a gift to the first Regent
a superb new cookstove for the Family Kitchen on the south
colonnade, which prepared Miss Cunningham's meals during
her residence in the Mansion. The colonnade was then in ruins,
and it was Mrs. Halsted too who raised by donations the funds
to rebuild it, thus restoring the symmetry of the west front. In
the early days she supplied one of the most amusing chapters in
the Association history by securing the donation in 1874 of a
cow, named "Lady Washington" by the benefactor—which
had to be shipped—free—from upper New York State to Mount
Vernon, had to be identified and claimed by her at Trenton,
and collected in Alexandria by Hollingsworth. Endless correspondence and complications arose from this inconvenient offering, and "Lady Washington's" progeny were still in evidence
when Dodge took over.

The announcement of Mrs. Halsted's sudden death at her
home outside Trenton while Council was meeting in 1891 was
one of the first functions performed by the new telephone,
which had recently linked Mount Vernon to the Alexandria
and Washington exchange, the expensive installation paid for
by Mrs. Hearst. It is interesting to find that when a few years
later the Association felt able to assume the cost of the annual
telephone charges they discovered that this most generous of all
Vice-Regents had already paid the bill for that year, in advance.
The "unsightly" poles of course caused criticism, and the wires
were laid underground in 1910.

Mrs. Halsted's loss was keenly felt by the junior Vice-Regents, and Mrs. Ella Washington wrote, with her usual turn of
phrase: "It is hard for those of our colleagues who come to us
in this bright period of prosperity to realize in full the utter
darkness of those days of adversity through which our sister
friend worked so nobly."

Lately this room has harbored the Eltham bedstead originally secured by Mrs. Ella Washington for the Yellow Bedroom, which was deemed too small for its display. The leather trunk at the foot of the bed, brass-studded and bound with iron, was used by Martha on her journeys to winter headquarters, and was presented in 1928 by Eliza Custis Law's granddaughter. Inside the lid is pasted a yellowing paper in Eliza's handwriting:

"Washington, July 4th, 1830

My dear Brother who I love much, George Washington Parke Custis, has made me a present of this trunk. I write these lines to tell my dear grandchildren I prize it most dearly. It was that in which the cloaths of my sainted Grandmother Mrs. Washington were always pack'd by her own hands when she went to visit and spend some time with the General, whenever the Army were in quarters. I have stood by it as she put in her cloaths sadly distress'd at her going away—& oh how joyfully when she returned did I look to see her cloaths taken out, & the gifts she always brought for her grandchildren!—no words can express how I loved her—she, and all else most fondly beloved are gone to their proper home among the Angels—my darling Grandchildren, three yet live, I leave this trunk to my Rosebud—it is fill'd with sacred Relics for my children—may God bless them!

ELIZA P. CUSTIS"

vii

The third-floor rooms are not now furnished or shown, but until 1943 on days when traffic was not too heavy on the stairs visitors were permitted to view the room over the General's Bedroom to which Martha was said to have retired after his death. The dreary little legend that she immured herself there till she died more than two years later, her only outlook towards the Tomb, seems to be apocryphal and does not accord with her lifelong commonsense and busy habits. He died in December, and the room has no fireplace and could not be heated except by charcoal brazier. It was of course the custom to close for a time the chamber in which a death had occurred, but there

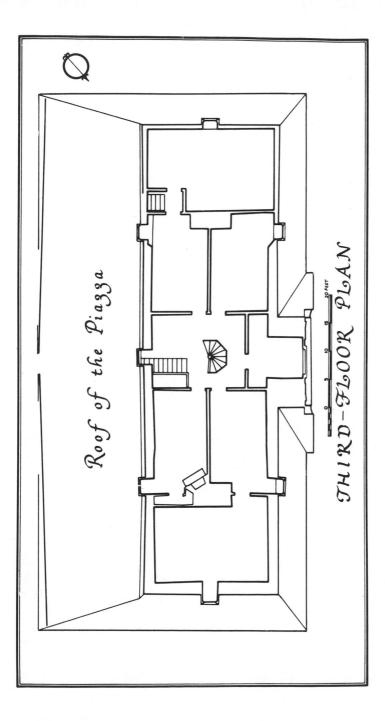

Roof of the Piazza

THIRD-FLOOR PLAN

0   5   10   15   20 FEET

were three comfortable rooms available to her on the second floor, as well as a bedroom on the ground floor behind the Dining-room. Her health became increasingly poor, and it is likely that with Nelly and a new baby in the house, her grief would have been set aside for her normal housewifely routine as long as she was able to pursue it.

Mrs. Martha Reed Mitchell (Wisconsin) asked for the room as early as 1873, "to furnish and occupy at Council time," and it was the first on the third floor to be restored. Mrs. Mitchell was a daughter of the pioneers and widow of a banker-congressman and railroad tycoon, generous with her check-book and popular with her colleagues. Described in the early days as "a mighty nice person," she more than deserved the tribute, having stood steadfastly behind the beleaguered Miss Tracy in the War years, and firmly supported the unhappy necessity, for Mount Vernon's sake, of the first Regent's resignation as her health failed. Mrs. Mitchell always laid her far-sighted plans with a qualifying "D.V."—God willing. She had stoutly opposed any pusillanimous appeal to an indifferent Congress for additional funds in times of debt and discouragement, and during one of many meddlesome attacks by outsiders on the ownership of Mount Vernon by a "passel" of women she wrote, with her bank account behind her pen: "We must not let the place go to anyone, even at any sacrifice!" And again: "Do not let us neglect to hold together and keep the place." That was the spirit which saved Mount Vernon.

Although in 1865 Mrs. Mitchell had written that as a result of the War strain she felt she ought to give way to a younger woman, and in 1868 she was "thinking seriously of resigning," she remained for almost another forty years. Her "steadfast, cool, and kindly judgment" was invaluable during the several crises caused by Miss Cunningham's disabilities. She was the only one of the twenty-two 1858 appointments to see 1900 —at eighty-two—having made the effort successfully to attend the 1899 Council, a year when their circle had for once remained unbroken by death or resignation. This was her last appearance at Mount Vernon, and her place was hard to fill. She was finally followed, in 1914, by Mrs. Hanks, another daughter of the pioneers, who was to become the seventh Regent.

Mrs. Hanks in her turn had felt obliged to resign in 1916, as she had been prevented from attending Council the first two years after her election. Her resignation was declined, and she scarcely skipped a year again, "her personal charm a rich endowment to Mount Vernon for forty years, five of them as Regent"—a post she was reluctant to accept. "I am too old, and haven't any ambition," she said, at sixty-nine. In 1948 she refused a second term as Regent because of an increasing deafness—at seventy-three—reclaiming her vice-regency for Wisconsin instead. In 1953, at the Association Centennial dinner, Mrs. Hanks, known to her intimates as "Molly," gave her reminiscences, going back to 1885 when as a child living in Washington City she had once glimpsed the second Regent, Mrs. Laughton, arriving at her father's house for a reception. Giving up even her vice-regency in 1956, she wrote, "My dear Madam Regent and Ladies—I resign in physical being only. My spirit will be ever with you. At the Council table, as you visit the Tomb or roam through the lovely gardens. But most of all, I believe it will be with you as you sit on the piazza in the approaching twilight, where one always feels the spirit of General Washington abiding in quiet and calm peacefulness."

In reply to telegrams from Council in 1959, expressing their love and remembrance, she replied promptly, "I haven't stood on my feet since last July, but your wires made me want to stand on my head. My dearest love and remembrance go to each and every one of you. . . ."

viii

Mrs. Margaret Mussey Sweat of Maine had modestly chosen the little third-floor bedroom in the half-story above the Banquet Hall, perhaps partly for its privacy, which she would share with a friend during Council. Its walls were finished in colonial buff, and she furnished it in the best of contemporary taste, with a four-posted bed, a mahogany bureau, a Persian rug, gay flowered draperies and pretty chamber china.

Mrs. Sweat was another of Miss Cunningham's appointments who could remember the vicissitudes weathered in the chaotic post-War years when funds were almost unobtainable and it was possible only to hold on, occupying the place by dogged representatives who at least tried to arrest the deterioration which the years of neglect previous to their ownership had made inevitable. "Pretty Mrs. Sweat" rhymed with *sweet* and was one of the handsomest of the ladies. Having a modest reputation as an author, she filled the post of Secretary for many years, while in her letters to her colleagues she left a vivid and touching account of the first Regent's decline and the desperate determination of the founding sisters somehow to survive as an independent organization and carry through the task to which they had dedicated themselves—the preservation and restoration of Mount Vernon.

For some idea of the labor of love involved in the Secretary-ship before the days of the typewriter, which did not arrive at Mount Vernon until 1891, one need only consult the Minutes of 1881, when the question of continued publication of an Annual Report was under discussion. Mrs. Sweat then described how when Council was over the Secretary sat down with a mass of rapidly written manuscript before her, to "the careful and conscientious rendering of the actual record, covering as it usually does, forty solid pages of manuscript." She continued, however, to discharge this onerous duty in her large, clear handwriting and with marked literary talent until 1887. In her letter of resignation (as Secretary, but not as Vice-Regent for Maine) which was read in Council, she reminded them that she had held the office since 1872, when ten Vice-Regents had assembled and the Report was a pamphlet of eight or ten pages—whereas now the attendance was doubled and the Report of the past year covered twenty pages, while the Minutes required forty-five. She protested that her request for "an honorable discharge" did not come from any unwillingness to work, but she added, "I confess I have often grown weary and turned away discouraged from the contemplation of the hastily prepared Minutes of Council which it was my duty to put in order after my return home. I have looked hard several times for an honorable loophole of escape, but have said to myself, and my friendly colleagues have said to me, that to resign when there was so much to do would be like a soldier leaving his post in time of battle.

But our battle with poverty, calumny, and perplexity is now over, and I am at liberty to seek my rest from this especial work. I leave to my successor the fruits of my honest toil in recording the precedents which will henceforth govern and instruct. I feel sure she will not have to grope, as I have had to do, amid uncertainty, for we have all learned how to work well in Council, and work well done is easy to record."

On the twenty-fifth anniversary of her appointment as Vice-Regent Mrs. Sweat presented the Association with twenty-five silver spoons. Her successor as Secretary was another veteran of many years' service, Mrs. Susan E. Johnson Hudson, appointed for Connecticut in 1870. Mrs. Hudson held the secretarial post for ten years, and wrote a spiky, illegible hand which looked well till you came to read it. It should be remembered that the first Secretary, Miss Tracy, was expected to make sufficient copies by hand for all the Vice-Regents and the record file, and that her first attempt to have the Report printed, in 1868, to spare herself this labor, was regarded as revolutionary, and deserving of reprimand by the Regent.

Mrs. Sweat, like Mrs. Hudson, was a confirmed traveller, and reported in 1893 from India and in 1904 from Italy. Her successor as Vice-Regent for Maine, in 1911, was Mrs. Richards, who probably occupied the third-floor room until she became the fifth Regent in 1927.

ix

Connecticut, the District, Florida, and North Carolina accounted for the four central third-floor rooms. The D.C. room contained a bureau from the Maryland Calvert estate, donated by the first Treasurer, the Washington banker, George Washington Riggs, whose son was the second Treasurer and whose spinster daughter Miss Janie was the beloved third Vice-Regent for the District, her mother having been the first. The second, Mrs. Barnes, declined in 1903 to alter the bed, supposed to have been an original Mount Vernon piece, by providing a new spring and mattress, on the grounds that "it would be vandalism, for the comfort of an occasional occupant, to modernize it." Mrs. Barnes, one of Miss Cunningham's appointments, was the widow of the Surgeon-General, a Mexican War veteran who

organized the medical department, such as it was, of the Federal
Army. In his official capacity he was present at Lincoln's death-
bed, and also attended Secretary Seward's wound. She was one
of the small group of Vice-Regents present at Dodge's first
interview with Mrs. Laughton, and had no doubt cast a vote
in his favor.

After refurnishing the Florida Room, the outspoken Mrs.
Denham objected some years later that it was only a passage-
way from the upper hall to Mrs. Washington's third-floor room
and to the stairs leading down to Washington's Bedroom, and
its use as a dormitory was discontinued, the accommodations
in the new Administration Building becoming available soon
after.

Mrs. Denham (1913–1948) was one of the characters. Always
saying and doing the gracious thing in her quiet, leisurely
"semi-tropical air"—most of her life was spent at Jacksonville
—she was the first to offer votes of thanks and was quick with
an apt piece of original verse. Her genius was the arrangement
of flowers, and she always did the table decorations for special
occasions and made delightful bouquets with paper collars for
presentations. In 1948 she insisted on resigning, after thirty-five
years, and in her witty little speech to Council at that time she
recalled how in her early days with the Association the new
Vice-Regents learned humility and self-effacement. "I remember so well," she said, "one occasion that left its lasting impression on my young soul. I was tapped on the shoulder and looked
up to see South Carolina sternly saying, 'I would like to speak
to you in the Nelly Custis room.' We went into the small parlor [Music Room] and she drew up two chairs and said, 'My
dear, you are very young and I want you to make a good impression. Your clothes are lovely, but I wonder if you can't put
something under the thin part of your waist so as to hide your
nakedness.' I simply gasped! For months I had been making thin
dresses and camisoles for the warm weather and now I must
cover it all. I told her I had thicker dresses, and she begged me
to be uncomfortable and wear them because I was a SOUTH-
ERN REPRESENTATIVE. So for the rest of my stay I suffered in a thick dress with the thorough approval of my colleague from Charleston. A year later she visited the Vice-Regent

for California, who fitted her out in a lovely wardrobe, and I
didn't say a word when the South Carolina lady returned to
Mount Vernon in lovely thin clothes revealing her aristocratic
shoulders."

South Carolina would have been Mrs. Elizabeth Allston
Pringle, (1901–1920) and California was of course the fairy
godmother Mrs. Hearst, to whom the refurbishment of a middle-aged dowd would have been a routine kindness accomplished
with infinite tact, good taste, and generosity. Like her predecessor Mrs. Pickens, Mrs. Pringle found her family fortunes ruined
by the War. Her father, at his death in 1864, had left to his
widow and several children a vast amount of property in the
Carolina Tidewater rice country, which became almost worthless in the post-War chaos in the South. After a brief marriage
which left her widowed and childless at twenty-four, "Miss
Bessie" undertook the management alone of the Chicora Wood
plantation near Georgetown, the only one remaining when the
estate was settled. She worked with "wage Negroes" and share-
croppers, and kept a diary recounting her daily trials and ad-
ventures, the humor of the loyal darkies, the death of a beloved
dog. Her book called *A Woman Rice-Planter* was published
in 1907 under the pseudonym of "Patience Pennington," and
was praised by Winston Churchill (the American novelist) because she had "accomplished one of the most difficult feats in
literature—to make the commonplace things of life interesting,"
for she had cast over this chronicle of a broken life the charm
and glow of her own radiant personality.

In her lonely life at Chicora, two miles from another white
woman, she taught herself solitude, and her piano became "very
nearly human in its companionship," and she wrote of playing
all one evening till one o'clock and then being too excited to
go to bed. A large moccasin snake encountered in her garden
represented to her only a fear which must be conquered, and
she walked on resolutely lest her peace of mind be forever destroyed by an unseen danger. "From being by nature a coward,"
she wrote, "I became very courageous, until I feared nothing
but a cow, and a drunken man." Her sister wrote of her "extraordinary insight, almost amounting to mind-reading," and
the rapier-like reproof she could administer. "A woman of rare

charm and accomplishment," said Mrs. Rathbone, "and at the same time a very child in joyousness, enthusiasm, and frankness."

It is to be hoped that in her strange friendship with the dissimilar Mrs. Hearst she found and recaptured something of the affection and luxury of which she had been robbed by the War. She apparently made more than one visit to the California home of Mrs. Hearst, the last in 1918, when her hostess seemed "more lovely and saint-like than ever," for although her eyes were giving trouble Mrs. Hearst's good works never flagged. She was finishing her twenty-fourth pair of fine woollen socks for soldiers. "She not only was never idle herself, but couldn't bear to see anyone else sit with folded hands," Mrs. Pringle recorded. "She called a maid and sent for knitting needles, wool, and the Red Cross book of directions for knitting socks, and it was a strong-minded person who would decline to attempt a sock at any rate. Three times a week all the maids and servants were sent into the vineyards to pick grapes so that they should be quite fresh, and great trucks were loaded with the beautiful and delicious bunches and sent to the camp forty miles away, with the request that those in the hospital should be served first. At Thanksgiving an invitation was sent for fifty privates to come to dinner at the Hacienda, a request being made to the Commandant that those who had no friend or other place to go should be preferred. They came and it was delightful to see their enjoyment of the grand dinner and the beauty of everything. After dinner the hostess in her lovely white lace dress rose and said a few words of greeting, and gave them her best wishes and her pleasure in seeing them, and a very shy young sergeant answered, expressing their thanks very awkwardly, but then proposed three cheers for her, which were given with a will."

The mutual attachment between these two women, so different in background and heredity, is another example of the magic amalgamation of the Mount Vernon endeavor. A second book, *Chronicles of Chicora Wood*, was published under Mrs. Pringle's own name in 1922. The great storm of 1906 and three bad crop years afterward destroyed forever the Carolina rice industry, though Mrs. Pringle continued to live at lonely Chicora, making an annual trip north to attend Council. At the time of her reproof to Mrs. Denham she was in her sixties, and a photograph shows a sweet-faced woman wearing the conventional widow's black, long-sleeved, with a little veil at the back of her bonnet.

Mrs. Denham flourished well into the memory of the current Vice-Regents. With her genius for organizing "occasions" she did much to enhance the celebration of the Association's 75th Council in 1941, though her suggestion that they all attend a gala dinner in colonial costume was not acted upon. The dinner given at the Mayflower Hotel in 1935 in honor of Dodge's fiftieth anniversary as Superintendent was first proposed by her, with a "purse" made up of a collection-box for an unspecified sum from each Vice-Regent, and "a banquet with toasts and general merrymaking." It is to be regretted that no further record of that memorable evening has survived. Actually there were two dinners—one at the Mayflower, attended by distinguished men and women and Government officials, and "a family affair" at Mount Vernon during Council, where little rhymes were read and little "inside" jokes were made amid much kindly and affectionate laughter.

The furniture of the North Carolina Room, which faced west on the third floor, was good mahogany a hundred years old, all gifts, as Mrs. Walker like many Southerners after the War was unable to provide from her own resources. An additional ornament, reported by her without comment at the 1897 Council, was a hornet's nest, of course uninhabited, presented by a Mrs. Sparkle of Charlotte—in memory of the title conferred on Mecklenburg County in 1781 by the frustrated Colonel Tarleton of the British Army.

Mrs. Walker had more than once offered the hospitality of her home near Guildford Courthouse to Miss Cunningham during the first Regent's gruelling journeys from Mount Vernon to the plantation near Columbia which was her home. In 1900 Mrs. Walker and Mrs. Mitchell were the only two remaining pre-War appointments made by Miss Cunningham, and she was often called upon to preside at Council "in her dignified and placid way," in the absence of the Regent. Like Mrs. Mitchell, she more than once threatened to resign, but remained in good health and vigor to read memorials to most of her contempo-

raries till 1908. They both lived to see the founder's dream
realized and fulfilled beyond her most extravagant early hopes,
and to enjoy the growing prosperity and peace and beauty of
Mount Vernon in the Association's care.

The remaining third-floor room was in the possession of Connecticut's Mrs. Hudson, where she had placed a handsome
carved four-posted single bedstead, a bureau, a writing-table
and a quaint shaving-mirror. Mrs. Hudson was to serve forty-
three years, until she died in 1914 at the age of ninety. Her
chief concern seemed always to be the comfort and welfare of
the current Superintendent—she had mothered Hollingsworth
almost out of his mind—and her early aggressiveness, deplored
by the gentler Southern spirits in the stormy 1870's, eventually
softened into "a gentle, refined, and courteous manner," in her
later years. Surviving Mrs. Walker, she was one of the last
direct links to the founder, with whom her relations had not
always been happy, as she had come too late on the scene to
have known the personal charm and irresistible drive of the first
Regent at the height of her powers. Mrs. Hudson, absent in
1886, would return to Council in 1888, and from then till 1913
she never missed a year, and was noted for always being the
first to arrive and the last to leave.

Martha's linen cupboard, with its unusual "cobweb" window
over the west door, was long used for storage of Association
papers and pictures, until in 1882 Mrs. Sweat moved that it
should be cleared out and opened to view.

x

Returning to the upper hall of the second floor, Dodge led
his visitors down the main staircase past the tall grandfather
clock on the landing, into the central Hall, which with a wide
door at either end provided the only air-conditioning in a hot
Virginia summer and was much used as a sitting-room in the
old days. The clock was in 1917 traced to a descendant of
Washington's brother Samuel in Dallas, Texas, and was recovered through Mrs. Maxey and the generosity of an anonymous "friend" who was probably J. P. Morgan, then a member
of the Advisory Committee. It was at first believed to have stood
there even in Lawrence's day, and throughout Washington's

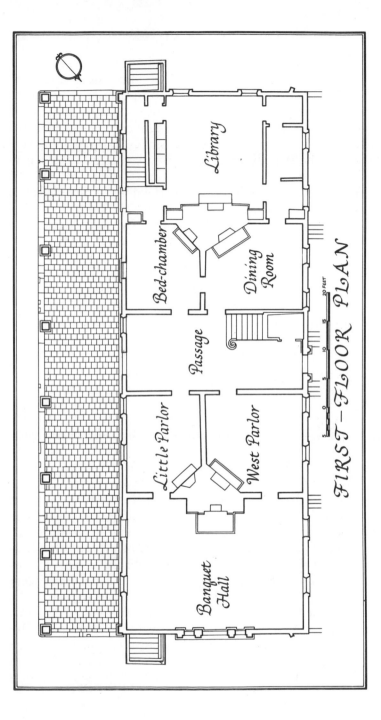

FIRST–FLOOR PLAN

Library

Bed-chamber

Dining Room

Passage

Little Parlor

West Parlor

Banquet Hall

5 0 5 10 15 20 FEET

life, and therefore would have had the longest history of any object in the house—but its maker's name insists on a later date.

The rubber treads on the stairs give an institutional air which is much deplored, but in view of the heavy traffic they seem to be unavoidable. In 1940 Goodyear rubber tile was installed to match the floor covering in the passageways—an inevitable concession to the steadily mounting attendance. In 1954 a barrier had to be devised to keep traffic in a single line, up and down simultaneously, and prevent overloading of the staircase. Removable weighted metal posts were made by—who else?—Wilfred Neitzey, according to a design by Mr. Macomber. Joined by an inconspicuous chain, these form a flexible barrier to control the crowd without tension.

Alabama (Mrs. Ella Smith Herbert, wife of Colonel Hilary Herbert a Civil War veteran who became Secretary of the Navy in 1893) asked for the Hall to be assigned to her State in 1882, and after her death only two years later her young daughter Leila continued the work her mother had begun. The Herberts seem to have had no connection with Upton, the first Superintendent, who was a Virginia man distantly related to the Washingtons. The Hall has always been a construction problem, and has several times been reinforced. In 1882 the Virginia architect Robert Fleming recommended the removal of the supporting wooden arch which had been installed in the 1870's to correct the sag of the second floor. Fleming substituted an iron girder resting on two polished wooden Doric pillars, one at either side. These were later removed under Dodge's supervision, and the supporting beam was altered again with an iron truss which could be hidden in the ceiling, and brick piers in the cellar were constructed to reinforce the foundation walls. Dodge found what he considered evidence of a partition across the Hall, which had been taken down probably during Washington's alterations in 1775. Several coats of dark paint were removed from the panelled woodwork, disclosing lighter tones, and an art student at Pratt Institute in Brooklyn undertook to reconstruct the design of some scraps of wall-paper found under several layers of subsequent dates. The copy was manufactured in New York and hung, though it has since been banished in favor of the whitewash finish so much used in Washington's time on the most elegant interiors, a more suitable background for the framed engravings, duplicates of those listed in the Appraisers' Inventory and mentioned in Lossing's account of the house published in 1859.

Mrs. Herbert raised $751 from her State donations, including $80.75 from a town called Selma, and after the repairs and painting were done she set about furnishing the area as it might have been arranged by Washington, with chairs and a sofa, genuine old pieces which she secured as a gift from a gentleman in New York. She traced and acquired the sword worn by Washington at the battle which resulted in the defeat of Braddock in the French and Indian War of 1755, when Washington was serving as a colonial aide to the British general, and when swords were not worn just for ornaments. Satisfied of its genuineness, Mrs. Herbert purchased it from Lorenzo Lewis's heirs at Audley. As she died before her work was completed, her husband came to Mount Vernon to see the sword installed in a glass case in the Hall, and to receive the thanks of the Council then in session, Mrs. Laughton presiding.

A few years later Mrs. Herbert's daughter Leila arrived as the third Vice-Regent for Alabama, bringing as a gift on her first appearance two dozen glasses. Youngest of all the Vice-Regents, an appealing blonde beauty, cultivated and travelled, with a social grace derived from acting as her father's hostess, Miss Leila found time to write a very creditable book about Washington's life at Mount Vernon which, although long out of print, remains a remarkable achievement in view of the limited source material available to an inexperienced writer at that time. She died in 1898, still very young, after a fall from her horse.

The expense of the work on the Hall was then assumed by Michigan (Mrs. Rathbone) whose annual contribution from the Detroit Mount Vernon Society was always a substantial sum. The Society, composed of Detroit matrons, each year gave a tea at the home of some well-to-do hostess who sponsored and financed the affair with appropriate decorations, refreshments, and a musical program. It was the custom in early years for the guests to attend in 18th-century costume, and Whelan sent out a big box of Mount Vernon flowers, which were sold to the guests. Michigan, as one of the later States, had not received a room of its own in the original allotment, and was anyway temporarily out of a Vice-Regent at that time, but Mrs. Rathbone was one of the most active and devoted of the Vice-Regents. In 1913 she gave an amusing account in Council of having addressed the Detroit chapter of the Children of the Republic, which listened without any apparent enthusiasm until at the end she was rocked almost off her feet by the club "yell": *"What's the matter with Mrs. Rathbone, RAH, RAH, RAH!"*

When she resigned in 1918 after thirty years, because she had moved from Michigan to New York, she was given honorary status and no other appointment for Michigan was made during her lifetime.

A niece of Mrs. Walker, Mrs. Lizzie Johnson Johnston, took up Alabama's responsibility for the Hall for thirty years beginning in 1900. Noted for her bubbling good humor and cheerful acceptance of physical infirmities, she was active in giving little talks to the schools and colleges of her State to awaken interest in Mount Vernon, and she urged in Council the need of a small history of the Association for children, which was never written. It was Mrs. Johnston's privilege to receive for Alabama the famous Braddock sash, with its continuous history from the time it was used as a stretcher to carry the dying General from the Monongahela battlefield. Washington, as Braddock's sole surviving uninjured aide that day, brought the sash to Mount Vernon, from where it descended through Nellie Custis to the New Orleans Butlers and thence to Zachary Taylor, who carried it to the White House. Passing to his daughter's heirs, it was purchased by the Association in 1920, with money presented as an expression of sentiment by a distinguished visitor the previous year. It was placed in a glass case in the Hall which already held Washington's sword, and the inscription on its card read: *"Purchased with money donated for a relic by Prince Tokugawa of Japan."* The Prince, on his way to France with an imposing suite representing the Red Cross of Japan after the first German War, was impressed to the extent of $1,000 by the reverence shown at Mount Vernon for the memory of Washington, a sentiment entirely comprehensible to a nation accustomed to honor its ancestors.

In 1921 the old black haircloth sofa in the Hall, dating back to Mrs. Herbert's New York donor, and upon which fatigued lady visitors were accustomed to catch their breath, was considered by Dodge so "unsightly"—a word in frequent use at Mount Vernon to this day—from wear and tear that he sent it "to town" to be re-covered in leather. The Hall settee was still a problem in 1954, when it was commented on by the Chairman of the Furnishing Committee, Mrs. Nancy G. Cabot (Massachusetts) in a paragraph in the Minutes which irresistibly illustrates the trouble, and the thought, and the humor which illumines the most routine deliberation of the Vice-Regents: "The settee in the Hall remains our most vexatious problem," she wrote in her Report to Council. "The Committee droops in front of it with discouragement. The necessary support of the stout and weary, its replacement with a fine old piece is out of the question. Itself a reproduction of late Sheraton, probably a reproduction of an earlier period would be the solution. Until such can be found, however, the Committee has decided that its appearance must be improved, and can be, by removal of its shabby leather and re-covering it with a sturdy, not expensive, fabric of a harmonious color and inconspicuous design suitable to the Sheraton period. A sample of our choice of fabric has been laid on the sofa for you to see."

Next year's Report noted that "in the Central Hall the utilitarian sofa so long an eyesore to past and present committees was refinished in the Mount Vernon shop, and covered with the sturdy fabric selected last year. Though not ideal, we feel that at least it has been rendered innocuous."

The sofa still stands, just inside the piazza door, not roped off and covered in black figured haircloth.

A small Queen Anne table, dislodged from the Music Room by the arrival of a new settee, was placed beside the staircase below the bannister with the chamber candle-sticks handily set out upon it for lighting the family to bed. In 1785, after Washington's return from the War, William Hunter, a London merchant and one of the many uninvited guests who experienced Mount Vernon's hospitality, recorded in his journal that after an evening's conversation about Congress, the roads, improvements to the Potomac, etc., in the company of Washington and a few neighbors over a few glasses of champagne, he "had the honor of being lighted up to my room by the General himself."

The old lantern which hangs from the Hall ceiling was believed to go back to Lawrence, the older half-brother from whom George inherited Mount Vernon, and it was returned in 1915 by Miss Mary Custis Lee. The Association's conscientious pursuit of authenticity has again updated a traditional piece to a later time—in the 1760's. When it was reconditioned in 1949 it was found, to everyone's surprise, to be made of tin, instead of the less perishable iron which had been assumed. A suitable candle was installed in it at this time.

The model of the Bastille which now stands on a marble-topped table in the Hall, was presented to Washington in 1795 by an English admirer named Slade, and is said to have been carved from one of the stones of the demolished prison. It was for a while exhibited by George Washington Parke Custis, with other mementoes, at the Patent Office in Washington City, from where it returned to Mount Vernon in 1870, probably at the instigation of Mrs. Robert E. Lee.

The key to the Bastille is perhaps the only object which is still exactly where Washington left it. It is one of the few things which remained in the house when the last Washington owner vacated it in 1860, he having presented the key to the Association. Originally it was sent to Washington by Lafayette in 1790, and must have been carried to Mount Vernon from Philadelphia and then affixed by Washington's order to the wall at the foot of the staircase. Other gifts from this devoted friend to his one-time General included a pair of Spanish asses, some exotic pheasants, and a pack of French hounds. The key still hangs in a glass case between the doors to the Family Dining-room and the Downstairs Bedroom. To illustrate the irresponsible busybody meddling and carping which has pursued the Association from the beginning, it should be mentioned that two separate attempts have been made in the Press to agitate the return of the Bastille key to France as an unsolicited gesture of good will. The Regent herself was once supposed to fly by chartered plane to Paris and personally present the key to the French Government on July 14th, Bastille Day, at a ceremony in which the promoter of the idea was himself no doubt planning to play a conspicuous part. It was explained to him with exemplary patience and tact that the Association had no right to dispose of George Washington's possessions on any pretext, and that an alternate proposal that the Regent should anyway fly to Paris with an expression of good will—and presumably an apology for Lafayette's own gesture of good will nearly two hundred years before—would be to no outstanding international purpose. The second attempt, as late as the 1950's, by a chronically dissident D.C. columnist, ended in a public expression by the President himself of his official satisfaction with the present custody of the key.

xi

The first room on the right descending the staircase is the Family Dining-room, assigned to South Carolina in 1880, and one of the most beautiful rooms in the house. Mrs. Lucy Holcombe Pickens was appointed in 1866, but was unable to attend Council until ten years later, after Miss Cunningham's death, when she still retained the "gentle, bewitching manner" and "the subtle spirit of fascination" if not the wartime beauty of her portrait which adorned the Confederate $100 note—though her life since then had become a heart-breaking series of sorrows.

When very young she had married the grandson of Andrew Pickens of the Revolution, who had rallied the militia at the Cowpens and led them again at Eutaw Springs. Francis Wilkinson Pickens was a wealthy rice planter and Congressman, appointed U.S. Minister to Russia in 1858. Lucy's honeymoon was spent among the European courts, where her sensational beauty was soon famous. Her only child, a daughter, was born in St. Petersburg, and the family returned home in time for Pickens to become a fiery secessionist, and he was Governor of South Carolina when Fort Sumter was fired on. He died in 1869, and the Negroes remained faithfully on the ruined plantation which his widow made a brave attempt to run as he had done. She was said to have a mysterious kinship with flowers, and as Chairman of the Greenhouse and Gardens Committee she made the gardens her especial concern, though she somehow raised the funds to furnish the Dining-room during the 1880's.

Its handsome stucco ceiling and mantelpiece had been exe-

cuted when the room was redecorated under the supervision of
Lund Washington while the General and his lady were at Cambridge. The correspondence between Lund and the harassed
Commander-in-chief at that time is touching and illuminating,
for Washington often paused as it were between skirmishes to
set down his anxious queries as to the progress of the work, and
Lund felt his responsibilities very keenly and wrote in detail of
the problems confronting him in Virginia. "The ceiling is not
clumsy," he reassured Washington in October, 1775. "I think
it is light and handsome. It is altogether worked by hand, which
makes it tedious. . . . The stucco man agrees the ceiling is a
handsomer one than any at Colonel Lewis's, although not half
the work on it." This was a reference to the house now known as
Kenmore at Fredericksburg, which was built for Washington's
sister Betty by her husband Fielding Lewis, and which remains
a masterpiece of 18th-century elegance. Preserved and restored
by the Kenmore Association formed in 1922 to save the house
from annihilation, and maintained by a Board of Regents, this
beautiful mansion is open to the public, and a service of tea
and gingerbread in the kitchen is included in the price of admission. The last home of Washington's mother, for whom
Betty assumed responsibility after 1772, stands at the end of a
path running from Kenmore's garden. It was restored and
opened to the public in 1929.

The ceiling of Washington's Dining-room resembles those
in a contemporary book of designs which must have been
available to his nameless workman, whose leisurely performance
so fretted Lund at the time. It is of remarkable beauty, entail-
ing fine hand-work by which bits of wet pressed paper were
applied in chain-like arabesques of great delicacy to form an
exquisite pattern of interlocking curves and beading like tiny
leaves, which were then touched with gold leaf. Photographs
of the Mount Vernon ceiling laid beside illustrations from the
book show the work of a craftsman superior to the original in
airy grace and imaginative detail, well worth the irksome
amount of time spent in completing it while Lund fumed
among the ladders and scaffolds. This is the ceiling which occupied Wilfred Neitzey in 1960 when the plaster was found
to be cracking away from the wood lath which held it. The

risky work of restoration was undertaken by Mr. Macomber, under whose supervision the cracks were minutely widened and undercut, so that new plaster could be inserted. At the same time the unsuspected gold leaf was revealed under many coats of paint, and a similar effect was recaptured with gilt paint laid on by Neitzey. The mantel-piece was found to be of carved walnut which had been painted over at the time of its installation with the warm putty color it now wears again.

The original dining-table has not been traceable, but the one which stands in the room is a Virginian contemporary, found by Mrs. Harrison at Richmond in 1944. Because of Hitler's war a general retrenchment was in force, and a reluctant decision was made to forego the expense of its purchase, but the necessary funds were supplied by Miss Failing, the Vice-Regent for Oregon. Miss Failing was often in delicate health, and could not face the rigors of the Mount Vernon accommodations in the early years of the 1900's, but she attended Council faithfully, staying in Washington where she had a nurse, a maid, and a doctor in attendance, and making the daily trip to Mount Vernon by boat, and later by motor, to place her wisdom and humor and often her purse at the disposal of the Association. Her belated arrival after Council had assembled was often greeted with affectionate applause, for she had a remarkable capacity for friendship with her diverse colleagues. In 1936, when the unexpected death of the Regent, Mrs. Richards, left them startled and rudderless, looking to her as their senior, Miss Failing firmly declined the succession because she did not feel "competent" to fill the post—though she continued as Vice-Regent for another ten years. In a gracious gesture at the next Council she placed the Regent's ribbon around Mrs. Towner's neck, with a traditional little speech: "As Dean of the Mount Vernon Ladies' Association of the Union I have the privilege of giving to you the Regent's badge of office. With it goes the trust and confidence which we all feel for the future and a deep appreciation of what you have done for us in a difficult time, which you have filled with much competence and faithfulness." A broken hip in 1945 added to her disabilities, and she died two years later, having served thirty-eight years. She always gave, they said then, assessing their loss, "a sense of being aloof from the ordinary wear and tear of existence," and she left them a bequest of $1,000 in her will.

The table, which replaced a very respectable one of not quite the right period, which had replaced a drop-leaf pedestal type which would not do at all, carries the mirrored plateau, which was purchased for Washington in Paris on his order in 1790 by Gouverneur Morris, American Minister to France during the presidency. The plateau and the bisque classical group which accompanied it were among the many treasures returned to Mount Vernon through Mrs. Goldsborough, and were first exhibited in the Banquet Room in 1895. Morris, that genial, knowing charmer whose wooden leg, acquired in a Philadelphia carriage accident, was no handicap to him with the pretty ladies, did considerable shopping for Washington abroad, including a gold watch required to be similar to the one Jefferson had procured in Paris for James Madison some years previously (25 guineas enclosed)—in addition to the plateau, of which only the middle and two end pieces, of several sections, are displayed on the table, along with the bisque ornament and Waterford candelabra. This table garniture was used at the Philadelphia presidential mansion, and was brought back to Mount Vernon in 1797 to grace the dinner-table there. It was an expensive whim, and Morris could be depended on to choose only the best. "You will perhaps exclaim that I have not complied with your Directions as to economy," he wrote to Washington at the time, "but you will be of a different opinion when you see the Articles. I could have sent you a number of pretty Trifles for very little Prime Cost, but the Transportation and the Freight would have been more, and you must have had an annual Supply, and your table would have been in the Style of a *petite maitresse* of this City, which most assuredly is not the Style you wish. Those now sent are of a noble Simplicity, and as they have been fashionable above two thousand years, they stand a fair chance to continue so during our time."

The inlaid Hepplewhite side-board until recently seen in the Dining-room was returned to Mount Vernon, like the bedstead, by Mrs. Lee, very early in the Association's history. The recent discovery of a similar piece has caused the removal of Mrs. Lee's gift to the Banquet Hall, where Washington is known to have had a pair of side-boards, and a smaller side-table now occupies its place. For a while the Lambdin portrait of Miss Cunningham hung above it, to be replaced by that of Washington's half-brother Lawrence, purchased from the descendants of the last Washington to own Mount Vernon. Lawrence was moved to the Library on the acquisition of the framed engravings which duplicate those listed in the Appraisers' Inventory as hanging on the walls of the Dining-room at the time of Washington's death.

The handsome ladder-back Chippendale chairs are mostly originals, part of a shipment of household goods purchased by Martha in Philadelphia on her way home after the War ended in the autumn of 1783. They have been accumulated by the Association from different sources and supplemented by similar pieces of the same period. The high-chair in the Windsor style was probably purchased by Martha at the same time, and would have been for the use of little Nelly and George Washington Parke Custis during their childhood at Mount Vernon after the Revolution, though it is unlikely that it often appeared in the grown-ups' dining-room in those days. It was presented by Miss Failing in 1911, very much "worn and battered" then, but authenticated by the Relics Committee before she acquired it from Mrs. Daingerfield Lewis, the wife of Nelly's great-grandson. It was repaired to such a degree of perfection that there is a legend that Dodge thought it necessary to scuff up the footboard with sand-paper for the sake of realism.

A door in the south corner of the Dining-room leads to the Pantry and the outer door through which the food arrived from the detached Kitchen via the south colonnade. Here in the Pantry, which was presided over by the colored butler or steward named Frank, the table china and glass in daily use were kept. Washington's favorite blue-and-white Nankin ware was mentioned in his invoices from the time of his marriage, and a few cherished pieces of this service have survived and are now in the Museum. By tradition, the Washingtons presented to their Philadelphia friends the Samuel Powels, a corresponding china service at the time of his final retirement to Mount Vernon in 1797. More than a hundred pieces of the Powel china are now displayed on the shelves of the Pantry, through the generosity of the eighth Regent, who placed it there on indefinite loan in 1951. After serving the two allotted terms as Regent, Mrs. Powel resumed her vice-regency for Rhode Island, having become Mrs. Albert Harkness by a second marriage. In her 1952 Report to Council she related a charming incident which occurred during her sojourn in England that summer, when she attended the Garden Party at Buckingham Palace. Princess Elizabeth and her husband had visited Mount Vernon, accompanied by Miss Truman, during their American tour the previous November. They were met at the west door by the Regent, Mrs. Powel, and the assembled Vice-Regents, who were presented to the royal party and accompanied them through the Mansion, and were photographed with them on the lawn above the river. To the Regent's surprise—though it would be to no one else's—her striking good looks had made a sufficient impression on the royal memory so that many months later she was cordially recognized quite out of context in the Buckingham Palace garden, even before her name was given.

Also in the Pantry is the small square black walnut table, country-made, on which tradition says that the Washingtons' wedding breakfast was served—assuming that it was ever brought to Mount Vernon from the Custis residence called the White House on the Pamunkey where the marriage took place. It was left here on loan by a descendant of Mrs. Washington in 1945. The mahogany wine-chest which holds six glass bottles is believed to be one imported by Washington soon after his marriage in 1759. It appears in both his invoices and the Appraisers' Inventory, and its price— £17.17—caused him to complain to his London agent: "Surely there must be as great a mistake or as great an imposition as ever was offered by a Tradesman." In the "tobacco economy" which existed in Virginia prior to the Revolution, most of the planter's cash income was derived from the sale of his tobacco crop to a merchant in England. The colony exported little else, and the planter's credit with his English merchant was expended to satisfy his varied household needs. Under these circumstances, delays, losses, and impositions were inevitable. The wine-chest was returned to Mount Vernon in 1911 by a niece of Mrs. Goldsborough.

On special occasions, such as Christmas and Easter, the table in the Dining-room is laid with the old china and glass in the dessert-wine setting, or by using one of Washington's menus, with the dinner service and even artificial food. One of the distinguished visitors in 1960, Mme DeGaulle, was delighted with this additional detail. Visitors from abroad, where houses much older and grander than Mount Vernon abound, are nevertheless impressed by the fact that Mount Vernon is one of the few places in the world where the home of a great man can be found looking practically the same as it did during the lifetime of the owner. They are deeply moved by the very quality of reality to which the Association has given so much thought and effort—presenting an 18th-century home, frozen in time like the Sleeping Beauty, seeming capable of resuming at any moment its former daily routine in the presence of its original inhabitants.

xii

Next to the Dining-room, with a connecting door between, is the room which has enjoyed the most varied history of any in the house, the Downstairs Bedroom. After the addition of the south end was completed this apparently became Martha's Sitting-room, to which she could retire, no doubt with relief, when the house was full of company, and from it she had access to the Library and the private stair to the Bedroom. Because of the increased size of the household when they returned from the presidency, it reverted to a bedroom, easing the necessity to accommodate a couple of secretaries—Colonel Humphreys and Tobias Lear—as well as Washington's nephew Lawrence Lewis, who acted as his manager, the young Custises, and the innumerable overnight guests mentioned in the Diary. Although the rooms were stripped of furniture when the last Washington moved out in 1860, Miss Cunningham furnished this one as her bedroom, to avoid climbing stairs, with the adjoining Dining-room as her sitting-room.

Having been allotted to Georgia—Mrs. Eve—by 1883 it had been renovated and furnished for the use of Council and Committees, but in a style which was sharply criticized by a lady visitor who wrote for *Century Magazine* in 1887: "In most of the rooms some attempt has.been made to restore at least the epoch in the furniture selected; but one—Mrs. Washington's Sitting-room—is furnished with a tawdry set of modern ebonized furniture covered with red and yellow plush. Nothing could be more out of taste, especially in combination with the bar-room window-shade of yellow and pink." The judgment seems harsh in the circumstances, and the writer was of course unaware that the choice was probably not Mrs. Eve's, for she would have had to accept gratefully any donation at the time in order to put the room to use at all, as her personal fortunes had been destroyed by the Civil War and she had next to nothing to spend.

There had been a slight passage at arms shortly before Dodge's advent, when Mrs. Hudson, already in possession of the northeast room on the third floor known as Connecticut's, which she occupied as a bedroom at Council time, laid claim to the first-floor Sitting-room also, alleging that in her absence it had been "thoughtlessly taken away" and assigned to Georgia. Miss Harper as peace-maker "deprecated the tone of Mrs. Hudson's letter of protest," and hoped that nothing of the kind would happen again, reminding everyone that Connecticut did not need two rooms, and the Sitting-room remained in Georgia's possession. It was later to suffer again from an inappropriate but expensive gift from an Augusta donor—another plush atrocity which was tactfully disposed of by the Superintendent after Mrs. Eve's death.

By the end of the century the Association was in a happier position to discriminate, and the Furnishing Committee wrote: "When Mount Vernon first came into the possession of the Association it was quite empty, and all bits of furniture or relics were gratefully accepted; but as it is now well filled, and as the appreciation of old things is constantly increasing, the Committee ask that great care be taken to find articles suitable for the different rooms, and that they should always be consulted when changes are made."

In 1911 another weeding out was advised by the Committee to limit by degrees some of the overcrowded rooms to articles proved to have a connection with Washington, though even now a few fine contemporary pieces have been added to dress the rooms, not as unauthenticated relics but as examples of what it would have been possible for Washington to own.

Tireless, if tactless, in her zeal for Mount Vernon, Mrs. Hudson after a trip abroad in 1902 presented a hive of Italian bees for the Kitchen Garden, and five young peafowl. In 1907, after yet another sojourn in her beloved Italy, she reported: "At my villa on the Island of Capri I gave a reception on the 22nd of February which was well attended by American and English residents. Views of Mount Vernon were distributed to the guests assembled under the folds of our flag. 'To the memory of Washington' was drunk, standing, and in silence." Always concerned for the welfare of the employees, she invariably proposed to provide support for the old and feeble, long before there was any organized pension arrangement such as now exists.

It was not until 1946 that Mrs. Coolidge (Massachusetts) found evidence that the room had been used as a bedroom in 1799, and a decision was made to refurnish it from the other rooms and the pieces in storage, in accordance with the Association policy of restoring the house as it was when Washington saw it last. Mrs. Mary Lurton Van Deventer (Tennessee) offered her own bed, which was dated about 1780 and resembled the one in Washington's Bedroom. Tennessee has always been interesting, from Mary Middleton Rutledge Fogg, the first Vice-Regent, on. Mrs. Van Deventer, whose generosity could hardly go further, gave her reminiscences at the 1953 Council, when everyone took a long look backward on the one hundredth anniversary of Miss Cunningham's first impulse to rescue Washington's home from his impoverished heirs and make it a place of national pilgrimage. Mrs. Van Deventer referred with humor to her first arrival as a new appointee in 1921, the year before Mrs. Danforth's, and described the formidable assemblage of her elders in Council, some of whom had recourse to ear-trumpets. As Mrs. Leary had found nearly fifteen years earlier, the senior Vice-Regents were not always as cordial to a shy freshman as they might have been, and her first entrance was always an ordeal overshadowed by the memory of the beloved colleague whose place she was required to fill, so that she experienced always a paralyzing sensation of having a great deal to live up to. Dodge, on the other hand, with his infinite courtesy and

kindness of heart, always went out of his way to put a newcomer at her ease.

The Council of 1921, which was Mrs. Van Deventer's initia-
tion, was indeed an impressive one, though its most outstanding
achievement was the decision to extend the new electrification
to the Kitchen, and to commission plans for a fire-proof Relic
House or Museum to be built inside the shell of the old Store
House in the north lane. Miss Comegys was Regent in 1921, the
rather overwhelming Miss Longfellow was the senior Vice-
Regent, and further down the list were Mrs. Pringle, whose
reprimand to Mrs. Denham was not long past, and Mrs. Maxey,
an ardent supporter of women's suffrage, on whose motion in
1903 Miss Cunningham's Farewell Address was incorporated
into the printed Reports and Minutes of the Association, as it
is to this day, and who was to become a loving friend to Mrs.
Van Deventer for the next eighteen years. In her tribute at the
time of Mrs. Maxey's death in 1939 after forty-three years as
Vice-Regent for Texas, Mrs. Van Deventer said: "It is difficult
for those of us who have come as Vice-Regents to Mount Vernon in this bright period of prosperity to realize in full the
constant anxiety in the hearts and minds of our predecessors,
concerning the safety and future of the home of General Washington. The changes which Mrs. Maxey witnessed during her
vice-regency were many. When she came into the Association
telephones were a rare luxury, a primitive one on a party line
having been installed at Mount Vernon just a year before; good
roads and automobiles non-existing, and no electric lights or
power at Mount Vernon." It was Mrs. Maxey who first suggested "illuminated" or colored post-cards, and she offered to
raise in Texas funds to erect a suitable gate at the Railway
Entrance—which is now the north gate—and later began there
the construction of the brick wall which has now been extended
around most of the Mount Vernon acreage.

A small chest of drawers was borrowed from the Yellow
Bedroom upstairs for the transformed Sitting-room, to be added
to Mrs. Van Deventer's bedstead, along with a handsome dress-
ing-glass from the Conrads, and Miss Cunningham's portrait by
Lambdin was brought from the Dining-room to hang over the
mantel-piece of what had once been her bedroom. In accord-

ance with the tradition that nothing not pertaining to Washington should be given place in the Mansion, this portrait has since been retired to the Little Museum in the East Quarters, in favor of an equestrian portrait of Washington by one of the Peales, which was displaced from the Music Room by changes there. It is a standing grievance, nobly borne, of all the current Staff and curators that every time Council meets, and the ladies have finished rearranging things in the Mansion, all the post-cards and catalogues have become obsolete.

One of the many "supposed" Mary Ball pieces, a wing-chair freshly re-covered in damask, was soon dislodged by a Hepplewhite armchair procured by Miss Longfellow, whose lifelong home in Cambridge was the one-time Craigie House, which served as Washington's Headquarters during the first winter of the Revolution. Miss Longfellow's chair was believed to have been in use there at the time of Washington's occupancy. Presumably one of the oldest pieces in the house, though not owned by Washington, the Ball wing-chair has come to rest in the Library.

xiii

From the Downstairs Bedroom past the little stairway leading to the Washingtons' own quarters on the second floor, visitors came to the Library, that sunny sanctuary Washington created for himself below his Bedroom, from which he could reach the Dining-room, the piazza, and the grounds without passing through the rest of the house. It is a large, bright room, with two south windows, one wall consisting of a ceiling-high bookcase. Here he kept his private papers, did his accounts, wrote his innumerable letters, and accumulated a sizable collection of good editions from Gibbon to Chastellux, and a sprinkling of the innocuous Gothic novels which were apparently enjoyed by Martha and Nelly.

Bushrod had used the room to dine in, and it still functioned in that capacity throughout the Civil War and during Miss Cunningham's subsequent residence in the house. It continued as the Vice-Regents' dining-room until the present Administration Building was put up in 1929. It was practically unfurnished when Miss Longfellow attended her first Council as

Vice-Regent for Massachusetts in 1880, and she asked at once for the privilege of adopting it. The architect Fleming, already at work on the Hall, was engaged to repair and paint it, and she undertook the search for the missing books as well as the furniture. The shelves were then full of Association papers and old copies of the short-lived *Mount Vernon Record*—Washington's books had been dispersed by Judge Bushrod and his nephew who followed him. Most of them had been sold in the mid-1800's to the Boston Athenaeum, where they remain. Some volumes which escaped this sale continued for years to turn up in private collections and sales, often with Washington's book-plate and signature. The price of these items has by now risen to an almost prohibitive figure, but the Association has acquired by gift and purchase some eighty such volumes, which have been returned to the shelves of the first wall-case. Miss Longfellow's valiant effort to regain for Mount Vernon the Athenaeum collection was unavailing, but thanks to the Appraisers' Inventory it has been possible to acquire one by one many duplicate editions of books he owned at the time of his death.

"Grave Alice" of *The Children's Hour* had early encountered tragedy when her mother's light summer dress caught fire from hot sealing-wax in the library of the spacious house in Cambridge where she sat writing letters. Subsidized largely by Miss Longfellow's will, the house is now open to the public as a memorial to the happy family life which was somehow built there out of a mutual sorrow and devotion by Mr. Longfellow and his children. He was himself badly burned in attempting to save his wife, who died a few hours later. Miss Alice was then eleven, and found herself responsible for several brothers and sisters as well as the stricken poet. The Longfellow hospitality was such that she used to recall how as her father's hostess she would count the hats on the table in the hall in order to organize the dinner-table and the menu.

In 1891, unable to attend a sale of Lewis family memorabilia at Philadelphia, she authorized Mrs. Laughton to purchase on her behalf books for the Library up to $300. Some of Washington's own volumes were thus secured, such as *Henry Hume. Loose Hints Upon Education, Chiefly Concering Culture of the*

Heart, Edinboro, 1782, with Washington's autograph on the title page. *James Harvey's Meditation and Contemplation,* London, 1750, with his mother's autograph in each of the volumes, one of the rarest in the Washington family. Allen Ramsay's *Tea-Table Miscellany,* Edinboro, 1760, Cook's *Voyages,* and Boswell's *Antiquities.* Washington's own edition of Gibbon's *Roman Empire* with his bookplate and autograph was secured as a gift by Mrs. Maxey just before her death in 1939.

In 1905 the Association was forced to draw "temporarily" on the sacred Endowment Fund in order to purchase the "tambour Secretary and book-case" which Washington had brought home with him from Philadelphia, and at which he had written out his will in the summer of 1799, at that time bequeathing it and its attendant circular chair to his old friend and physician Dr. Craik. Miss Longfellow, again ill and unable to attend Council, sent her personal check for the full amount to restore the precious reserve fund. The desk was then recovered from Dr. Craik's heirs in Kentucky, who expressed regret that they were not in a position to donate it, but hoped some day to be able to refund the money—and it returned to its present place against the west wall of the Library. The revolving chair which belonged to it was regained the same year from Andrew Jackson's heirs, by contributions from five Vice-Regents.

After Mrs. Ball's death Miss Longfellow was for a few years the dean of the Vice-Regents, and her reminiscences on an evening during Council in 1919 enthralled the younger members who heard her, and who ten years later were to mourn the loss of "her dignified and beautiful presence, her richly endowed mind, her keen sense of humor." If she had been able to attend in 1929 it would have been her fiftieth Council as Vice-Regent.

The large terrestrial globe was not removed from the house when the last Washington left it, being presented to the Association by him in 1860, along with the Bastille key, and it has therefore a continuous history of residence at Mount Vernon since Washington installed it there on his return from Philadelphia in 1797. It had been delivered to him in New York from London, and must have travelled with him to Philadelphia and thence to Mount Vernon on his final homecoming. It was probably obsolete before his death, but careful restoration in recent years has preserved it in fair condition, though Dodge once commented that it somewhat resembled "the one-horse shay" and was falling apart.

The telescope, surveying compass, and ducking gun were all his, with authentic histories. The portrait of Lawrence is thought to have hung in this room during George's lifetime, as it does now. The tall gold-headed cane is the one given by the Association in 1858 to Edward Everett, in recognition of his efforts towards raising the original purchase money, and was returned to Mount Vernon by his granddaughter in 1911. Mr. Everett gave a series of lectures on Washington, travelling at his own expense from Boston to the Mississippi to the deep South, and added some $60,000 to the original purchase fund. The head of the cane is beautifully engraved with the Washington coat of arms, and was doubtless in use during the presidency. In the Longfellow house at Cambridge there is a similar tall cane, which was owned—and carried—by Miss Alice, who in her later years became an imposing figure, given to striking costumes and a tardy, dramatic arrival at Council, in a chauffeur-driven Rolls-Royce, to "make an entrance." The story goes that she kept a second car, a mere Pierce-Arrow, for the chauffeur's use on minor errands around Boston. Her interest and her generous donations were shared by Radcliffe College, which remembers her with the same affection she inspired at Mount Vernon.

As part of the Bicentennial preparations begun in 1931, the South Porch was removed from the Library end of the house, freeing the room from the gloom of the overhanging porch roof. Miss Tracy had always tried to get rid of it, and it was disparaged by Mrs. Eve in the 1870's as an excrescence erected by Judge Bushrod, but it had been many times mended and cosseted at some expense, until in 1932 it was suddenly gone.

xiv

Crossing the central Hall in front of the staircase, the visitors came to the Music Room, or East Parlor, its windows shaded by the piazza facing the river. Ohio's Vice-Regents, seeming always well-to-do, have had this room in charge since Mrs. Elizabeth Lytle Broadwell, who was niece to Mrs. Laughton, began its restoration in 1878, by organizing a Mount Vernon

Aid Society in Cincinnati, and it soon became one of the gems
on the ground floor. She engaged Emmart & Quartley to put the
room in perfect repair "without changing a hinge, lock, or
board," and then had furniture *made* in reproduction of what
Washington was believed to have had there, so that in 1879,
Mrs. Sweat as Secretary wrote: "If the whole Mansion could be
as thoroughly and successfully restored as the Ohio Room has
been, the ghosts of Washington and his familiar friends might
almost be won back to the home of their earthly forms."

When Mrs. Broadwell discovered that Washington had called
it the Music Room, she reclaimed Nelly's harpsichord from the
Banquet Room where it had stood hitherto, and also exhibited
with it what was alleged to be Washington's flute, though on
his own evidence he was not a performer on any musical instrument, much as he enjoyed hearing music played. When in 1789
the talented poet-composer-politician Francis Hopkinson sent
him a copy of "Seven Songs" dedicated to Washington, the tactful recipient wrote, with his sometimes rather ponderous courtesy: "But, my dear Sir, if you had any doubts about the reception which your book would meet with, or had the smallest
reason to think that you should need any assistance to defend it,
you have not acted with your usual good judgment in the choice
which you have made of a Coadjutor; for should the tide of
prejudice not flow in favor of it what, alas! can I do to support
it? I can neither sing one of the songs, nor raise a single note
on any instrument to convince the unbelieving, but I have however one argument which will prevail with persons of good
taste, I can tell them that it is the production of Mr. Hopkinson. With the compliments of Mrs. Washington added to mine
for you and yours, I am, etc."

The Minutes for 1909 record "an unusual request" from an
aged doctor who had "an ardent desire to play upon Washington's flute"— an indication of a courteous reply in the negative
would be a safe guess. A few years later Mrs. Broadwell expended
considerable time and energy tracing down a violin which was
supposed to have been Washington's, but which was probably
purchased for Jacky Custis, perhaps to accompany his sister
Patsy on the spinet. Its price was excessive and she abandoned
it, along with a cut-glass punch-bowl which was a more likely

prize. Since then no less than four other violins have been offered as Washington's, one of which was at least still in the possession of the family. It is possible that Jefferson's famous skill with that instrument had in some way been allocated to his non-performing contemporary, by one of the vague cross-overs which abound in the public mind.

Patsy Custis died young, before the Revolution began, and her niece Nelly's first music lessons were doubtless on Patsy's old spinet. The harpsichord was ordered from London in 1793 as a gift to Nelly, while the Washington family was still in the presidential mansion at Philadelphia. When they returned to Mount Vernon it travelled there, by the water-route with the other heavy luggage, and after Martha's death it accompanied Nelly to Woodlawn. From there, when that household was broken up by the death of her husband Lawrence Lewis, it went to her brother's house, Arlington, long a sanctuary for all Washington treasures. It was sketched there by Benson Lossing in the 1850's, and after George Washington Parke Custis's death in 1857 Nelly's widowed daughter-in-law presented it to the newly organized Association. It was therefore the first of many familiar Mount Vernon furnishings to return, seemingly almost of their own volition, like homing pigeons, to the house where they had been the daily companions of its master. Where the harpsichord spent the Civil War years has escaped mention, but as it had already been designated for the Association it must have stood, along with the globe, ghostly and silent in the bleak house which was in Miss Tracy's care during that time.

Writing to Mrs. Sweat in 1868, Miss Cunningham complained of the depredations committed by the post-War visitors during her own tenancy as care-taker: "The cornices are constantly broken off, even the ivory on the keys of the celebrated harpsichord are taken off, though a man stands in that room to protect the things exhibited there." And in 1884, with reference to the gates which had to be installed in the doorways of the rooms, Mrs. Sweat as Secretary recorded that "the Vice-Regent for Ohio, wishing the public to observe the many interesting objects in the Music Room which has been restored under her care, was rewarded by having an important piece of the ornamentation of the fine old clock on the mantel torn from its setting and carried away. Also, not long since, a boy was captured on his way to the boat, with one of the balusters he had pulled from the staircase in the main Hall." It was necessary for Mrs. Alice Key Dandridge Irwin to replace the broken and missing ivory keys in 1913—they were fortunate in finding old ivory of the exact shade to match the originals. At the same time the broken strings, stops, and pedal-rods were repaired, though no attempt was made to put the instrument in playing condition for fear of snapping the remaining original strings. The music-book, open on the rack, with Nelly's name on the cover, was presented in 1921 by Miss Annie Burr Jennings of Connecticut. There is also a receipt, dated 1768, "for teaching Miss Custis a year's music." This would have been Nelly's aunt, the tragic Patsy, who died six years before Nelly was born in 1779. A notation on the back by George Washington Parke Custis says that the handwriting was Washington's.

Miss Jennings was always outstanding among the Vice-Regents. Her home was at Fairfield, and Yale University shared with Mount Vernon her boundless enthusiasm and devotion. When in 1940 it fell to Mrs. Denham to read a memorial to Miss Jennings, she said: "At the football games or the crew races she was a brave, lovely figure in her gowns of Yale blue—recognized wherever she went. The walls of her home held mementoes of stirring events connected with Yale, as well as dozens of rare pictures of the life of Washington."

The Windsor chairs in the Music Room have needlepoint cushions worked in the red-and-yellow cockle-shell pattern of the original ones by Martha, whose "yellow-bottom chairs" were mentioned by Joshua Brooks in the record of his visit to Mount Vernon in 1799. The reproductions have been duly "distressed" into a suitably used-looking condition by being exposed to direct sunlight on the lawn behind the Admistration building and then sat upon for days by the Staff in their respective offices.

The vice-regency for Ohio has usually been a family concern, going by nieces. Mrs. Broadwell was among the later appointments made by her aunt, Mrs. Laughton—women who had never seen Miss Cunningham, but were none the less devoted to Mount Vernon. She was aunt to the seventh Vice-Regent for

Ohio, Mrs. Lily Broadwell Foster Livingood, who bore Mrs. Laughton's first name. As late as 1956 an album of photographs of Mount Vernon taken by Mrs. Livingood in 1925 was returned by her niece and forms a valuable part of the Mount Vernon record.

xv

Next to the Music Room is the handsome West Parlor, called by Washington the Blue Room, which has always been finished in that color, as is shown by a letter from Washington to Tobias Lear, the Secretary who assisted in the family's final removal from Philadelphia in 1797. "In my last from Elkton," he wrote, "I mentioned the want of a Carpet for my parlor at Mount Vernon—and observed that as the furniture was blue, the ground or principal flowers in it ought to be blue also; and that if Wilton Carpeting was not much dearer than Scotch I should prefer it. Mrs. Washington says there is a kind different from both and much in use (Russia) if not dearer or but little more than the former I would have it got. The room is about 18 feet square, and the Carpet should have a suitable border if to be had."

None of Washington's Mount Vernon rugs has survived, but the 1942 Minutes record that "after years of fruitless search" during which the floor was left bare, they had come at last upon an 18th-century collector's item, "offered by a dealer who against much discouragement from the Regent had brought it for inspection at his own expense. It proved to be the long-sought hand-woven Wilton with earlier type tapestry background in the desired coloring." The expert declared it to be an irreplaceable specimen, and in spite of the high price it was unanimously decided upon.

The West Parlor became the responsibility of Illinois under the first Vice-Regent, Mrs. Elizabeth Willard Barry, whose great-uncle was once President of Harvard. She was succeeded by one of her lady-managers, Mrs. Mary Carver Leiter, wife of a partner of Marshall Field's early ventures. The furniture which she caused to be made for the parlor in the proper 18th-century style remained in use until well into the 1930's.

Mrs. Leiter's beautiful eldest daughter Mary was the heroine of one of the few successful transatlantic marriages between

American heiresses and British peers, a fashion which a few years earlier had endowed the future Sir Winston Churchill with an American mother, and was to wreck the life of the unfortunate Consuelo Vanderbilt, who was coerced by her ambitious mamma into unwilling union with Churchill's cousin, the ninth Duke of Marlborough. Mary Leiter's marriage with Lord Curzon was without any doubt a love match, after a long, discreet courtship, and she shared with him the glittering vice-regal throne of India, a position which her unusual beauty and dignity adorned with great credit, though the climate of India was responsible for her early death in 1906. Her mother, who travelled to India and to London to witness her daughter's splendor, was laughed at both at home and abroad for her malapropisms, most of them probably invented, and she was anyway the author of two little volumes of Biographical Sketches of the Generals of the Continental Army, which are worthy of respect. Her other two daughters, also famous beauties, both married into the British nobility. Lord Curzon, always theatrical, was broken-hearted over his wife's death, but recovered to carry on a spectacular affair with Elinor Glyn before marrying a wealthy widow in 1917.

Mrs. Leiter showed good taste and discretion as Vice-Regent for Illinois, and in 1909 supported Mrs. Hearst's proposal for the erection of a suitable separate house for the Resident Superintendent, which was finally accomplished on Mrs. Richards's insistence in 1936.

Mrs. Carpenter, who so annoyed Miss Comegys, succeeded Mrs. Leiter, and copied a canvas-stitch chair-cover for the room. In 1940 she presented some valuable old blue Canton china to replace broken pieces of value. She was followed in 1949 by her nephew's wife, Mrs. Elizabeth T. Isham.

The Chippendale card-table, laid out for a game of loo with ivory fish-counters and 18th-century cards, fits the description in a 1785 invoice of Washington's, and was presented in 1897 by Mrs. Goldsborough, authenticated as an original Mount Vernon piece. The picture above the mantel-piece seems to be the "neat landskip" ordered from England by Washington in 1757 with measures to fit the space, when he was improving the house before his marriage. Lafayette is said to have played whist on the tilt-top table on which the silver tea-service is set out, and which was presented by Mrs. Broadwell. The silver tea-tray had the adventure of being seized during the Civil War by the Federal Government, having been in Mrs. Lee's possession. It was returned to her daughter, Mary Custis Lee, as late as 1896, and was purchased by the Association from her estate. The tea-set in the "Chinese porcelain" so popular in Washington's time has come back in three different lots from Martha's descendants, and has the deep saucers from which it was quite proper to drink, while the tea cooled. The famous broken mirror, repaired by Dodge and Jimmie Rouse in 1928, hangs over the Hepplewhite card-table against the west wall. The Argand sperm-oil lamps, of which there were once fourteen, were acquired by the Association from the Upshur family, descendants in the Peter line. The most charming portrait in the house is that of Fanny Bassett, Martha's favorite niece, painted by Robert Pine at Mount Vernon about the time of her marriage to George Augustine Washington after the Revolution. The half-length portrait of Washington, in uniform, was painted by Peale during the War, and came by bequest from the Boudinot family.

This beautiful room, upholstered in blue, somehow does not photograph well from any angle, and must be seen to be realized.

xvi

From the West Parlor a door leads into what Washington called the New Room, as it was not finished until after his return from the War, though it has somehow since then acquired the rather unsuitable name of Banquet Hall. Granted that Washington built it in order to accommodate the numerous guests, invited or unexpected, who took advantage of his hospitality, it was unlikely that the room was reserved for special occasions which might be called banquets, and probably the family meals were often served there, depending on the number of extra plates required. Like the addition on the south end, it had been erected in his absence, with Lund directing the workmen.

When Washington arrived home at Christmas time, 1783, the New Room lacked even a mantel-piece, but this was soon supplied by what was almost a chance acquaintance—a travelling Englishman named Vaughan, who had an American wife and American sympathies, and went out of his way to meet the victorious Commander-in-chief during Washington's triumphal

Perspective drawing of Mount Vernon, published soon after its purchase by the Mount Vernon Ladies' Association; showing the Summer House in the foreground, the Tomb on the left, the old Stable and the Kitchen Garden left center, and the south colonnade. The wharf is off to the left.

Mount Vernon today, from the north, showing the Palladian window in the Banquet Room, and the north colonnade leading to the Office.

The north colonnade, between the Mansion and the Office, from the courtyard, with the scarlet honeysuckle trained along the arches as directed by Washington in 1785.

The piazza, with the thirty Windsor chairs presented by the Vice-Regent for Louisiana in 1891.

Early morning at Mount Vernon, 1965. Five guards assemble outside the Watch Room before the gates open.

The old Greenhouse, part of which was erected with Government indemnity funds in 1869, and the first restoration of the Quarters.

The Greenhouse today, reconstructed in 1950-1951, after study of Washington's specifications for the one he built in 1785-1789, and the second reconstruction of the Quarters.

The north lane, looking toward the circle on the west front, past the Store House and Watch Room.

The wharf and shelter, always the concern of California, rebuilt through the generosity of Mrs. George Hearst.

The Central Hall in the 1890's, showing the wooden Doric columns inserted in the 1870's to support the weight of the second floor.

The riverfront, or Sea Wall, which was completed in 1902, largely by contribution from Mrs. Hearst.

Mrs. Phoebe Apperson Hearst. Second Vice-Regent for California, 1889-1918.

Mrs. Justine Van Rensselaer Townsend. Third Vice-Regent for New York State, 1876-1891, and third Regent, 1891-1909.

Miss Alice Longfellow. Second Vice-Regent for Massachusetts, 1879-1928, in the study of her home at Cambridge.

The Library, in early days, showing the brass rail which protected the exhibit from the souvenir-hunters—the globe, which has remained in the house since 1797, the tambour-desk which returned in 1905 through the Vice-Regent for Massachusetts, and the circular chair which was purchased in the same year with the aid of the Vice-Regent for Kentucky.

Miss Harriet Comegys. Second Vice-Regent for Delaware, 1888-1909, and fourth Regent, 1909-1927.

The Library today, with many of the original editions restored to its shelves.

Miss Leila Herbert. Third
Vice-Regent for Alabama,
1894-1897.

Mrs. Emma Reed Ball. Third
Vice-Regent for Virginia,
1874-1919.

Mrs. Ida Richardson. Third
Vice-Regent for Louisiana,
1880-1910.

Miss Emily Harper. First
Vice-Regent for Maryland,
1866-1891, from a portrait by
Sully.

The Banquet Room in the 1880's, showing the colossal Peale canvas of "Washington Before Yorktown" obscuring the west window, and protected by wire netting which for a time also encircled the mantel-piece; the relic-cases, later removed to the Museum; the make-shift furniture, and the undraped Palladian window.

The Banquet Room today, with the reconstructed window-draperies of dimity and green satin, and the Sheraton chairs.

The Family Dining-room, showing the Custis children's high-chair, presented by the Vice-Regent for Oregon in 1912, the original side-board returned by Mrs. Robert E. Lee in 1874, and the Lambdin portrait of Miss Cunningham above it.

The Dining-room today, showing the contemporary table presented by the Vice-Regent for Oregon in 1943, with the plateau and garniture sent from Paris by Gouverneur Morris in 1790, presented by the Vice-Regent for Maryland about 1895.

The visit of the late King George VI and Queen Elizabeth in 1939. Mr. Wall on the far left, the Queen, and Mrs. Roosevelt behind Mrs. Towner who is on the Queen's left.

The visit of Queen Elizabeth II, then Princess, and Prince Philip, in 1951. The Regent, Mrs. Harkness, at left, wearing the Regent's badge and ribbon.

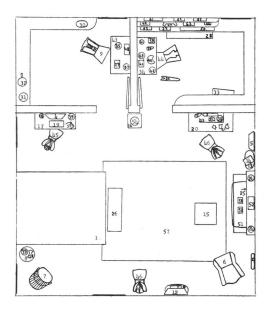

Floor-plan of Washington's Bedroom, from the Curator's 1958 Furnishings Catalogue. Each piece is numbered and colored for reference to source, authenticity, and history.

The Central Hall today, showing the Bastille model and the key.

Washington's Bedroom in the early 1930's, showing wall-paper which was found to be of too late a date and removed.

Washington's Bedroom today, with the windows restored to their original proportions, the hand-woven rug, and one of Washington's trunks.

The Music Room, or East Parlor, showing Nelly Custis's harpsichord and music-books, and reproductions of Martha's needlepoint cushions on the Windsor chairs.

The Custis Bedroom, showing the crib with its netted canopy.

"Our wizard, Jimmie Rouse,"
about 1912.

Harrison Howell Dodge.
Third Superintendent, 1885-
1937. From a portrait by his
daughter Anna, now Mrs.
Elvin Heiberg.

The guards, about 1933. Front row: Lacey, Simms, Ayers, Utterback. Back row: Rogers, McCally, Deavers, Permar, Costello.

The second fire-engine, presented by Henry Ford in 1936.

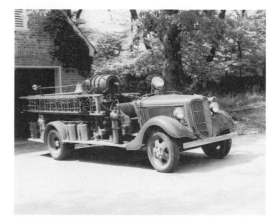

The Family Kitchen today.

journey homeward in the autumn after the peace treaty was
signed. Washington apparently warmed towards the admiring
stranger sufficiently to talk of his beloved house on the Potomac
and the work going on there. Vaughan begged the honor of
presenting for the new dining-room a mantel-piece from his
house in England, and Washington probably took the offer as a
generous impulse born of a convivial evening and acquiesced.
He was doubtless more surprised than pleased when the mantel-
piece actually arrived, in ten large packing cases, early in 1785.
His letter of thanks said that he considered it "too elegant and
costly by far for my room and republican stile of living." But
since it was there, all the way from Wanstead, England, it was
duly installed, complementing by its pastoral figures in high
relief the agricultural motif in the ceiling decoration of the room.

The following year Vaughan sent a mantel garniture of three
Worcester porcelain vases to complete the gift. After being separated for some time, the three pieces are now reunited to stand
where Washington must have placed them nearly two hundred
years ago. The familiar Stuart portrait of Washington over the
mantel in this room is the "original copy" by Stuart himself
which was presented to the Association by Mrs. Richardson in
1904. In order to prevent souvenir-hunters from chipping off
bits of the high-relief carving on the mantelpiece itself the Association for a while kept a wire netting around the entire fireplace, extending out into the room to protect the hearthstones
from—it is a matter of record—tobacco-juice. The head of a
marble lamb once noticeably missing is now back in its place,
but other small projections have been broken off. The mammoth
canvas by Rembrandt Peale depicting Washington and his horse
before Yorktown, which Dodge found in possession of this
room, was finally removed in 1902, when Mrs. Ball arranged that
the Corcoran Gallery in Washington should house it indefinitely
"on loan." It too had had to be protected by a wire netting, but
had suffered from exposure to the window which it obscured,
and continued for years as a recurrent worry and responsibility,
requiring expert nursing.

In the 1880's the center portion of the elaborate stucco ceiling
fell, and the repair work by Emmart & Quartley was done
at the expense of Mrs. Townsend, Vice-Regent for New York
until 1891, when she became the third Regent. She was the

widow of an Albany physician, and after her husband's death maintained a home in New York City, where she had organized several amateur theatrical entertainments of *The Sleeping Beauty* and *The Mistletoe Bough*, raising thousands of dollars for the Endowment Fund, that separate hoard dreamed of by Miss Cunningham to be held in reserve as a cushion for the maintenance and repair expenses which increased every year. After further repairs in 1920, the ceiling of this room let go again in 1941 and the room had to be closed for three months. The Mansion Committee (Mrs. Denham, Chairman) expressed itself as "stunned by the catastrophe"—which occurred only a few days after Council had adjourned. But it was found that what fell was not the original ceiling but the former repair job, and the cove with its graceful Adam-style decoration has never been damaged. A man was found in Washington to undertake the tedious work of restoring the design of the central part. Appreciating his responsibility, he performed with loving care. Mount Vernon's William Miller, who first came to Mount Vernon at the age of sixteen in 1907, and is now the senior man in the Shop, undertook with his assistants the wearisome and difficult job of removing the many coats of paint from the delicate design of the woodwork and walls, which were then done over in the shade specified by Washington in a letter of 1787—"buff of the lightest kind, inclining to white"—and the decoration of the frieze and pilasters were picked out again in white. When the room was reopened it was much admired.

In 1951 it was again renovated under Mr. Macomber's supervision, and the question of wall-paper or paint arose. At the time the Yorktown painting was removed Dodge had found behind it a small piece of wood-blocked wall-paper border and bits of green wall-paper, which had apparently survived the first Association repairs. This had been preserved, and during the 1951 work more scraps of green wall-paper were discovered around the woodwork of the Palladian window, which could be matched to Dodge's. Washington had written for samples of wall-paper in 1787, when he specified buff woodwork. Miss Cunningham had had the room painted what she called "French grey," which was said to go well with the original color of the cornice. After lengthy conference it was decided in 1951 that the 18th-century method of hanging white wall-paper and then painting it the desired color should be followed, and the room emerged in its present delicate shade of green picked out in white. Joshua Brooks had mentioned "white chintz curtains with deep festoons of green satin," which seemed to many of the current Vice-Regents an odd combination of fabrics, but it has been successfully carried out.

Council always met—and still does—around a long table in the Banquet Room, the public being temporarily barred from passage through the room, an inconvenience to everyone. There was at least one instance when Council was adjourned in order that visitors might have access to the room, and another when it convened in a new committee room across the way in the restored Quarters, but felt so uncomfortably uprooted there that it voted to return to the Banquet Room as before. The transformation in 1951 was something of a shock to the more conservative membership, not all of whom approved—so that the Regent (Mrs. Powel) remarked reassuringly in her Report: "I would add that each time I see the room I MIND IT LESS!"

The search for dimity for the curtains in the Bedroom and Banquet Room became almost comic in its many doubts and frustrations, but satisfactory material was at last accomplished in 1953, when at the Centennial Council Mrs. Cabot in one of her amusing Reports answered the vexing question: "What *was* dimity in 1790?"—a stout cotton-ribbed material with a modicum of translucence—and a precious sample of a surviving specimen in the possession of the Boston Museum of Fine Arts was escorted "under proper guard" (never *mailed*) to a weaver in New York, complete with magnifying glass to aid him in the analysis of the weave. It was patiently after many trials reproduced on a hand-loom out of a scarce single-ply yarn, and 100 yards was dispatched to Richmond to be made into curtains "which would have looked familiar to Washington."

The "slatted shades" or Venetian blinds at the large window were recommended by the Mansion Committee in 1917, and Mrs. Furness asked that a gift of $50 sent to her by the Colonial Dames of Minnesota, to be used "as needed" at Mount Vernon, should be devoted to the cost of the blinds. By 1927 what Dodge referred to as "old fashion Venetian blinds" had been installed in all the downstairs rooms. The use of Venetian blinds is sometimes queried, as though they were a modern invention, but when the matter was gone into by the Committee which re-furbished the Mansion in preparation for the 1932 Bicentennial it was determined that Venetian blinds had been in general use before 1767, and that Washington had ordered them in 1787.

The handsome Chippendale tripod torchères or candle-stands appear in the Appraisers' Inventory, and were purchased at the sale of furniture after Martha's death by the inventive and con-troversial amateur architect-author William Thornton, who is believed to have designed both Woodlawn and Tudor Place—and of whom it was said after his death: "his company was a complete antidote to dullness." They were returned to Mount Vernon in 1887 by the same Campbell brothers who presented the Deer Park in memory of their mother, the third Vice-Regent for Missouri.

Research revealed that the room had originally contained two Hepplewhite side-boards, each with a pair of knife-boxes and a gold-framed mirror hung above it, and twelve Sheraton chairs. The matching side-boards for years appeared almost impossible to achieve, but to everyone's satisfaction a suitable contemporary to the one long exhibited in the Family Dining-room was dis-covered in private ownership in the spring of 1966, and the two are now installed on the north wall, with the Palladian window between—while a smaller table has been placed in the Dining-room, to advantage. The knife-boxes, two of several owned by Washington, were acquired at a sale of Washington items about 1830 by the daughter of the rector of Alexandria Christ Church, which Washington attended in his later years, and they were re-cently returned by her descendants. The mahogany Sheraton-style chairs are an adaptation by the Philadelphia cabinet-maker John Aitken of a design in his published drawing-book, and Washington ordered two dozen in 1797.

No "Banquet Room" table appears in the Inventory, and it seems likely that Washington may have used a removable trestle-table, as Council does for their meetings. To the best of anyone's knowledge the spacious room now perfectly represents what Washington had to wait so many weary years to enjoy, at the end of his long service to the infant country which looked to him as its father and inspiration.

The Outbuildings

3

The question of who was the "architect" of Mount Vernon is frequently raised, and cannot be easily answered except to say that there was none. The master-builder in those days was qualified to design as well as to build, and Washington employed a man called Going Lanphier, who for years exasperated both Lund and the General in every possible way, but must have been a competent workman in view of what he accomplished under their constant nagging and exhortation. But the plan, the vision, and the ultimate achievement was Washington's own, based perhaps on English books of architectural design which were available to him, and on his observation of other men's homes from which he accumulated and adapted certain features which appealed to him. But while the James River mansions all bear a family resemblance to each other, and even the Potomac houses like Gunston, Marmion and Rippon are in the same general style, Mount Vernon stands more or less alone, four-square, like some of the others, but with noticeable deviations, like the corner fireplaces and the piazza, from the rest.

The exterior finish, instead of the neighborhood brick, is of pine siding, bevelled, painted, and then sanded, to resemble blocks of stone, and is unique—Washington called it "rustication." The suggestion has been made that he got the idea of the high piazza, also unique in his era, during his boyhood voyage to the West Indies, the only time in his life that he ever left the shores of America. The roofs are of hand-rived cypress shingles and the piazza is paved with sandstone flagging which he ordered from England and which was laid originally about 1785. In time some of the stones cracked and chipped, and cement substitutes were made, until in 1914 Dodge had the astounding good fortune to locate through the Geological Museum in London the very quarry from which they had come—

on Lord Lonsdale's estate near Whitehaven in Cumberland. The manager there could prove that the Whitehaven boats had traded to Virginia for tobacco in the 18th century, with the stone going out as ballast.

It is interesting that Washington's purchase had been made from the notorious first Earl, affectionately known to his contemporaries as "Wicked Jimmy," and that Dodge's dealing would have been with the agent of the equally notorious fifth Earl of the second creation, the magnificent Hugh, called "Lordy" by his tolerant tenantry, and who survived in Edwardian splendor with flamboyant yellow liveries, yellow motor-cars and racing colors, long after the modern world had begun to turn drab and unprivileged, and Whitehaven Castle had been sold to become a town hospital.

A sample of the stone was sent to Mount Vernon and was verified at the Smithsonian. Dodge ordered a sufficient supply so that a complete replacement stock—about 1,500 stones—could be stored in the wine-vaults beneath the piazza. The 1914 shipment was delayed by the first German war, and did not arrive till 1916. Because they qualified as "dressed stones" the U.S. Treasury Department required payment of duty, thus conforming to the long established Government policy of treating Mount Vernon and the Association as some kind of uncalled-for step-child of doubtful ancestry for whom it could grant no favors and make no concessions. About 100 stones were at once made use of as replacements for the cement imitations. These were renewed again in 1921, and individual stones, cracked by frost or worn by the tread of feet, are still replaced from the remaining stock, which was replenished from the same source in 1965.

The eight evenly spaced square columns which support the piazza roof were in such disrepair when the Association acquired the place that extra raw timbers had been put up beside them to take the weight of the roof. In the autumn of 1860, just when the future Edward VII as Prince of Wales paid a visit, made a speech at the Tomb, and planted a tree in the grounds, the repair job to the piazza columns undertaken by the first Superintendent, Mr. Herbert, defaced the east front of the Mansion. By 1893 Herbert's columns had begun to rot from the inside, and had to be replaced again, one by one—they had stood for more than thirty years and Washington's originals had lasted more than twice that long. At the same time dry rot was discovered in some of the heavy oak sills, so that Dodge reported the whole house resting on a thin shell of sound-looking timber which would soon give way. He brought in a civil engineer for consultation, and a great deal of work was done under his supervision by the usual Mount Vernon employees.

The gimcrack balustrade which for so long rode the front edge of the roof above the piazza was not a part of Washington's plan and does not appear in the drawing made by Benjamin Latrobe during Washington's lifetime. It was apparently added in the 1830's, when the money could have been better spent on upkeep, and was conscientiously repaired by the Association several times over, always a futile expense, until in 1934 it was attacked by Mrs. Romayne Latta Warren (Michigan) as Chairman of the Mansion Committee and condemned by Council. Like the South Porch it then vanished practically overnight, causing any view of the Mansion in which it appears to "date" by about thirty years.

The weather-vane on the cupola, repaired by Neitzey in 1947, was minutely described by Washington in a letter to his nephew George Augustine in 1787, when it was sent back from Philadelphia to be installed. "I do not suppose there would have been any difficulty in fixing it without directions but I have requested the maker to give them and they are sent accordingly," he wrote during some homesick interlude in the proceedings of the Constitutional Convention which had called him out of his happy retirement after the War. "The wood part of what is sent must receive a coat of white paint; the spire if that is not the case already, must have that of black. The bill of the bird is to be black, and the olive branch in the mouth of it must be green. These last two are otherwise by mistake. Great pains (and Mr. Lear understands the compass) must be taken to fix the points truly. Otherwise they will deceive, rather than direct, if they vary from the north, south, east, and west. . . ." Detailed directions for the use of compass and plumb-line were enclosed.

It is interesting that during the 1947 repairs to the cupola the weather-vane did not have to be altered—the original setting done in Washington's time still read true.

Until 1891 iron benches were placed on the piazza for the use of fatigued visitors, and then Mrs. Richardson donated the thirty Windsor chairs mentioned in the Appraisers' Inventory. She had got them hand-made in Connecticut, and they were fastened together in groups of three or four and painted green. In 1953 an item appears in the Minutes which would give Washington pleasure: "Tuesday evening (October 27) being unusually mild, the Regent and some of the Vice-Regents walked to the Mansion and sat on the portico, enjoying the full moon on the autumnal foliage and the quiet river." It was exactly one hundred years since Miss Cunningham, from her sick-bed in Philadelphia, had written her first letter to a Charleston newspaper launching her apparently hopeless campaign to raise $200,000 for the purchase by a still nebulous organization of women of the decaying home of the first President.

The colonnades also are an unusual feature of Mount Vernon —arched and paved covered ways curving out from each end of the Mansion to join it to the first outbuilding, or dependency, the Office on the north, the Family Kitchen on the south. Their construction caused Lund considerable anguish while Washington was at Cambridge. They were still building in 1778, when he was short of workmen, and Washington was still inquiring about their progress in '81, from his Headquarters on the Hudson. In the spring of '85, when he had got home again, his Diary notes the planting of scarlet honeysuckle at each column of the covered ways, and from Philadelphia during the Constitutional Convention, he wrote of his desire that the honeysuckle should be nailed up and made to "spread regularly over the parts which are painted green."

"There is no repairing the colonnade, for the wind left not a vestige of it, but levelled it to the ground," Miss Tracy wrote the Regent in the spring of 1861, after reporting that the south end had blown down. That there was no shelter between the Library, which she used as a dining-room, and the Kitchen all during her war-time residence at Mount Vernon must have been one of Miss Tracy's major trials, but it is not mentioned again, and the colonnade stayed down until 1874, when Mrs. Halsted raised the funds to erect another. Both sides were reconstructed by Dodge, on the original pattern, in 1904, and remained with some patching up until 1956 when Mr. Macomber undertook extensive alterations to both the north and south curves to make them conform to a photograph taken about 1854, before the destruction of the south end. The effect of the colonnades, to an imaginative visitor arriving from the west gate, as many of Washington's did and as today's traffic is directed, is that of gracious open arms extended in hospitality.

The history of the individual dependencies, except the Kitchen and the Office, is scanty. When Dodge arrived in 1885 there were fifteen buildings, all ancient and in need of repair, some of them mere cottages outside the present Exhibition Area, housing nineteen resident employees, including children. Early in its administration the Association was advised by the usual busybodies to remove all subsidiary buildings entirely, even those belonging to the Mansion life, as unworthy of preservation. This was done at nearby Gunston and at Stratford farther down the Neck, and except for the kitchens those of the James River mansions have largely disappeared. But once again at Mount Vernon foresight and respect for tradition prevailed, and they were made use of for storage and housing, while retaining their original names—Kitchen, Smoke House, Spinning House, Wash House, etc.—as in Washington's time. The round-the-clock guards made use of some as dormitories, literature and souvenirs were sold from another, and refreshments were served in a tent affixed to the Kitchen. As fast as funds permitted they were vacated in favor of newly built bungalows well hidden from the Exhibition Area and designed for the use of the employees and their families. These houses gradually acquired electric light, screened porches, and bathrooms, and the occupancy hazard to historic buildings was reduced. At present the number of extra family dwellings has dwindled to three, besides the Resident Director's house.

In the 1930's, with public interest and attendance increasing, a committee was created to direct the restoration and furnishing of all the Mansion's dependencies to complete the picture of Mount Vernon as Washington knew it. This program was interrupted by Hitler's war, and was resumed in the late 1940's under the supervision of Frank Morse, who seems to have arrived by a happy accident, to become one of the most valuable people Mount Vernon has ever contrived to attract to its service. He found awaiting him a considerable backlog of miscellaneous treasures and plain old junk in uncatalogued storage, which has now been sorted out and added to by his field-trips into the hinterlands to find and purchase forgotten odds and ends in old barns and attics—so that every now and then another outbuilding is opened to view, more or less complete with its 18th-century contents arranged as for daily use. The Appraisers' Inventory at the time of Washington's death has been of course very helpful, but without Mr. Morse's specialized knowledge and patient curiosity it would have been inadequate.

Beginning with the first building on the north colonnade, which was known to Washington as the Servants' Hall or House for Strangers—a sort of guest-lodging for casual visitors and white servants, and the overflow from the Mansion at crowded times—we come to the spacious and picturesque Office of the Resident Director, with secretarial quarters in the two upstairs rooms which once served Hollingsworth, Dodge, and Young as dormitories above their offices on the ground floor. It had also functioned as an office for Washington's secretaries Humphreys and Lear, while they put his official papers in order after the war, and for the historians like Sparks and Lossing who were allowed by Bushrod and his heirs to consult the files. The ground floor room next to the colonnade, with its enormous brick fireplace, was for a time believed to have been used as a kitchen when the banquets were served in the New Room, as Washington always called the large north addition—but as that would have entailed two full kitchen equipments it seems not to have been practicable, and certainly when Dodge lived there with his family their meals were still prepared across the way in the Family Kitchen and carried over to be eaten in this room.

The same kitchen arrangement when Washington dined in state implies a procession of much admonished young colored servants, some of them doubtless quite small, precariously conveying hot covered dishes across the west front or through the length of the Mansion to some sort of temporary pantry possibly set up in the Music Room, from where they could be brought to the table by the butler—and one wonders about bad weather, and rain in the soup, to say nothing of stumbles, spills, and off-stage crashes.

When the two upstairs rooms of the Office building came to be slept in by Dodge and Young and their families it was "deemed advisable" to add two dormer windows in the rear roof, and Dodge remarked in 1890 that "the ventilation thereby secured makes these rooms comfortable in summer, which they scarcely were before"—and scarcely were afterwards, in a Virginia heat-wave, for in 1947 air-conditioning units were installed in the upper rooms for the comfort of Worth Bailey, the Museum technician who then worked there, and who suffered acutely from recurrent undulant fever. Mr. Bailey was a versatile man who had worked at Norfolk, Jamestown, and Williamsburg, and could apparently do anything from devising charming little tail-pieces for the *Maxims* booklet and designs for the envelopes enclosing the flower-seeds on sale, to a revision of the Swords and Military Equipment catalogue and the re-arrangement in 1941 of the Museum built in 1929. He resigned in 1951 to become curator at Woodlawn, which had recently been purchased by a non-profit organization to preserve and show it. This beautiful house, standing on a hill which once gave a view to Mount Vernon, has since been turned over to the National Trust, and is open to the public.

The building next to the Office and separated from it by the north lane has always been known as the Gardener's House, though it has seldom been occupied, except briefly, by a gardener. When Lund was overseeing its construction in 1775 there was some reference to Washington's intention that it should serve as a hospital for the people on the place, but it was variously used for spinners, shoe-makers, and tailors, until in 1793, again in Washington's absence, the Dutch gardener John Christian Ehler applied for permission to move his family into it, as it had an upper room, "which a decent woman would require." This was granted, but Ehler, who drank, left Mount Vernon unlamented a few years later.

About 1893 Dodge was reporting repairs to the Gardener's House which would make comfortable dormitories for two of the night watchmen, with the back room as a guards' office and housing for the portable fire appliances and chemicals, telephone, etc., and an extra small bedroom above. In 1911 it was again rearranged as a Watch Room, which it is still called, Post Office, now located at the north gate, telephone station, and guards' changing room, and for a while post-cards and literature were sold there. In 1926 Mrs. Hanks, then Vice-Regent for Wisconsin, heard that the guards' quarters were somewhat spartan, and recommended the addition of five comfortable chairs, a reading-light, etc. The gardener association occurred briefly again when the present horticulturist used the front room as an office while the new Greenhouse was being built. When he took possession of his new quarters on the second floor of the rebuilt Greenhouse the Gardener's House was again overhauled, providing more ventilation and locker space for the greater comfort of the guards, whose hours are long and whose dispositions stand up to all trials and emergencies.

In the meantime it had become by degrees the nerve-center of the Mount Vernon Security System, which to the initiated visitor seems to approximate that of Fort Knox. It began in 1878 with a thing called the Burglar Alarm Telegraph, which was installed at Mrs. Townsend's expense ($225) and which connected the Tomb with the bedrooms of Hollingsworth and Nathan, but gave no immediate protection to the Mansion at the same time. The first night watchman—required to be unmarried and resident—was engaged in 1892, at Mr. Dodge's discretion. In 1916 the old alarm system was found to be beyond repair, and new wiring was done, this time for the Mansion as well, so that anyone tampering with a lock or relic-case would cause a bell to ring, when the house would be closed by the guards till the offender was found. A new alarm at the Tomb was also connected with the Watch Room. In 1936 portable flood-lights with concealed outlets in the lawn east and west of the Mansion were provided as protection against "malicious approach." When the relic cases had all been removed from the Mansion to the Museum which was built in 1929 the alarm system became obsolete, and an "Electric Eye" was advocated during the 1940 Council. The following year the Eye was installed and working, and the Vice-Regents were invited to witness a demonstration of its "uncanny performance."

Till December, 1941, the night man in the Watch Room and the man on patrol in the grounds had no direct communication with each other. But while a bombing of Mount Vernon was an extremely remote possibility, its proximity to the capital area brought it at once under the D.C. precautions. Chief Engineer Jimmie Rouse, then in the twenty-eighth year of his Mount Vernon service, was as usual equal to the occasion. The Watch Room was blacked out, a direct wire from the Alexandria alarm center was connected, and extra night patrols were set up. Making use of the existing telephone cables, Rouse then devised a communication system whereby the patrol could transmit a signal, visual and audible by a red light and a simultaneous buzzer, to the Watch Room from each of the seven stations on his beat. In reverse a red light could be turned on at each station to signal the roving guard to report to the Watch Room by telephone.

Arrangements were made for underground depositories for important possessions, and a priority list of these was prepared in case it became necessary to move quickly. Otherwise Mount Vernon proceeded much as usual through its eighth war. In May, 1942, when things were fairly jumpy elsewhere, Mrs. Towner, who as Regent always had the gift of the necessary word, said in her Report to Council: "As we meet today in this tranquil spot we are deeply conscious of a world in turmoil, of a world at war. We cannot fail to be aware of conditions which have increased our responsibilities immeasurably, and which may in the near future make unpredictable demands upon our resources. During the last few months it has become necessary to give careful thought to possible emergency disposal of our priceless Washington possessions and to consider many problems directly due to the unprecedented conditions brought about by the war. At the same time it has never been more important so to conduct affairs at Mount Vernon that all who visit here may continue to feel the inspiration of Washington's character and life. Twenty-five years ago we faced a similar crisis, and our records bear witness to the place Mount Vernon then held in the minds and hearts of those who came to us at that time from the four corners of the globe on missions incident to the first World War. May we meet the present crisis with courage and fortitude."

By 1943 the rationing of gasoline and oil began to tell, and attendance dropped again to the 1918 level—even the boat stopped, as it had done in the Civil War. The army had to be dissuaded from establishing a searchlight and anti-aircraft emplacement on the hill just north of the Mansion, when a site west of the Highway proved to do just as well, and with some difficulty a 24-hour air-watch in the cupola was discouraged as "unpractical."

"These are grim times," the Superintendent remarked in his Report, "but there is here a combination of faithful service, wise counsel, and unity of purpose which assures the future of Mount Vernon." Professor Bailey's undulant fever kept him out of the Army, and sent him to the hospital, but Walter Densmore of the office Staff was lost to the armed services for several years, to be returned intact from Japan in 1947, releasing Mr. Wall from his war-time round-the-clock duty. And by 1948 a return to normal was signified by a general increase in salaries and the home-coming of other employees from far-flung active stations. The following year the attendance rose again to the pre-war figure.

After the War Emergency ended, irresponsibility and vandalism were noticeably on the increase, and Doberman dogs with the guards as handlers were added to the night-patrol. These trained guardians are handsome and well-behaved, but not friendly.

Security also involved fire-protection, which at Mount Vernon is a long and lively story, animating Dodge's Reports for years. "There is nothing that fills my mind with more apprehension when I am from home than Fire," Washington wrote to his manager James Anderson in 1791, while enduring the last year of his second term as President. "I request, therefore, that every charge and every precaution against the bad effects of it may be given and used during my absence to guard against the danger of it." And it is indeed a miracle that the Mansion has survived candles, whale-oil and then kerosene lamps, open fireplaces, and a primitive coal furnace, to stand for more than two hundred years. Dodge's first problem was adequate storage for water, to replace the three cisterns hitherto designed to be supplied by rain-water piped off the roofs, and a small portable suction-engine worked by two men, which delivered a half-inch stream half way up the roofs, and exhausted its operators within ten minutes. The water to fill the cisterns was of course wholly dependent on the rainfall. Mrs. Halsted had sent some "fire extinguishers" which could not be trusted, and the idea of an elevated tank to hold water at a sufficient height for adequate pressure was rejected as "too unsightly." A steam pump was then located near the river to force water to the cisterns in the event of a drought, and water mains were laid to the Mansion and other buildings.

In 1891 the Holloway Chemical Fire Engine System was installed by sinking in a concrete vault near the sun-dial in the west forecourt four cylindrical copper caissons filled with water in which a quantity of bicarbonate of soda had been dissolved, and which were surmounted by a glass bulb charged with sulphuric acid. When by turning a lever the acid was emptied into the alkaline water below it generated carbonic-acid gas which furnished the pressure to force water through a hose with a cut-off nozzle. In the vault under a metal trap-door in the lawn of the west front circle the hoses were coiled on spools connected with the tanks, nozzles upwards within easy reach. At the same time the water supply was ensured by piping to the cisterns and the deep well back of the Kitchen, and a pump with a quick-steaming boiler was housed in a small brick building behind the Store House on the south lane built to receive it. When the work was finished Dodge was able to point out with pride that there was nothing in sight above ground to disturb the appearance of the original surroundings of Washington's home.

A demonstration was given for the Vice-Regents on the west lawn, by erecting a structure of old boards and straw which was set ablaze. Within 6 minutes there was steam pressure to operate the pumps, and the fire-corps, consisting entirely of Mount Vernon employees, ran out the hose and played the water upon the flames, which were extinguished in 26 seconds. Turned upon the Mansion roof, the hose threw a stream higher than the cupola and weather-vane. There was only one qualification to everyone's satisfaction. A competent engineer was needed to operate the little steam-engine which delivered the water from the cisterns, and no one at Mount Vernon was considered suitable for this responsibility. James Ringold Archer, who had accompanied the Holloway installation, was therefore retained, and the Association was to benefit later from his mining-engineer training, when he planned and executed the drainage of surface water from the hill on which the Mansion stands, ending the periodic landslides towards the river.

Archer was a Princeton man, long known to Dodge, and who lived with his mother, who kept a select girls' school in Washington City until her death. Short and stocky and dapper, says Mrs. Heiberg, he was always something of an eccentric, given to mysterious absences which lasted for days, so that Dodge's Diary would note: "Archer in eclipse"; "Archer back again, thank God," etc. His appointment in 1907 as a permanent member of the resident Staff was designed to hold him down a little, though he remained a likable enigma even after his sudden death in 1924 in the Washington hotel rooms he inhabited alone.

In 1914 the steam-pump was exchanged for an Otto oil engine which drove a triplex pump to force the water through 3-inch mains to centrally located fire-plugs. In 1923 a reservoir holding 250,000 gallons of water was constructed on the hill north of the Mansion—to be supplied from the river by a piston pump driven by a kerosene engine housed in a building on the river's edge. Mains ran from the reservoir to a centrifugal pump and gasoline engine hidden in the basement of "that little orphan structure on the north lane called the Ice House," which was no longer practical for storing ice. This engine had a self-starting device which operated within 7 seconds of pressing an electric button in the Watch Room, and the Ice House pump delivered 750 gallons per minute at 100 pounds pressure to the fire-plugs in the grounds. Hose carriages and extra apparatus were stored on the ground floor of the Ice House, level with the lane and behind a quick-acting bolted door. This unfortunate little hump-backed building which plays such a useful part in the Mount Vernon security organization has been disparaged as not having been there in Washington's time—its brick is of too late a date—and he is thought to have had a blacksmith's shop where it now stands, of which traces were found in 1937. It may have been constructed—for ice—by one of the later Washingtons, when ice was still "harvested" in the creeks and even taken from the river, in happy ignorance of the dangers inherent even then in that supposedly less polluted water. As late as 1920 Dodge reported cutting and storing 33 loads of ice, though electric refrigeration was then already proposed.

Archer trained young Jimmie Rouse to take over the engine work, and in 1923, as almost the last service of his twenty-seven years, he was to devise a system of perforated pipes concealed in the roofs of the Mansion and adjacent buildings with connections at ground level for the chemical fire-truck hose. When the chemical truck was operated the pressure caused by the carbonic acid gas would force the water from the tanks up through the pipes and spray it out into the areas where it was needed. In 1936 a carbon-dioxide installation, complete with new pipe, replaced the Holloway mixture, to eliminate the chance of water damage. This system was operated from the same vault in the west circle by the sun-dial. From the stationary gas cylinders pipes then radiated to the principal buildings, connecting with the perforated pipes concealed under the shingle roofs, whence carbon dioxide gas could be liberated in sufficient volume to smother a fire in its incipiency.

In August of 1923 the Association received a handsome gift from Henry Ford, described as a "specially made auto-chemical engine, mounted on a Ford chassis, handsomely finished—the double tanks, containers, recharging units, lantern, bell, etc., being heavily nickel-plated. Extension ladder, hose, axes, etc., add to its efficiency." This amounted to making portable the installation under the sun-dial grass plot.

The Garrison Automatic Fire Detecting System went in in 1927, presented free of all cost including installation and repairs by the Company. This device not only announces the presence of fire or an overheated area, but gives its location, both visual in the Watch Room and audible by horns and bells, with a different sequence of signals for each location. A second, more powerful, up-dated fire-engine arrived from Mr. Ford in 1936, when Dodge reported in the Minutes: "The Garrison Fire Detecting System, as well as the Sterling engine, is tested daily, and the chemical tanks are periodically recharged. We are always ready!"

Hidden away in the Minutes for 1941 is the amusing answer to the legitimate query as to how Mr. Ford was first moved to

make so valuable a contribution. Mrs. Denham happened to recall, almost by-the-way, that when Mr. Ford was one day recognized among the visitors in the grounds, the astute Mr.
Dodge turned in a false alarm—the sight of the man-propelled equipment which promptly appeared so wrought upon Mr. Ford's
sensibilities that he, as one might say, "came through." Twice
over.

All this preparedness has fortunately never had a really serious
work-out—except for brush-fires and a small Service Area blaze
—but in June of 1954 a careless passenger on the boat let fall a
lighted cigarette into the dry top of the east cluster of piles at
the wharf. One of the Embrey boys, living the enchanted life of
the employees' childen whose homes are inside the gates of
Mount Vernon, spotted the fire and gave the alarm which
brought the crew and equipment in earnest—not before the
flames had crept up the roof of the wharf shelter and burned a
few shingles. The fender piles at the nose of the wharf had to be
replaced at some expense, and matching shingles were turned
out in the Mount Vernon Shop. Since so relatively little damage
resulted, the excursion was probably a welcome excitement for
all, and young Embrey, after his brief glory, grew up to be a
guard.

There is no doubt that Dodge enjoyed his false alarms, and
fire-drills were called at any hour of the day or night to keep
everybody on their toes. In 1927 the Fire-chief of San Francisco, on his way to an International Convention of Fire-chiefs,
visited Mount Vernon incognito to make a personal sneak inspection. So well had the Association concealed from view the
modern equipment which Washington certainly never envi-
sioned, that the delegate from San Francisco saw nothing but the
six leather fire-buckets which were Washington's only safeguard
besides the buckets of salt stored in the attic and kept ready to
be poured down whichever chimney flue happened to catch fire.
He therefore reported to the Convention that he had found
Mount Vernon shockingly ill-prepared for fire, and a resolution
of censure on the Association was "indignantly passed." When
the consequent Commission of Investigation and Remedy arrived and made themselves known, Dodge addressed them im-
perturbably: "Gentlemen, you have taken me completely una-

wares, even as accidental fires are apt to do. Nevertheless, I will proceed to convince you that the Convention was erroneously informed as to the status here. Let us have a demonstration at once and see what will happen. If some one has a stop-watch, please note the elapsed time from my sounding of the alarm to the arrival of men and equipment."

It was the noon-hour, and most of the men had scattered for lunch, but Dodge pressed the button. The bewildered visitation was immediately engulfed in the ensuing stampede of the fire-crew to their posts, and in 54 seconds the chemical fire apparatus reached the Mansion, and ladders and hose were ready for action. In 7 seconds less than 2 minutes four lines of water hose were laid and the pressure was on—furnished by the Sterling engine in the Ice House. The visiting firemen looked at each other in astonishment and said: "Let's go home!" But Dodge was not done with them. "Gentlemen," he said, "an explanation is necessary. For over forty years I have been responsible for the safe-keeping of Washington's home, and I have steadfastly aimed to do this with every means procurable. To equip the establishment with every essential improvement that the present age requires, without marring the picture of that real simplicity which pervaded Mount Vernon originally, necessitated the *hiding of every new appliance.* I am indeed gratified by the statement of the Fire Chief of San Francisco—that he found nothing here with which to fight fire—for it proved that my efforts of concealment had fully succeeded. May I hope that you gentlemen will clearly report this?"

The gentlemen had very little choice.

ii

The small square building next on the north lane from the Gardener's House is labelled Store House, and has been variously known as the Salt House and the Carpenter's Shop, though Dodge's carpentry was done in a shed beyond the Kitchen Garden on the opposite side. It stood derelict for years until a decision was made to remove the clumsy glass-topped exhibition cases from the Dining-room, Music Room, Banquet Hall, some of the upstairs bedrooms and the Hall, in order to restore the Mansion's "domestic character"—make it less like a museum and

more like the home Washington lived in. Housing for the "relics"—a gruesome term for which *treasures* might be a better
word—was then urgently required.

As far back as 1869, when the Association had only about
five such articles to display, Miss Cunningham had said that
there should be a Museum for the "souvenirs of Washington and
other Revolutionary worthies." By 1875 there were enough
"relics" to fill two cabinets in the Mansion, and these continued
to multiply, by gift and purchase. They were stored at first
precariously in desks, bureaus, and the anachronistic display
cases in the various rooms. Each year at Council time the Relics
Committee carefully dusted, checked, and replaced them. In
1911 a committee was appointed to look into the matter of a
"fire-proof room" outside the Mansion to house these valuables.

It was not until 1922 that the Philadelphia architect M. B.
Medary was commissioned to draw up plans for fire-proofing the
north lane Store House as a proposed Relic House—finally
to be called a Museum in 1935. Recognizing that Washington
had had no such problem, but faced with the necessity to house
and display articles which had become precious only by their
connection with him, the Association first contemplated erecting
in what was called "the Greenhouse group" a fire-proof building large enough to provide accommodations on its upper floor
for a few members during Council. Medary discouraged this
plan, and recommended instead making use of the small structure already available, which could be made fire-proof but
would not provide dormitory space.

His view was accepted, and he furnished Dodge with "working plans" which were at once put into effect. Without altering
the outside shell and roof of the old Store House they built
within it a fire-proof room measuring 15 feet square, with a 10-
foot ceiling and an "unsightly" automatically controlled over-
head door as specified by the underwriters. It was furnished
with dust-proof and moth-proof cases lined with velours, and in
February, 1923, Dodge "personally and alone" transferred all
the relics from the Mansion cases to the new ones, checking
them against his lists and finding all correct and accounted for.
The alarm wiring was then removed from the Mansion.

Almost immediately, however, the new arrangement proved

to be inadequate—the space was too small, and everybody arrived there at the same time—ventilation was a problem—the collection was growing annually. By 1928 they were contemplating the construction of a fire-proof vault in the old Barn at the bottom of the south lane, which would double the exhibition space and utilize a so-far neglected area, and one day Council adjourned especially for an inspection tour of the Barn. It was at this time that notice was taken of the old graveyard where Washington's servants had been buried, and a "suitable marker" was ordered to be placed there. Miss Jennings at once offered to supply the stone.

Mr. Dodge called their attention then to an old plan of Mount Vernon, showing a building called by Washington the House For Families, which had stood behind the Spinning House in the Greenhouse group. It had apparently been taken down by him when the brick Quarters either side of his new Greenhouse were completed in 1793, and he established his experimental "Botanical Garden" near its site. A new building erected on its foundation would provide museum space and other accommodations as well, without doing violence to Washington's own scene. Before the 1928 Council broke up the idea was adopted and estimates were asked for.

The new Museum building, its exterior conforming to that of the Spinning House next to it, was completed and opened to the public before the year was out. Once again Dodge accomplished the move himself, and the cherished relics, no longer crowded, were "seen to great advantage." The Association's greatest treasure, the Houdon bust of Washington, acquired a new pedestal enclosed in a square glass box—details of its background, lighting, and environment were discussed for years, and many anxious alterations were made in its display. The great value of this likeness, which has always left the writer cold, is that it was taken from life, at Washington's prime, at Mount Vernon, between the War and the presidency, and its authenticity is undisputed.

The Museum building supplied on its upper floor another long-felt need. Six bedrooms and three bathrooms, with a separate entrance, supplemented by five more bedrooms with lavatories constructed over the Palm House, which seems to have

stood approximately on the original Greenhouse site, again reduced the occupancy of the historic buildings as living quarters.
(There was even then in the wind a project for what was to become the present Administration Building, facing the Quarters
from across the north lane.) The report of the Relic Committee
(Mrs. Hanks, Chairman) in 1929 is a fitting comment on the successful completion of the Museum, which had been paid for out
of the Association's own funds, without begging or borrowing:

"It was with a feeling closely akin to ecstasy that the Relics
Committee met for the first time in the wonderful new room
that Council has provided for its treasures in the restored Family
House. Its spaciousness and light give added lustre to the relics,
their beauty is seen adequately for the first time, and a comforting glow pervades our hearts with the knowledge that at last
they are both fittingly and safely housed. Those of us who date
back to the days when the relics were kept in the book-cases,
closets and secretaries of the Mansion, with the only records of
these priceless links with the past written in faded ink on odd
bits of paper, feel that little short of a miracle has occurred. The
dusting and verifying of our Washingtoniana has been accomplished with such ease and celerity the former arduous duty has
now become a pleasure, and they can truly be said to be in excellent condition."

The abandoned Store House was then equipped with steel
filing cabinets and became the Archives Building, thus making
documents, letters, and photographs hitherto kept for safety in
a Washington bank vault more available for reference and research work. This was the nucleus of the present Reference
Library in the Administration Building, which did not materialize until several years later, when the contents of the old Archives
Building were finally installed where source material for the
whole Mount Vernon story can now be found, with the aid
and consent of the Association and Staff. Empty again, the Store
House has undergone further study and alterations, and in 1966
was opened for exhibit with riverfront supplies, such as hand-
knotted seines festooned from the beams, barrels of coarse salt,
fishing paraphernalia, etc., as well as blacksmiths' tools, though
even the site of Washington's smithy has disappeared.

Meanwhile, the Mansion became a home again, and the Museum is a model of its kind, with unsuspected living-quarters above and inconspicuous public rest-room facilities below. But already the exhibition space is proving too limited, and hidden storage areas contain material worthy of display. The Association has long been plagued by an embarrassment of potential riches, and the unsolicited offerings range from numerous locks of Washington's hair enclosed in various mountings and of varying authenticity—one was even presented by that experienced collector, J. P. Morgan—to alleged family portraits and furniture, for some of which fantastic sums are asked by the current owner. Authenticity is the first requirement at Mount Vernon, and many objects when screened cannot pass that test, despite the honest convictions of the owner. The story of Dr. Craik's watch illustrates the care with which the exhibition has been formed. At the 1940 Council it is recorded that "Mrs. Barret [Kentucky] then showed to an entranced Council the watch which was held by Dr. James Craik while he counted the last moments of General Washington's life." The watch was the gift to the Association of the sixth-generation descendant of Dr. Craik, then living in Mrs. Barret's State. Mrs. Barret read an account of the present generation and those between the donor and Dr. Craik, and gave some details of the efforts to secure the gift. Mrs. Van Deventer's motion to "accept with great pleasure" was seconded and carried.

BUT in 1953 the Report of the Museum Committee contains the following paragraph: "The watch displayed in the Museum and known as 'the Dr. Craik watch' is to be removed from exhibition. Research reveals that it is a 19th-century piece, far too late to have had any association with General Washington. The watch is therefore recommended for removal."

And it went, although the Craik heirs were doubtless perfectly honest in a cherished family tradition.

The so-called relics—from old coins to old newspapers—hopefully offered for sale or as gifts sometimes have an amusing triviality; tiny squares of cloth purporting to be cut from Martha's dresses and mounted with care; even a piece of Washington's alleged christening-robe and his first short dress; a wineglass said to have been used at his christening ceremonies but proving also to be of much later date; and quite recently a dressing-gown supposed to have been worn during his last illness, its value claimed to be enhanced by the grisly assurance that it had never been laundered since then; cigar-cases and snuff-boxes, always suspect in view of the fact that he seems never to have used tobacco in any form; Bibles, bedspreads, towels, cracked china, buttons—all are courteously considered, investigated, and often returned with thanks as either unauthenticated or unsuitable for display. An offer in 1893 of a whole log hut, priced at $1,500 and said to have been used by Washington as a youth, was "deemed inexpedient." An offer in 1892 of a "memorial chair," bearing stars and other devices commemorative of Valley Forge, which was required by its donor to be enclosed in a glass case was declined "for want of space." A scarf-pin, said to have been Washington's and valued at $5,000 by its owner, was declined, as was a linen chemise supposed to have been worn by Martha, at $1,500. Another Stuart copy of the famous portrait, priced at $5,000, was respectfully declined. A sand-box, part of the 18th-century writing equipment, which was said to have travelled on Washington's saddle-bow with an attendant ink-horn, throughout his campaigns, was accepted as a gift from the Vice-Regent for Rhode Island (Mrs. Ames). Connecticut (Mrs. Hudson), who should have known better, recorded in 1898 the gift of homespun sheets and bed-hangings, the work of her grandmother who was the wife of an officer "who under General Washington led his men at Bunker Hill, Ticonderoga, and Danbury"—at none of which engagements General Washington was even present. Equally ill-informed, though possibly genuine in some sense, was the gift in 1932 of a camp-bed "used by Washington at Valley Forge." At Valley Forge, Washington had the use of a comfortable, though cramped, stone dwelling-house as Headquarters, where Martha joined him, and there is some doubt that he would have had need of a portable bedstead during that entirely static winter. General Washington's uniform sash was presented by J. P. Morgan in 1923, and after spending some time in the glass case in the Hall which held his swords is now in the Museum alongside Braddock's, which it resembles.

By 1910 there was such a growing and laudable desire on the

part of those who still possessed inherited true Washington heirlooms to have them returned to Mount Vernon, that a resolution was passed that only articles authentically owned and used by the Mount Vernon Washingtons or their immediate family could be given room; a decision which denied sanctuary to such seemingly deserving objects as a portrait of the General's kinsman, Colonel William Washington, which was offered by a descendant of his in 1902, accompanied by a drawing of the flag he carried at the Cowpens battle, which had been made for him out of a red damask curtain by a young Virginian lady who was living at Charleston when they met there, and whom William married at the end of the War in a romance largely forgotten by the historians. The innate pathos of helpless inanimate objects left behind by their owner's death is somewhat mitigated, if they can be proved genuine and suitable, by the loving care they are accorded here.

It was early decided that identifying labels on gifts bearing the name of the donor should be banned in the Mansion (though not in the Museum) as impairing the homelike appearance of the rooms, a regulation necessarily extended to include trees planted by visiting celebrities—they are recorded by number— to avoid defacing the grounds.

In 1939 the ten-year-old Museum building was completely renovated, with a new heating and ventilating system which also served the upstairs store-rooms and bedrooms now occupied by bachelor members of the Staff, and the Continental color motif was carried out in the blue velvet which lined the cases and the buff paint on the walls. The Houdon bust in its lighted, glassed-in niche was for a time balanced on the opposite wall by a portrait of Martha, copied by an unknown artist from the one by Gilbert Stuart, but it was on loan and has been replaced by a handsome display of old silver loaned by Dr. George Bolling Lee, grandson of Robert E., beautifully displayed against the blue velvet lining of its case. A full-length idealized portrait of Martha by Eliphet Andrews, designed to complement the full-length portrait of Washington known as the Lansdowne Portrait, was offered to the Association in 1905 and declined because of its apocryphal nature. It now hangs in the East Room of the White House in Washington. The only likeness of Martha as a

young woman at Mount Vernon is the charming Peale miniature
in one of the cases, along with those of Jacky and Patsy Custis.
Two lovely pierced ivory fans, belonging to Martha, one of
them recovered from the Conrad family by Mrs. Richardson in
1894, are to be seen in the Museum. The drafting instruments
displayed in their original carrying case, with a doubtful signature by Washington, date to the days when he did his own
surveying and mapped his boundaries and laid out sites for his
buildings.

The "Braddock sword" presented by Mrs. Herbert for the
Hall is now in the Museum. Other swords, all willed by Washington to his several nephews, have been returned by or acquired from their descendants—including the State sword with
the silver filigree pommel and guard, which he is supposed to have
worn on the day he resigned his commission in Annapolis at the
end of the War, and again at his inauguration as President; this
being another gift from J. P. Morgan, who was for several years
on the Advisory Committee of the Association, and once
brought his yacht to the wharf and took tea on the piazza.

Some pieces of the blue-and-white Chinese or "Nankin" porcelain table-ware which Washington preferred all his life, as
well as the Cincinnati china purchased by him in 1786 and bequeathed by Martha to George Washington Parke Custis, are
in the wall cases. The "States" china with Martha's cypher in a
gold sunburst was sent to her as a gift by a Dutch sea-captain
who retired from the China trade and came to settle in America.
The third china set with the interlaced GW in gold was made
in Washington's honor at Niderville in France, the owner of
that famous factory having been one of the volunteer French
officers at Yorktown. This was probably the first French china
to reach Mount Vernon, though it became the fashion after the
Revolution to use French china instead of English, and Washington acquired a quantity of Sèvres from de Moustier in New
York in 1789. There are four magnificent punch-bowls remaining of the many which Mount Vernon hospitality would have
required.

In 1946 Miss Helen Louise Sargent, Vice-Regent for the District and Chairman of the Museum Committee, remarked in her
Report on the opening of the extra "Little Museum" in the re-

stored East Quarters arranged by Worth Bailey, that "for the moment" there was enough exhibit space, but eventually the Association would have either to limit its acceptance and purchase of small articles or plan a larger exhibition space—outside the present Exhibition Area—"some twenty years from now." That hour has struck. But looking around the perfect grounds and familiar pattern of the present buildings, one wonders how and where such an addition could be placed—and hopes it will not be necessary after all.

iii

Proceeding along the north lane from the Store House, the visitors come to the Spinning House, once occupied as living quarters by the servants and employees of the Association, who were moved out into new accommodations built to receive them, so that the rooms could be converted into lodging for the Vice-Regents at Council time, long before the Administration Building was put up. It has since been altered back again, so that the changes made in 1892 have disappeared.

The Minutes for that year record that Minnesota (Mrs. Rebecca Flandreau) and New Hampshire (Mrs. A. R. Winder) had joined together to "combine utility with beauty in providing rooms for their own accommodation there," as Kansas and Colorado had already done in the old Quarters farther down the north lane to the west. At first only two rooms in the Spinning House were painted and repaired and "made suitable for occupancy," with a skylight in the upper room. Mrs. Flandreau had a ground-floor room, and at the same time she undertook to furnish the main room adjoining hers with an assortment of spinning implements of the right period which Dodge had discovered during a New England vacation and which were purchased by contributions from the school children of St. Paul.

In 1894 the interior was redesigned again, to make two rooms and a hallway on each floor, and five Vice-Regents for whom there was no room in the Mansion were then in possession, obviating for them the daily trip from Washington to Council—each being expected to share equally the expense of the renovation and to provide their own furniture. Besides the first two, the Spinning House sheltered Michigan (Mrs. Rathbone), Ohio

(Miss Mary Lloyd Pendleton), and Georgia (Mrs. Georgia Page King Wilder.) A portable heater was installed in the basement, connected to the chimney and with registers opening into the rooms. But the accommodations must still have been rather primitive, especially for ladies accustomed to the services of a personal maid, and accompanied by bales of luggage, as in the Minutes for 1925 the Household Committee requested for the Spinning House "windows arranged to open," hooks in the bathrooms, shelves to hold towels and soap-dishes, and bars at the sides of the bath-tubs.

Mrs. Leary, the first Vice-Regent for Washington State, was given Mrs. Flandreau's room, left vacant by her death in 1911, and she brought in her own furniture. "Dear Mrs. Leary" also gave the garden seats, and financed repairs on the causeway leading from the wharf. She was the first to propose that men in uniform should be admitted free, and in 1919 made a motion in Council that Miss Longfellow—whose weight was becoming a problem—should be permitted to bring her motor-car right up to the door. "Washington" was always proud of the fact that in twenty-two years, from the farthest corner of the continent, she never once missed a Council.

Miss Pendleton bore the same name as the first Vice-Regent for Ohio, and may have been her granddaughter. She soon married a man named Abney and removed from the State, thus forfeiting her vice-regency. Her next successor but one was Mrs. Alice Key Dandridge Irwin, which were also Pendleton names, and her father was a Virginian. Delicate health prevented Mrs. Irwin's regular attendance at Council, and the vice-regency for Ohio went back to the Laughton-Broadwell line in Mrs. Lily Broadwell Foster Livingood, who in memory of her aunt presented the furniture in her room to the Association for the use of all future Ohio Vice-Regents.

Similarly, Mrs. Page Wilder Anderson succeeded to the Georgia room after the tragic death of her mother in a motor accident, and in 1948 her daughter, Mrs. Page Randolph Anderson Platt, became Vice-Regent for Pennsylvania, where her marriage had taken her, making a record of three consecutive generations in Mount Vernon's service.

Mrs. Winder was followed by Miss Harriet Lane Huntress,

who was kin to Molly Stark, and lived at Concord, New Hampshire.

The basement bathroom was moved upstairs in 1930, and two more lavatories were added on the second floor. An extra rest-room for the public was provided in the basement in 1935. But none of these arrangements is visible now in the restored worka-day look of the Spinning House.

While the gift of a spinning-wheel specifically claimed to have been owned by Martha and used by her at Mount Vernon was accepted "with appreciation" in 1936, the picture of Wash-ington's lady spinning at her own wheel when the Spinning House was humming with colored maids trained for the task, is an unlikely one. Evidence was found during the 1953 restora-tion work that one of the ground-floor rooms had been used for living-quarters, and when the house was first renovated for the use of the Vice-Regents mention had been made that a new cottage was being built for the colored family which had to be moved out. The upstairs rooms were so drafty that the chinks between the wall-planks had been stuffed with rags, and a news-paper dated 1885 had been pasted over the cracks. Washington having referred to it as "the Servants' and Spinning House" is a further indication of its use as a dwelling-place, and the north ground-floor room has accordingly been furnished even to a trundle-bed, as though ready to be lived in, resulting in "a lovely crowded family look" which the Outbuildings Committee ap-proved. Recently an "infant basket" covered with the current cook's lace-trimmed white apron was added, and the place be-came so homelike that a visitor's lost child after frantic search was found serenely seated on the battered rocking-horse in the family room.

iv

Next beyond the Spinning House and the Museum are the East and West Quarters, flanking the Greenhouse in the middle, with doors on to the north lane. These structures, which were occupied by Washington's house servants and such workmen as the cobbler, had suffered from the original Greenhouse fire in 1837, and were sufficiently patched up at the time the Greenhouse was rebuilt in 1869 to allow the gardener to make use of the west end.

Owing to the increased demand for accommodations for members of Council, augmented by recent appointments and larger attendance, Mrs. Jennie Meeker Ward (Kansas) undertook in 1888 to raise in her State the money an architect named Bradshaw would require to rebuild "the old servants' quarters on the west of the Greenhouse" as recommended by Dodge in order to relieve the Vice-Regents who had no lodging in the grounds of the daily journey down the river from their Washington hotels to attend Council sessions. Two years later this reconstruction was accomplished, using all old bricks, and Kansas and Colorado (Mrs. Alice Hale Hill, collaterally descended from Nathan Hale and wife of Senator Nathaniel P. Hill) took possession, furnishing their rooms at their own expense. The erection of what became known as "the Kansas Quarters" also eliminated the worst of the old ruins in the Greenhouse area.

Doubt that the original buildings had been used as living-quarters by Washington's servants was dispelled by Richard Washington, who in 1897 was rising eighty. He was a younger brother of the last Washington owner of Mount Vernon and had married a Harewood cousin. He could remember as a child stopping at the old Quarters in the north lane to talk to the colored mammies of the period, Aunt Lucy or Aunt Polly, and the other old Negro servants. Born in 1822, his boyhood recollections went back before the fire which destroyed the original buildings.

Mrs. Ward was originally a New Jersey woman who had taught in the Trenton schools before marrying a professor from the Ottawa, Kansas, University. She accompanied him there, and continued her work with young people. Her reclamation of the West Quarters was so successful that she and Mrs. Hill were joined there by Mrs. Alice Lippincott (Pennsylvania) whose young and enthusiastic membership was lost when after furnishing a room for herself she died from a chill caught during a journey to Mt. Desert, Maine. She was succeeded by Mrs. Ella Waln Harrison, who served for a quarter of a century, and is remembered for more than one act of generosity and imagination. It was she who first proposed a "commons" or dining-hall for the Staff and visiting Vice-Regents between Councils, "at a suitable distance from the Mansion." This was the initial move, in 1914, towards the present convenience in the Administration Building, whereby a hot buffet lunch is served daily in a cheerful Chippendale dining-room for the Office Staff, privileged visitors, and any Vice-Regent who has happened to turn up.

By the end of the century Mrs. Ward's neighbors in the West Quarters dormitory were Texas (Mrs. Maxey), Pennsylvania (Mrs. Lippincott and later Mrs. Harrison), South Carolina (Mrs. Pickens and later Mrs. Pringle), West Virginia (Mrs. Sarah Boyd Pendleton Van Rensselaer), and she even offered to partition her own room to provide for Alabama (Mrs. Johnston.) In the same decade the old Quarters on the east side of the Greenhouse, likewise damaged by the 1837 fire, were restored for the Vice-Regents' use by New York (Miss Amy Townsend) and Ohio (Miss Pendleton), partly by contribution, partly from their own funds. This building matched the West Quarters on the exterior, and contained a large ground-floor room where Council could be held, with a smaller committee room at each end and four bedrooms upstairs. After Miss Pendleton's marriage and resignation her room was occupied by one of four who established themselves in the East Quarters with their own furniture—Miss Longfellow, Mrs. Graham, Mrs. Mary Polk Yeatman Webb (Tennessee), and Mrs. Ames. Both Mrs. Maxey and Mrs. Johnston moved from the West Quarters into the newer building on the east within a short time, and Louisiana (Miss Annie Ragan King), Mississippi (Miss Mary Govan Billups), and Indiana (Mrs. Walcott) had rooms there at various times. Miss Longfellow was taken ill during Council in 1898 and remained confined to her room. In a letter to her sister she recorded that she had had a comforting call from Mrs. Pickens—"such good company"—and that fresh flowers were sent to her room each day from the garden. Dodge took note of it in his Diary: "All the ladies have left except Miss Longfellow, kept here by illness —has trained nurse and every attention," he wrote on May 8th, and on the 31st, "Miss Longfellow departed for home today. 3 laborers cutting off volunteer rye on grass lot. Stout mowing west lawn broke shafts of mower and had to quit." Mount Vernon rolled on.

Miss Townsend, who raised most of the funds for this extended project, was appointed during Mrs. Townsend's regency, but seems not to have been closely related. Her other contributions were many and generous, and included repairs to the dilapidated Pohick Church where Washington's pew is marked with a brass plate, and where Dodge is buried—but Miss Comegys, as Regent, writing to her friend Mrs. Rogers, had a complaint about Miss Townsend: "She is one who *never* remembers Council actions, and who does *not* consult her Minutes, but depends upon the Regent for promptings."

Council was duly held in the new East Quarters room one year, as an experiment, but though it escaped the curiosity of the public passing through the Mansion and peering in at the Banquet Room doors, it seemed very strange to everyone. Before the session ended the question was put: *Shall Council remain in the East Quarters?*—and the vote was overwhelmingly Nays. The year 1898 found them back in the Banquet Hall, where they have met ever since.

v

"If we only had a greenhouse we could make a great deal by the sale of cuttings," wrote Miss Tracy to the first Regent in 1866, "but now we lose nearly all every winter." Washington's building had burned down about thirty years before the Association took possession, and although some sort of make-shift glass-house had been erected by his heirs the site was still an unpicturesque ruin of smoke-blackened bricks when Lossing sketched it in the late 1850's. Another fire took place there during the Civil War, and there was then some attempt to rebuild with bricks which Mr. Herbert had on hand, in the hope of preserving what historic plants remained.

In 1869 a new greenhouse was constructed with money which would have been better spent on repairs to the Mansion; money wrung from the Government in compensation for the total stoppage of the boat from Washington City as a Federal war precaution, and the resulting loss of income from visitors. But Miss Cunningham in 1869 was carried away by the prospect of having hothouse grapes as well as flowers to sell, and allowed the work in the greenhouse to proceed till the money suddenly ran out. This 1869 structure was repaired, altered, and added on to for years, with appropriations from various States at one time or another, and its heating apparatus was a constant anxiety and hazard.

An adjoining rose-house was built in 1888, financed by Miss Pendleton, about to become Mrs. Abney, on what was believed to be the foundations of Mrs. Washington's forcing-house, and additional foundations were discovered during the work on the West Quarters restoration in 1889, when "the old greenhouse" was reported in need of repairs. In 1916 it was disparaged as being unlike anything Washington might have had and a suggestion was made that it should be taken down, as—moreover—it was presumed that Washington himself would not have approved the sale of plants and seeds from his garden. The 1869 building remained, however, with various auxilliaries, an incomplete and "unsightly" area, when in 1935 under Mrs. Richards's regency the first modern sketch plan for a complete reconstruction of Washington's building was made—only to be blocked by the unhappy realization that the demolition entailed must displace the Vice-Regents whose bedrooms were in the adjoining restored Quarters. Again in 1940 a study was begun "with a view towards restoration," under the direction of Walter Macomber, this being the project which first brought his experience and talents to Mount Vernon. The plant-sales room was removed from the Greenhouse to the gardener's cottage, and the excavation of the central portion of the group was begun.

At a meeting of the Buildings Committee at Mount Vernon on December 3rd, 1941, attended by Mrs. Hanks, Mrs. Berry, Mrs. Powel, and the Regent, who was then Mrs. Towner, Mr. Macomber reported on his findings as to Washington's own plans and correspondence, and the insurance documents of 1802 before the fire. It at once appeared again that the proper reconstruction of Washington's Greenhouse would require the razing and re-erection of both existing Quarters buildings, in which many of the Vice-Regents were accustomed to be domiciled during Council. This would make necessary a provision somewhere else—possibly in a new building outside the Exhibition Area—of lodging to accommodate Council members during session, but would allow the Quarters to be rebuilt as the original servants' rooms on the west, and on the other side of the central Greenhouse block extra museum and exhibition space would be gained. The eleven Vice-Regents who would be rendered roomless when the Quarters came down would have to make the journey down from Washington each day, or accept some kind of makeshift housing at Mount Vernon. There was also some doubt as to the wisdom of attempting so extensive an enterprise as both Greenhouse and Quarters at the same time, in view of a European war and a probable scarcity of materials.

Feeling inadequate to such a drastic decision on the spot, the Committee recommended a special Council to be called in January, 1942, so that more Vice-Regents might have an opportunity to express an opinion. Pearl Harbor intervened, and the first excavations were filled in with gravel to await the end of the War, though the general clean-up already accomplished was ruled an improvement. The dwellers in the Quarters were again reprieved, and smaller renovation jobs, such as the Wash House and Store House on the south lane went forward instead.

By 1949 the Greenhouse project which had been at the back of everyone's mind since it had wilted in 1935 in favor of the Vice-Regents' convenience and finances depleted by the Depression, came up again. Mr. Macomber was fortunately still available, and in August, 1950, he received the commission to proceed. Thus on the eve of its hundredth anniversary the Association had weathered wars, depressions, and ignorant criticism to find itself in a state of solvency and permanence sufficient to justify a further step towards the realization of the original dream—Mount Vernon as Washington knew it. Furthermore, it was able to embark on the biggest and most impressive job of its history without drawing upon its jealously guarded reserve fund, and although its Treasurer "was unable to resist his annual warning regarding the spending of money, he was quite philosophical about it, and the Ladies' ignoring his counsel, but his advice as to our curtailing expenses was no less emphatic than in past years." Even Treasurer Baird could not call it extravagance, and they had earned the right to proceed.

Mr. Macomber's first task was to devise an alternate lodging for the members of Council, which entailed a new building to be erected outside the Exhibition Area and screened by trees at the end of a service road running north from the north lane, near the modest brick house built in 1936 for the Resident Director and occupied since then by Mr. Wall. The two-story cream-colored stucco building known as Unit I could accommodate fourteen Vice-Regents in attractive small bedrooms with bathrooms, in complete privacy from the Exhibition Area, and it included a large ground-floor room as lounge and committee room. This emptied the old Quarters and made possible at last the authentic reconstruction of the Greenhouse group, though it was at once apparent that a second such housing unit would be needed, in view of the increased membership and more regular attendance at Council. Plans for a second bedroom Unit (III) to face the first one across a grassy yard were authorized and it was ready for occupancy in 1955, when the Vice-Regents' furniture was moved into their respective rooms. Mr. Macomber's genius for comfort and charm is evident in the pillared arches and woodland setting of this small isolated group. The central or Unit II portion is still lacking for the kitchen and other household equipment which now resides only in the Administration Building, where meals are still served to Council. The first occupant of Unit III was a Carolina wren, who raised and launched her family unmolested in one of the unfinished ground-floor rooms, while the carpenters and electricians walked carefully around her little home. On the suggestion of Mrs. Irene Tarr, first Vice-Regent for Oklahoma, the term *Unit* was dropped in favor of naming the new buildings *Cunningham* and *Tracy* respectively—which occasions such amusing statements as that there are termites at *Cunningham* and a bell has been installed in *Tracy*. They are both linked to the world by telephones and fire-alarm wired by Harry Rouse as engineer. The common room at *Cunningham* was furnished as a gift by Mrs. Louise Loughborough of Arkansas, who had served on the Buildings Committee.

Returning to the Greenhouse, which is the greatest single piece of restoration undertaken by the Association, the Regent's Report for 1951 remarks that it "rose with serene dignity and grace above the box-bordered parterres in the Flower Garden, and one feels the 'rightness' of it there, mutely eloquent testi-

mony to the slow and painstaking, but fruitful, research put
into the plans for this reconstruction by the architect, chairman and committee." Washington's plans and specifications
were largely contained in his correspondence with his former
aide, Tench Tilghman, whom he requested in 1785 to investi-
gate for him Mrs. Charles Carroll's famous Mount Clare greenhouse near Baltimore. A late 18th-century painting of Mount
Vernon from the northeast showed windows in the second floor
of the north side of the Greenhouse, but there was little reference to the interior arrangement of the flanking Quarters
except for the fireplaces in each room, though it appeared that
the first reconstruction half a century previously had been very
similar to the more recently studied plan.

The question has been raised as to where Washington's slave
population lived, and the obvious answer is that what were
probably small wooden cabin dwellings had long disappeared
before the Association acquired the place and that no indication
even of their location remained. They were also probably widely
scattered over the five farms on land which has now been built
over. But there is reason to assume that the Mansion Negroes,
numbering about sixty, had many of them been housed in the
Quarters, warmed by the constant Greenhouse fires and flues,
and certainly more sheltered and convenient than in the huts
and cabins to which the field Negroes were accustomed on this
and other plantations. The present arrangement of the West
Quarters as reconstructed for the second time by the Association funds has for exhibition purposes a "family" room with
quilt-covered bunk-beds and rough wooden tables and chairs.
A fire is kept burning on its hearth, for it has been realized
that the smell of woodsmoke must have always hung over
Mount Vernon in the days before cooking was done by electricity. Next to it is the shoe-maker's shop, which Washington
is known to have had there. The second-floor rooms were
designated by him for the use of white servants, probably those
of his guests, and stairs led up from the lower rooms. The upper
floor of the restoration became after a time the offices of the
horticulturist, and the west end of the West Quarters is still
the Sales Room, where the Association literature, post-cards,
and plant cuttings are on display.

The east room on the ground floor of the East Quarters has been finished as a supplementary or "Little Museum" for special exhibits, and the one west of it was equipped with a cot and toilet for the accommodation of "fainting ladies" among the visitors, who might be overcome by the heat or the cold or too much standing around. It has seen surprisingly little use, even in the humid Potomac summers.

The interior of the Greenhouse is furnished with movable plank tressels for potted and tubbed plants, designed in period by Mr. Macomber and executed by the Mount Vernon Shop— so that delicate plants like oleanders and hibiscus and lantana can be moved in and out in the autumn and spring. There is also a collection on high shelves of old gardening paraphernalia, bell glasses, pots, tools, and baskets collected by Mr. Morse.

A great many of the old brick weathered to the proper rosy hue used in the construction of the Greenhouse were obtained from the Commission for the Renovation of the White House in Washington, as that work was going on at about the same time. A service greenhouse and cutting-garden is hidden away beyond the machine shop and the Service Entrance on the west below the public road, where the flowers are grown for the floral arrangements in the Mansion. "Nothing at Mount Vernon is ever complete," according to the Minutes, "and as the years pass and more information comes to light it can be added to the sincere basic study, conscientiously shown in the structure today."

vi

The Administration Building, once called the North Quarters, was by far the Association's most important early undertaking, before the Greenhouse, in the way of additional construction, and was necessitated mainly by the need of dormitory space, and the wish to remove the cooking fires from the old Kitchen on the south colonnade, in the perpetual anxiety about any fire at all near the Mansion. Moreover, convenience had compelled the Vice-Regents to go on using the Library as a dining-room, though they were aware that the room should be kept as a Library for the visitors to see.

At the 1929 Council Mrs. Richards as Regent made the first official proposal, after several years' debate and consideration, to construct with Association funds a brick building similar in its exterior to the restored Quarters in the north lane, but containing a modern kitchen, dining-room, servants' rooms, living quarters for Dodge and Young, and more bedrooms upstairs for the Vice-Regents during Council. General approval of this by no means new idea was finally won at that session, though Mrs. Van Deventer made known "very forcibly and emphatically" her opinion that Council should continue to hold its meetings in the Banquet Hall, as "preserving for all time in the minds and hearts of the Council the proper atmosphere created by the Association and memories received and here experienced."

Mrs. Danforth's valuable reminiscences recalled that some of the Vice-Regents had become attached to their old familiar inconvenient lodgings here and there in the Spinning House and Quarters, and over the Museum and the Palm House. A few of them even retained the privilege of sleeping in the Mansion, "though," she added, "they had to be out of their rooms from 9 to 5 every day but Sunday, leaving them with no evidence of occupation in sight, had no plumbing, and the 'necessaries,' as General Washington called them, were about a city block distant. The new building also provided living and dining space which had been drearily met before by sitting round the poorly lighted Council table evenings, and using the jammed Library for meals. The Council table is still in the so-called Banquet Hall, but a building now under construction [Unit I] will free the Mansion of any use by the Association and all the Vice-Regents who have been used to meeting within its walls will feel as if bereft of home." They did. And Council still convenes around a long table set up each year in the Banquet Hall, though no one has slept in the Mansion for years.

With the Association's usual dispatch and fidelity to tradition, the new North Quarters on a site outside the Exhibition Area in the field bordering on the north lane and opposite the restored Quarters was ready for inspection within a year's time. No architect was needed, as the plans drawn by Dodge from the old Quarters were followed by the builder. Second-hand rosy-hued bricks procured in Alexandria gave the appearance of mellow age and dignity, and this facsimile of the original Quarters, now almost hidden by a tall hawthorn hedge, contained something like thirty rooms including nine bathrooms and two lavatories, a modern kitchen and adequate dining space for Council, besides a comfortable lounge for committee meetings and afternoon tea. On the second floor, lighted by dormer windows, it provided more storage for records and files, and overnight accommodation for the Regent and Vice-Regents in small bedrooms with a bathroom between each pair. The new building was successfully hooked into the existing hot-water heating system with its own thermostat, telephone service, and fire-detection.

In March of 1930 Dodge and Young moved out of the cramped little rooms over the Office which they had inhabited for forty years, and into ground floor rooms in the new Quarters, while there was a general exodus of servants and equipment from the old Kitchen to the new, and the Sales Room was removed from the Kitchen to the Gardener's House. The bedrooms above the Office were inherited by Mr. Wall and Julian Washington, grandson of the last private owner of Mount Vernon. Julian, with a useful knowledge of stenography and book-keeping, worked for a few years as clerk and financial secretary with the junior Superintendent, and it was through his mother, Mrs. Lawrence Washington, that many valuable Washington papers or transcripts came into the Mount Vernon files.

Young's retirement in 1934 because of ill-health left young Mr. Wall as Dodge's chief assistant and mainstay, and he occupied with his family Young's former rooms in the new building, until the brick house for the exclusive use of the Resident Director, as he is now called, was built. This dwelling had been suggested as far back as 1909 by Mrs. Hearst, who offered $1,000 towards its cost, but there was some objection in Council and Dodge showed little interest in the project, so the proposal had been tabled for more than twenty years. When it was brought up again in 1935 by that great innovator, Mrs. Richards, who felt that Mr. Wall's accommodations were inadequate, it was unanimously approved and a site was chosen in the edge of the woods on what is known as the Landon Lot.

The interior of the Administration Building has been slowly remodelled and adapted to meet growing administration needs, and at present it houses the Business Office, the Vice-Regents' lounge and dining-room, an up-to-date kitchen with freezer and dishwasher, pantries, and an adjoining lunch-room for the guards, besides the Reference Library, Reading Room and curators' offices. The latest upheaval there took place in the spring of 1966, when only the Regent's upstairs bedroom suite was retained as living-quarters, while all the other second-floor rooms were converted to the use of the library staff and its filing cabinets and typewriters, with a reading-machine for microfilm inhabiting what was once a bathroom.

The Reference Library was first suggested in 1930 by Mrs. Richards, when it was decided that space in the new building should be devoted to published works relative to Washington and Mount Vernon, available to the staff and to accredited researchers, and separate from the books in Washington's Library in the Mansion. Mr. Wall did much to build the basic list of reference books and to co-ordinate those already spread around in his own Office and other administration rooms. The present comfortable central Reading Room, created out of what once served the Regent as an office, is now shelved to the ceiling for a useful collection of books on 18th-century furnishings, architecture, and biography relative to the Washington family; substantial sets of historical societies magazines and cyclopedias; Association annals, and Washington's Collected Writings in thirty-nine volumes as edited for the Bicentennial by Dr. Fitzpatrick of the Congressional Library, and interleaved with material accumulated by the library staff since its publication.

Now that it has become known that a Reference Library exists at Mount Vernon, the inquiries telephoned or written in to the Librarian range from the scholarly or journalistic to the downright ridiculous, but all are dealt with as politely and helpfully as though the staff had nothing better to do than listen to long-winded amateur genealogists whose fourth-generation great-uncle once caught a glimpse of Washington at Valley Forge; and always the slow, tedious, rewarding work of research and authentication and cataloguing goes on, and on, and on.

vii

Returning to the circle on the west front of the Mansion, the first building on the south colonnade, designed to correspond to the Office on the north, is the old Family Kitchen, which saw nearly two centuries of continuous use before becoming an exhibition area as part of the over-all restoration program. In Hollingsworth's time it had served with a tent-annex as a lunch-room for visitors, with waiters in white coats and food prepared by Sarah, selling milk and fruit grown at Mount Vernon. This was in a way a concession to prevent the public from picnicking in the grounds and even in the Mansion with food they had brought with them, but it never paid and was done away with in the late 1880's, though milk, eggs and fruit continued for a while to be sold from the Kitchen, along with post-cards and souvenirs.

With the arrival of the railroad in 1891 traffic gradually shifted from the wharf to the north gate, where the main entrance is now. Here the man named Gibbs had established a sort of restaurant outside the gate, with a stentorian promoter who as each train arrived rang a hand-bell and exhorted the public through a megaphone to avail themselves of the refreshments. The Association protested against the noise, and the megaphone was removed, and signs advertising the restaurant were not permitted inside the grounds. In 1932 the present unobtrusive concession building was set up by the National Park Service outside the north gate, purveying adequate meals and the usual souvenirs and literature. Again, this is no part of the Mount Vernon Ladies' Association endeavor, which maintains its own small Sales Room for its plants and literature—no food—in the West Quarters.

Mount Vernon has steadily resisted periodic pressures to profit by the sale of "authentic" souvenirs, such as the 1894 proposition by a New England firm to manufacture chairs from wood "certified" to be from Mount Vernon trees, with a royalty of 50¢ on each chair to the Association—"Declined," the Minutes comment briefly. For a while canes fashioned from wood cut at Mount Vernon by the older employees were sold in the grounds, but that was discontinued. Even the sale of photographs of the place was restricted, by an exclusive contract with one photographer at a time, who had to agree not to sell or "commercialize" the pictures outside of the grounds, lest they become "commonplace." As time passed visitors were permitted to bring their own cameras inside the gates, on the understanding that the pictures were not to be sold or displayed except in private circulation. The ban on food sold in the grounds is firmly maintained, however, for fear a sanctuary would become a picnic resort. In 1946 it was arranged that the outstanding photographer Samuel Chamberlain should take both black-and-white and color photographs of Mount Vernon, some of which were to be used in the handsome new edition of the Guide-book ordered for that year, and Walter Densmore on the Staff soon began to do kodachrome photography for the catalogue and Sales Room. When he became Business Manager and Assistant Director, photography was added to the duties of the horticulturist, Mr. Fisher, whose flower portraits are of unusual beauty.

In 1900 Miss Amy Townsend had undertaken to restore the 18th-century look of the Kitchen, and brought from England an old dresser, and some copper and pewter ware said to be contemporary with Washington. Dodge visited the James River mansions and made drawings of articles in their kitchens, and a smoke-jack and turning-spit were installed. The building was cleaned and plastered, and sleeping-rooms were fitted up on the upper floor for the use of the extra maids and cooks who came in at Council time. Running water was brought in in 1910, and an electric range was introduced in 1922 to eliminate the open fire in the cook-stove. After the removal of the preparation of meals to the Administration Building in 1930 the Family Kitchen became part of the Exhibition Area. In 1939 a collection of Mount Vernon's old kitchen utensils was brought in by Miss Agnes Peter, and an electric burglar alarm was wired in for their protection. Ten years later the Kitchen was briefly closed for further reconstruction. The policy of the Buildings Committee has always been to avoid "those frustrating and inhospitable NOT OPEN signs, and further never to close more than one room or building at a time, which the public is accustomed to seeing open."

The Kitchen proved to be one of the most puzzling of the research jobs, having been used and re-used by Washington with new chimneys on an earlier shell, and there is mention in 1783 of white-washing the room above the kitchen, probably for the use of servants. In 1958 it came on the Outbuildings

Program, and the visitors' perennial question of where the Washingtons' dishes were washed was answered when the small room next the larder was set up as a scullery, with kettles and large copper basins for hot water, and even dish-towels drying on a line. The spits have been connected with the smoke-jacks and a plate-warmer stands beside the hearth where a wood fire is kept burning.

Mount Vernon menus have survived from 1797 and '99 and give a picayune modern appetite some idea of what the Kitchen was expected to produce—and Washington's table was by no means as extravagantly provided as those of many of his contemporaries.

> Leg of boiled pork—top of table
> Goose—bottom of table
> Roast beef
> Round cold boiled beef
> Mutton chops
> Hominy
> Cabbage
> Potatoes
> Pickles
> Fried tripe
> Onions
> Etc. Wine, porter, and beer at dinner
> Table cloth wiped
> Mince pies
> Tarts
> Cheese
> Cloth off
> Port
> Madeira
> Nuts
> Apples
> Raisins

A recipe for "a great cake," copied out by Martha Parke Custis for her grandmother Martha Washington was acquired in 1930. It begins: "Take 40 eggs and divide the whites from the yolks . . ." and goes on to add 4 pounds of butter and 4 of powdered sugar, 5 pounds of flour, half a pint of wine and "some French brandy." Two hours would bake it.

viii

Next to the Kitchen is what has come to be called loosely the Butler's House, when actually it was where a man named Butler lived for a short time as manager of the Home Farm, during Washington's absence—and of whom Washington wrote in 1793 with his endearing irascibility: "He may mean well, and for ought I know to the contrary may in some things have judgment, but I am persuaded he has no more authority over the Negroes he is placed [sic] than an old woman would have."

But mainly the building seems to have functioned as another Store House, for kitchen supplies, with lodging for an overseer. Later it was occupied by the guards on night duty, with a public rest-room in what had probably been the root-cellar. It was also for a time a so-called first-aid station, which was very little needed by the hardy visitors for whom it was thoughtfully arranged by the housekeeper in the early 1900's. Its actual restoration was begun in 1948, when the "overseer's room" was simply furnished with bed and bureau, chairs and a table, and a wall mirror. Within the next three years it too came under the Outbuildings Program designed to reclaim all the historic service buildings to a lived-in appearance, by collecting and disposing the humble furnishings of the period in their one-time setting. Mention was made by the Committee that "as most of our equipment seems to be either made by Mr. Morse or picked up by him at a bargain, we do not envision any great expense."

Second of the smaller buildings on the south lane is the Smoke House, which was opened to view in 1935, and the smell of a hickory wood fire in the pit was added to the artificial meats hung from the rafters. The wax representations of hams, shoulders, sides of bacon, etc., had a tendency to melt in hot weather, and even fell from the hooks to the floor, and rubber meat was contemplated as an alternative. In 1956, it having been discovered with some chagrin that as then modelled all the hams had come from the same side of the hog, molds were made for both rights and lefts, and the exhibit was reconstructed. "You may be fascinated to know," runs the Report of the Outbuildings Committee to Council, "that the wax comes from the candle-ends disposed of by the Washington Cathedral." Possibly at the instigation of Miss Ellen Tyler, who was then Vice-Regent for the District.

The addition of some large casks for pickling, a sousing vat, and slaughtering equipment helped to furnish it more realistically, and the building received a fresh coat of whitewash in 1957.

The Laundry or Wash House stands next to the Smoke House in the south lane. It had been remodelled in 1911 so that cots could be placed there for the extra waiters required during Council. Actual restoration began in 1943, when the interior trim was given a coat of the paint called Spanish Brown, later changed to grey-green, and the old brick floor was scrubbed and repaired. The big copper cauldron was added in 1946, with shelves, stools, and small appurtenances. Evidence that soap was made on the place, as well as bought, was plentiful, and an original soap-jar was acquired, which in the old days was probably kept under lock and key, its contents being a precious household commodity.

Finally the equipment was completed with a drying-frame, a slat-board for the laundress to stand on, benches for the tubs, and even hand-irons. Washington is known to have purchased a mangle, but nothing of its kind has been found. Small identifiable garments in the 18th-century style hung up on a line to dry add to the interest and the humor of this exhibit.

ix

The restoration of the Coach House was first undertaken by Mrs. Rathbone in 1894, when it was reconstructed from almost total ruin to house an alleged Washington coach which had been located through a correspondence between Dodge and a man named Brownfield, who believed he had traced it to the winter quarters of a circus in Philadelphia. Brownfield presented the vehicle to Mount Vernon and it was placed on exhibition in 1895. Doubts of its authenticity remained, and much interest was aroused by a photograph of another coach which was submitted to Dodge with a letter from a descendant of Washington's friend Samuel Powel of Philadelphia, establishing that while the coach in question—the second—was not actually Washington's, it was the twin to his, and having been in the Powels' possession it had undoubtedly carried him through the streets of Philadelphia during the presidency.

Washington's famous "white chariot" in which he made the southern tour in 1791 had been built to his order in Philadelphia and it stood up nobly to the bad roads and weather of the long journey. Presumably the return of the Washington family to Mount Vernon in 1797 was made in that chariot, which then resided in the Coach House during the remaining two years of the General's life. George Washington Parke Custis purchased it from the executors and used it himself around Arlington. Its last owner was the Virginia clergyman Bishop Meade, who in excess of admiration for the first President allowed the chariot to be broken up and the pieces distributed as souvenirs, or sold for the benefit of the diocese of Virginia. But Mount Vernon was not complete without a coach, and the Powel vehicle, of undoubted pedigree, was therefore acquired in 1902, through Mrs. Rathbone and the Detroit Mount Vernon Society. The Brownfield coach was returned to its donor and its replacement remained on exhibition in the Coach House at Mount Vernon for roughly half a century before its rehabilitation was begun under the guidance of a specialist in coaches, Colonel Paul Downing, the actual work being done by the usual Mount Vernon geniuses.

First the ancient vehicle was carefully dismantled, measured, and photographed, and many layers of paint and varnish were removed until the original color scheme could be determined. Minor repairs and replacements were made, in particular the coachman's seat, which was known to have been lowered and altered for the convenience of an aging coachman in the Powel family. The woodwork was given as many as sixteen coats of fresh paint and varnish, with painstaking rubbings between, to achieve the density and gloss of the period. The handsome blue Kersey hammercloth and blue leather upholstery were made from materials approximating the remaining bits discovered in the crevices, a new lamp was made to duplicate the one surviving—lamps being something of an innovation at the time the coach was first made. The Regent found among her family heir-looms a piece of carriage-lace or binding, left over from some original carriage-job of the right period, which could be re-produced and added to the finish, and handsome carved beading so closely matched that the join can hardly be found was fitted into the gaps. The final touch was the footman-holders, which were lace-covered leather straps with tassels, attached to the rear of the body, to which the footmen could cling as the coach rocked over the bad roads and pavements.

The next requirement was of course harness, which was a problem that could not be solved by collecting, as 18th-century harness was no longer available. Reproduction was the only solution. Adequate source materials, published and documentary, were not lacking, but harness-making was a vanished craft. Mr. Morse and his craftsmen on the Outbuildings staff decided to revive it. Harness-makers' tools were illustrated in the old cy-clopedias, with text explaining their uses, and they could be devised or reproduced by altering tools of other crafts which were not too dissimilar. No attempt was made to record the total time spent on this project, but 3⅔ miles of thread were used, all hand-stitched. Three hundred and forty-two brass fittings were cast to special patterns at a small local foundry, buffed in the Mount Vernon Shop, and worked into the harness. Felton's *Treatise on Carriages and Harness* (1805) was a de-pendable guide to style and an aid in developing techniques. The finished harness for six coach horses made a handsome display in the coach compartment of the stable, reposing on proper racks as though ready for use; and the effect of readiness was suitable, as the harness has been tested and found flawless in service.

Mr. Morse's report to Council touched briefly on the several difficulties, such as the difference in size between 18th- and 20th-century horses (which had to be taken into account if the harness was to be worn by today's larger breed, as it has been); the tools for hand-sewing leather, which had to be found or made; and the patterns to be cut out for both leather and brasses from 18th-century manuals. The opinion of Council was that Mount Vernon could be justly proud of the harness which hung, three sets to a side, on appropriate pegs on the Coach House walls.

By 1957 ten saddles had been added to the exhibit, including the war saddle copied from equestrian portraits of General Washington, with its pistol housing and leopard-skin saddle-blanket. And with the saddles were displayed the proper number of bridles, horse-blankets, sweat-scrapers, buckets, etc., and four curry combs patterned on one excavated in the stable area and reproduced by Wilfred Neitzey and his assistants in the Mount Vernon Shop, along with the whips.

In 1953 Mrs. Frances Packette Todd (West Virginia) presented to the Association a two-wheeled riding-chair—a vehicle with a single seat like a Windsor chair set on a platform, with a narrow platform behind it for the small colored boy whose duty it was to jump down and open gates for his master to drive through. Few of this type of vehicle have survived, and next to the Powel coach it was of great importance as an acquisition. It was originally owned by Washington's one-time patron, Lord Fairfax, at Greenway Court in the Valley, and was purchased from his nephew by Mrs. Todd's great-grandfather in 1812, Mrs. Todd herself being descended from Washington's brother Samuel. Since it is known that Washington possessed such a vehicle, it is proper that the Fairfax riding-chair should be displayed in the stable at Mount Vernon.

The brick Barn which faces the Coach House across a cobbled yard is the original structure built in 1782 to replace the one which had burned down in Washington's absence. It was saved from dilapidation in 1874 by a $50 contribution from each Vice-Regent at that time, and was repaired again in 1889. Washington spent so much of his life in the saddle that it was thought appropriate in 1933 to open the horse-stalls and mule barn to view, and in 1957 further reconstruction of the stable area was done under the supervision of Mr. Macomber.

In an open-faced shed behind a fence alongside the Coach House there has been assembled a collection, begun in 1946, of old farm implements, wooden hay-rakes, a horse-hoe, a stone-roller, a watering-cart, etc. By 1921 farming at Mount Vernon had been largely abandoned as unprofitable, except for the meadows which still produce a hay-crop. What has always been called "the Tomb lot" was kept planted in crimson clover for its artistic value.

Dodge's first-year planting had provided provender for the animals then on the place, and the silo built at his desire was considered a success. Until 1897 milk was sold to visitors by the glass, and butter was made in the Dairy. But "The refractory character of our clay soil baffled the best efforts of even General Washington to wholly correct it, nor have we, his successors, yet solved its vexing problems," Dodge reported in 1934. Lime and other commercial resoratives had been applied, and crops of cowpeas, buck-wheat, and coarse hay were rotated and ploughed under, and the meadows were re-seeded. A team of farm horses was kept for "local color," cows graze even now behind fences in the lots behind the Tomb, and the spring of 1967 brought 4 enchanting black lambs. But farming, as such, is long abandoned, as not worth the expense and labor. "We adhere as far as possible," wrote Dodge, "to Washington's preference for the landward outlook from the Mansion to stress the effect of far-reaching meadows, as now seen."

Among the obsolete buildings demolished by the Association as of too recent date was the old Milk House or Dairy, which operated in Miss Cunningham's time but was taken down in 1947 as not being even on the site of Washington's, which was in what he called the Spring House "below the hill." Bushrod's Summer House, which stood over Washington's old dry well storage for ice, overlooking the River, was kept in repair till 1936 and then was removed as being foreign to Washington's landscape.

The Machinery

4

Electricity and motor transport have come to Mount Vernon, but in the beginning it was only on sufferance. The Mansion's wiring for illumination and vacuum cleaning is now on a cut-off switch in the Watch Room, and is kept turned off except when in actual use for lighting Council or for cleaning. The parking lots are well out of sight outside the gates and behind the Administration and Service buildings, and are screened by planting.

Mr. Archer, the resident engineer in charge of drainage and wharf operations, presented a revolutionary proposal in 1916 —the fiftieth anniversary of the first Council presided over in person by Miss Cunningham. He wanted to install the Edison system of storage-battery electricity to light the Mansion, Office, Quarters, and other buildings used as dormitories. The Vice-Regents were at once shocked into the objection that electric light in Washington's house would be incongruous. Archer replied reasonably enough that the kerosene or coal-oil lamps then in general use were as unknown to Washington as the Edison electric bulbs could be, and much more of a fire hazard. Mrs. Harrison (Pennsylvania) and Miss Townsend (New York) remained unconvinced by even that clinching argument, even in view of the fact that no visible change need occur, the lamps and the small batteries to which they were attached being removable when not needed. Archer further explained that the low-voltage storage-battery was endorsed by insurance men everywhere, and that in the trial installation of lamps already set up in the Council Room and Dining-room the batteries were concealed under the tables, supplying a 32-watt illumination—rather dim by present standards—from covered wires. The cost was not considered exorbitant, in view of the safety factor, and Mrs. Hearst, attending for the eighth time since her appointment, promptly offered to contribute what amounted to practically the whole of the estimate. Mrs. Brown (Rhode Island) made the motion that "Mount Vernon should be electrically lighted by the Edison low-voltage storage system, as recommended for safety by Mr. Archer," and Delaware (Mrs. Victorine E. Foster) seconded. Mrs. Harrison voted the only No. Mrs. Leary and Miss Failing between them made up the balance of $625 needed for the installation, and no appropriation of Association funds was required.

As usual, once the decision in Council was taken, action was prompt and effective. Mr. Edison himself was magicked to Mount Vernon in person, and assigned his chief engineer to direct the work. Dodge's Report the following year announced —along with improvements to the Ha-ha wall at the west end of the Bowling Green and repairs to the Banquet Hall window casing: "The Edison electric lighting system, as a precaution against accidents by fire, has taken the place of the dangerous candles and lamps which formerly were used for lighting the Mansion and adjacent buildings. Mr. Edison gave his personal advice in the installation of this system, and his chief engineer directed the work. A small dynamo driven by a kerosene engine generates the electricity and stores it in portable batteries"— which had to be recharged every day during Council use.

The further cautious development of the electrical system at Mount Vernon is complicated to tediousness, but it appears that in the beginning when the first hook-up to an outside power-line was made for the purpose of running the fire-pumps, drinking-water pump, etc., the power supply was often interrupted by the extra demand made by the trolleys climbing the hill outside the gate. This was sufficient to throw the circuit-breaker and stop the main pump, which lived in a small building near the river shore. Then someone had to go down there and re-start it. At the 1921 Council it was moved and carried that electricity should be introduced into the Kitchen for cooking purposes. Mr. Archer was sent to Orange, New Jersey, to consult Mr. Edison, to whom all things were possible, and with the aid of his engineer a new plan was laid out approving an "isolated plant without any connection with an outside source of electricity." Archer then journeyed to Dover to explain this innovation to the Regent, who directed that the work should proceed. It was completed in time for the 1922 Council, when a 50-horse-power Otto Engine was housed in the building on the riverfront with larger storage batteries capable of taking over in the intervals when Mount Vernon was robbed of outside power by the trolleys. The wires were all laid underground, safe from the electrical storms which come roaring down the Potomac, and the wiring for lighting fixtures was put into rigid conduits, abolishing the flexible cables already in use. All the work was done under the direction of Edison's engineer by Mount Vernon's Rouse-Miller-Thomas team, "who have been commended for their intelligent efficiency by all of the experts engaged in the installation of the Edison Power Plant," Dodge reported, and the Association acknowledged its debt to Mr. Edison for "patriotically giving his advice for the benefit of Mount Vernon." Dodge added: "The successful installation of this improvement marked an era in our utilities which, I feel, Washington would have been glad to see."

The new electric range gave no trouble to its operators, and the Kitchen was no longer in summer "a fiery furnace," which was appreciated by the servants who worked there. The electric refrigerator was supplemented by a cold-storage compartment built into the old Milk House behind the Kitchen. The lighting power was noticeably increased, as was that for pumping water. The same year the new reservoir up on what was called, from its donor, the Gould Lot, was filled with river water, and Archer's perforated pipes for fire-fighting were completed.

Mount Vernon was thus independent of any other power source until 1925, when Dodge rendered a complete report on the electrical service as generated by a 100-horse-power Diesel engine using kerosene as fuel. The situation had by then seemingly reversed itself, and he advised a return to Company power, with the Diesel as auxiliary for emergencies. Technical details were not lacking to confuse Council, though they probably gathered that it would be advisable to rely for power henceforth on the Alexandria Light and Power Company, which would have to run their lines to Mount Vernon at considerable cost—worth while to them only if the Association agreed to buy Mount Vernon's whole supply and reduce its resident equipment to the position of stand-by. Intricate financial details indicated that the cost of the new arrangement was not greatly in excess of what their own system required, considering the expense of fuel, etc., and the necessity for constant maintenance.

As if to underline what had not been regarded as an urgent decision, there were two serious break-downs of the Diesel engine on which they had been depending for their power—once just after the 1926 Council had adjourned, and again just before the 1927 Council was due to convene, when an important bearing ceased to function and an expert from the Philadelphia factory had to be called in. "Had the break-down occurred *during* Council, imagine the dilemma!" Dodge exclaimed, and went on to explain that to avoid the possibility of being "stalled" again, the advice of mechanical engineers to utilize current from an outside power corporation had been heeded, and the laying of a triple line of electric cable encased in steel conduits for a distance of over 2,000 feet was already going forward. The following year extra lines were laid and meters installed to supply electricity to the employees' cottages in the grounds.

The final change-over from direct to alternating current bought from the Virginia Public Service was made in 1935, and an entirely new telephone system went in at the same time, with a switchboard in the room adjoining the Office. This has now been banished completely out of sight, and operates mysteriously in an upstairs office room via a handsome gadget like a typewriter with light-up keys in each office. The expensive reconstruction for alternating current resulted within two years, as predicted, in cutting operating costs in half.

ii

An even more urgent problem than the lighting of the Mansion was its heating apparatus, necessary as much against damage from damp as for the comfort of visitors and its occasional occupants during the early Councils. The dangerous old coal-burning furnace installed in 1878 through Mrs. Halsted's efforts and re-set under Dodge's supervision ten years later was by 1900 discarded in favor of a new hot-water system, planned by a Boston firm and located in a subterranean boiler room excavated 400 feet from the Mansion, from which underground pipe-mains in terra cotta conduits extended to the Office, Watch Room, and other Outbuildings used by the employees, as well as to the Mansion itself. Each building was separately valved and could be cut off from the circuit as desired. The increased comfort and benefit to the Mansion was at once appreciated, the heat being radiated through grills in the hearths and under the stairs. It was expensive—and it still burned coal. But it worked for twenty-three years, when new "Ideal" boilers with automatic regulators were installed by the same expert who had supervised the original work. Electric stokers and thermostat controls were added in 1930, and six years later in the summer of 1936 the construction of tunnels for the heating mains and the work on the reconstructed electrical installations disfigured the grounds west of the Mansion. Water, telephone, and electric lines are now carried through the tunnels, as well as heat. But the pungent smell of wood-smoke still hangs over Mount Vernon, even in summer, as it must have done in Washington's time, for the fireplaces in the Quarters and some of the Outbuildings are kept burning as they would have been then.

An all-steel Service Building had been erected in 1926 in the Valley beyond the North Gate, where the employees' cottages were grouped. Within a few years it was found necessary to increase the size of this building and a larger one was constructed around it, the final result being the present inconspicuous Power House complete with its own heating-plant. It contains a carpentry shop with power-lathes, saws, and other tools, storage for paint and other inflammable materials, garage space for several cars, and the auxiliary Diesel generator—which the writer has seen in smooth operation within minutes of a blackout caused by a summer thunderstorm. Designed after similar 18th-century utility buildings, and constructed by a Richmond firm from old bricks, with a slate roof, the Power House stands inside a separate Service Entrance, protected by a mechanical wooden arm which can be raised and lowered by a man from inside the building. Apparently nobody but light-minded historians is amused by the inscription in black letters on the white-painted barrier: STOP AND BLOW. The 1936 Ford fire-engine, polished and groomed like a favorite charger, occupies its own small brick dwelling across the hard-top lane which leads up to the Exhibition Area.

iii

In 1866, when the War's end restored the boat service from Washington to Mount Vernon, and the little steamer *Arrow* resumed its daily trips, Miss Tracy had purchased for $34 a derelict army ambulance which, drawn by Mount Vernon horses, carried infirm visitors up the steep slope from the wharf to the Mansion, with a stop at the Tomb on the way. In 1869 it required a new oil-cloth cover, which was accomplished by the gardener Craig, and in 1882 it was replaced by what Mrs. Laughton called a boat-wagon, made to order in Philadelphia and driven by a Negro coachman. Its seats ran along the sides and it could convey eighteen or twenty passengers, at an additional fee of 10¢. This was also the vehicle in which the Vice-Regents rode to Pohick Church on Sundays during Council.

In 1904 Mrs. Sweat reported that a gentleman visitor had professed himself to her as "shocked" by the shabbiness of the conveyance provided to and from the wharf. "I explained to him that the Association would not object to exchanging it for a handsomer one, under proper conditions," she added. "He replied with enthusiasm and promised to send a new carriage soon after his return to Columbus, Ohio. He gave me his card and repeated his promise. I wish I could also report the arrival of the carriage." Dodge was then authorized to dispose of the old wagon, which was thought too heavy for the horses assigned to it, but no bids resulted and a new one would have cost over $500. He gave the old vehicle a coat of fresh paint and "a pair of handsome and powerful Percherons" were purchased to draw it. This must have been quite a sight, with a venerable coachman on the box and a colored lad guarding the back steps, but no photographic record of it survives. The 10¢ fare for a ride was removed in 1913, and younger horses were purchased to replace those which had been in service eight years. At the same time a pair of mules presented by Kentucky in 1903 were retired from farm work to a "good home" in the flat country on the Maryland shore.

The Minutes relate that on Sunday, May 14, 1916, "being a

cold and rainy day, several of the gentlemen in the neighborhood placed their automobiles at the service of the Regent and
the Vice-Regents, which was very thoughtful and a decided
improvement over the transportation to church by the coach."
In 1924 Dodge's Diary says: "Showery all this A.M. Took 19
Vice-Regents to Pohick Church, parishioners kindly sending
autos for them. Rained hard this P.M." The picture of Dodge,
leading his flock of Mount Vernon ladies into the little church,
is a beguiling one.

The aging Wharf-wagon was again re-painted and new harness was provided in 1911, it was overhauled in 1930, and in
1936 Dodge wrote its brief obituary: "To accommodate passengers for whom the walk from the wharf to the Mansion
would prove too tiresome, we have always had a vehicle at the
landing. For 50 years it was the same horse-drawn coach, but
it became obsolete and an auto-car now serves more conveniently." As there was no storage space at Mount Vernon for
the faithful veteran, it was with the Regent's approval given to
Henry Ford for his historic village at Dearborn, Michigan,
where motorized vehicles are banned.

The death in 1951 of Robert Pulley, who for many years
before his retirement in 1944 had been the coachman on the
horse-drawn bus between wharf and Mansion, brought another
small era to an end. Nowadays a station wagon usually meets
the boat, but finds few passengers as a hardy generation of
visitors takes in its stride the upward slope past the Tomb on a
smooth gravelled road. Mrs. Danforth in 1935 donated the price
of two non-motorized wheel-chairs for the use of the elderly
and infirm.

In 1921 a Ford tractor was sent down "to be exhibited and
tried," apparently something of a curiosity, for Council turned
out to see it work. This was followed by the two Ford fire-
engines in 1923 and 1936. Meanwhile, visitors in motor-cars
were multiplying fast, and cars were being hired by the more
progressive Vice-Regents to ease the journey down from Washington at Council time—notably Miss Jennings and Miss Townsend as early as 1916, when the road was still bad. Mrs. Troup
(Nebraska) seems to have been the first Vice-Regent to fly in
to Washington to attend Council—which she did at the age of

eighty-four in 1940. Sight-seeing motor-busses were operating in 1923, as boat and railway travel declined, but it was not until 1929 that Council authorized the purchase for its own use of a "handsome Buick limousine to accommodate seven"—which was at once acknowledged to be a great convenience, and soon a Ford car was ordered also, to spare the lordly Buick general run-about work.

The journey down from Washington has now been cut to less than an hour by an enterprising hydrofoil operator, in love with his machine, which plied between the wharf at Mount Vernon and the Washington pier, during the summer of 1966. Accommodating less than two dozen passengers, it is hardly a threat to the boat which still makes the summer cruise down the river an old-fashioned treat in a hasty modern world.

iv

The first shadow of things to come fell over Mount Vernon in October, 1918, when two young officers flying an airplane from Richmond to Washington City ran out of fuel and landed on the westward lawn to replenish. A railroad contractor outside the gates supplied them, but a strong wind prevented them from clearing the tree-tops on their take-off, and the machine was wrecked, though the men were able to walk away from it. As usual Dodge's Diary provides no illumination on what must have been at least an exciting day. The entry is buried in a closely written page with a too-hard pencil, recording the illnesses and occupations of employees on a busy Friday. The plane landed at 12:45 in Field #7, he says. But one of the Rouses was at home ill, and Simms had gone to town to be measured for a new uniform, and the leaves wanted raking—the two airmen must have found a somewhat preoccupied reception for their adventure.

The following year it was suggested by heaven knows whom that a flight of several airplanes should dip down and drop flowers on the Tomb on February 22d. Dodge protested to the Secretary of War about the possible risk to historic buildings and the flight did not take place. In 1925 a low-flying reserve officer from Bolling Field was officially rebuked. In 1923 the

first air photographs were taken—without permission—and
again in 1927.

By 1946, with another war over, a survey counted 85 planes
in an 8-hour period, flying directly over the Mansion, and 71
more which were visible and audible—20 per hour. Even at
night they came, at an estimated 1,000-foot level. A protest to
the Civil Aeronautics Board brought a suggestion that an executive order from the President would be effective. In 1947 a student pilot made an emergency landing in the west field and
broke his propeller, demonstrating the continuing hazard, and
extra fire-fighting equipment was purchased. Mrs. Bolton
(Ohio) Congresswoman as well as Vice-Regent, arranged a
meeting with the Air-Space Subcommittee, which resulted in an
informal agreement "to protect the home and tomb of Washington not only against accident but against the disrespect of low-
flying planes."

The year 1951 saw a further increase of flights which could
only be considered dangerously low, and Mrs. Bolton appealed
to the Secretary of Defense. In 1957 there was an incident in
which helicopters "seemed to be looking in the second story
windows" of the Mansion, and it was decided that the Regent
should write the President in the name of the Council, to request
that Mount Vernon might be declared a "forbidden area," with
a ground radius of one mile and an elevation of 5,000 feet. Mr.
Eisenhower expressed himself as deeply concerned, and it was
hoped that the new airport at Chantilly might lessen the encroachment by the heavier commercial planes, though helicopters continued to be a threat, and repeated pleas to different
authorities afforded only temporary relief. The *Pilots' Manual*
carries a request (in very small print) that "the immediate vicinity of the Mount Vernon estate" should be avoided.

It would take only one small miscalculation, one flaming
wreck, costing only one of thousands of expensive machines and
a reckless boy's life, to reduce to ashes the irreplaceable cherished record and symbol of a great American ideal.

The Grounds

5

The choice of a site for Mount Vernon, often attributed to George Washington himself, was made by his father, who brought his family to live for a short while on the bluff at his Little Hunting Creek property, which was later, as the heritage of George's elder half-brother Lawrence, to become Mount Vernon. Exactly when the Washingtons came to Hunting Creek or how long they remained there is not known. They were living at the place called Wakefield, down the Potomac at Pope's Creek, when George was born in 1732, the first child of his father's second marriage. By the time he was seven years old they were established on a farm near Fredericksburg on the Rappahannock, where his father died in 1743, and where his widowed mother continued to live with his younger brothers until all were grown, in the mid-1760's. Wakefield, at Pope's Creek, became the heritage of the eldest son, Augustine, called "Austin." The Little Hunting Creek property was the portion of the second son Lawrence, from whom after his widow's re-marriage it passed to George in 1754. The Pope's Creek house burned down about 1780, while in the possession of "Austin's" son, and by the hundredth anniversary of George's birth only the kitchen chimney and traces of the foundations remained.

A fine reconstruction of an early 18th-century plantation house has been accomplished there by the Wakefield Memorial Association, organized in 1924. The house as erected near the family burying ground on the placid shore of the creek, with the assistance of John D. Rockefeller, Jr., who made Williamsburg possible, is now administered by the National Park Service. It is perhaps a little grand to represent Washington's birthplace, though Augustine Washington, Sr., was a man of some substance, able to send his two eldest sons to England for schooling, as was the fashion among his contemporaries. The children of his second wife were left more or less dependent on her after his death, and had to make their own way.

At the time of his marriage to Anne Fairfax in 1743 Lawrence occupied the Little Hunting Creek house and named it Mount Vernon. George spent much of his boyhood there, as a close attachment existed between him and the invalid half-brother whose only child to survive babyhood was a delicate girl who died in 1752. George enlarged and rebuilt Lawrence's house before his own marriage to the widow Custis in 1759, adding the third story, and had begun the additions on the north and south ends when he was called away by the Continental Congress in 1775. He went straight from Philadelphia to Boston to take command of the American army there, and the work at Mount Vernon was continued under the management of his cousin Lund, all through the years when the Revolution prevented George from once inspecting its progress. When at last after eight years' absence he was able to return home, much of the finishing remained still to be done in the Banquet Room and the new Library. In 1784 he was able at last to begin laying out the grounds in "serpentine walks" either side of the Bowling Green, devoting himself to the imaginative transplanting and arrangement of the shrubberies and groves which surround the house. It is thanks to his enforced absences, however, that so much evidence remains, in the form of letters between himself and Lund and his later deputies, to assist the Association in the restoration and maintenance of both house and landscaping as he left it at his death.

Included in the original Association purchase were some 200 acres of land, but it soon became obvious that that was not enough to protect it from commercial encroachment, the specter of which haunted even the first Regent. In 1877, in spite of the Centennial year prosperity, there were not sufficient funds to buy from the heirs of the last Washington owner the 33 acres of rising ground beyond the Mansion on the northeast, where it was rumored some speculators intended building a resort hotel. Ten years later the Association was still in dread of an undesirable neighbor there, as well as of the proposed railroad from Alexandria, which it was feared would dump large crowds of sight-seers at a terminus near the land gate of Mount Vernon and by cheap fares subtract revenue from the boat, hitherto the main means of access. The question was raised in Council as to the Association's legal power under its charter to purchase additional land, and it was decided to ask protection by the Virginia Legislature against commercial encroachment, and also to secure a charter right to buy protecting land at the boundaries. The immediate anxiety was then allayed in spectacular fashion by the first instance of Dodge's genius for attracting good will and support from those best able to confer it.

His Diary, like Washington's, was always proof against emotion or drama, and the entry for June 7, 1887, is as wilfully colorless as usual. But as he grew older he liked to tell stories, and in 1932 he wrote in book form an informal account of the Mount Vernon history as he had lived it—so informal as to be without an index, and to amount to only a collection of anecdotes, interesting because of their source, but undocumented and showing some lapses of memory. But here the Diary entry was expanded to allow the reader a glimpse of what really happened that momentous summer.

Mr. Lawrence Washington, son of the man who was finally induced to sell Mount Vernon to the Association, had been born in the room where Washington died, and was a babe in arms when Miss Cunningham in 1856 travelled through prostrating summer heat to Mount Vernon to plead with his parents to reserve to her still nebulous organization the right to raise money to purchase the estate. In his thirties, and with a family, Lawrence was in need of funds and instructed his agent to sell the remaining land on the Potomac not included in the Association charter. The 33-acre hill was offered to the Association in 1886 and again in 1887. Not satisfied to await the Legislature's decision on charter technicalities as to the Association's right to purchase more land if and when they could afford it, Lawrence Washington advised his agent to find another purchaser and close a deal. That this sale was about to be accomplished Dodge discovered by a chance encounter in Washington, after the adjournment of the 1887 Council, when the ladies had scattered to their homes. He acted with his customary verve and decision. He went at once to Mr. Washington's agent in Alexandria and "finally persuaded" him to give an option for the first refusal of the property for one week.

Before he was out of the office, the prospective purchaser arrived with a cash offer for the lot overlooking Mount Vernon. The agent's integrity allowed Dodge to escape with his seven days' grace in his pocket, and a seemingly hopeless problem to redeem it in time. "That very day," his later account proceeds, "a really remarkable coincidence occurred. Mr. Jay Gould of New York with his wife and three children came to Mount Vernon on their private yacht. It was their first visit, and was therefore especially enjoyable to them. I made every effort to enlighten them on the various phases of Washington's home. On leaving, Mr. Gould invited me to accompany him to the yacht, and when some distance from the wharf, scanning the riverfront of the estate, he asked what extent of shoreline was owned by the Association. This being pointed out to him, he inquired why the prominent hill to the northeast was not included in the estate, remarking that it seemed important to acquire it, if for no other reason than to safeguard the Mount Vernon property against the possibility of undesirable neighbors or unsightly modern buildings. When it was explained to him that the Association was prohibited [by its charter] from buying additional land, Mr. Gould asked if anyone should offer to donate the lot could it be accepted. When I assured him that it could, he requested me to buy the lot at once, send the bill of costs to him for payment, and he would execute a deed of gift to the Association. The only stipulation he enjoined was that his connection with the transaction should not then be made public. The Regent was quickly communicated with, and confidentially apprised of all the circumstances which thus cleared the way for the acquirement of this long wished-for tract. The purchase was quickly consummated, and later a deed of gift to the Mount Vernon Ladies' Association of the Union was joined in by Mr. and Mrs. Jay Gould."

Even here, the account is somewhat over-simplified. The Diary allows a thin crack of elation to show, in an underlined sentence, but there is no doubt that Dodge's composure was equal to Gould's, which was famous, during that amazing boat-ride and its dazzling consequences. He wrote, in the little pocket-size notebook, with a sharp-pointed pencil: "Jay Gould's yacht 'Atalanta' stopped here at 12:30. He and family shown every attention. *On leaving he donated $2500 to purchase 33½ acres.* Rain this afternoon. Stopped work at 3 o'clock. Sent George Ford to Alexandria to mail special letter to the Regent telling her of the Goulds' gift."

Unanswered questions form a rising tide of exasperation with so much self-possession. At least he gave up work at 3 o'clock, perhaps to dance a saraband in the privacy of his office.

Not a word about his experience aboard what was said to be the most luxurious craft afloat, where he was doubtless given lunch during the off-shore cruise. The *Atalanta* was appreciably longer than Astor's *Nourmahal*, and cost $1,000 a week to maintain, and her owner was a railroad millionaire who "outside his own home was considered the most ruthless and hateful man of his time." A one-time barefoot boy from upstate New York, he had worked a 16-hour day in a general store for his bed and board. Thin, weedy, and pallid, with tragic dark eyes, dyspeptic, tuberculous, and moody, he possessed a peculiar charm which had won him the devotion of a gently bred New York heiress and an unusually happy family life. Yet he had not hesitated to ruin his best friend financially, and then provided handsomely for the widow of his victim. He was socially ignored by the Vanderbilts and the Astors, but inhabited a mansion on Fifth Avenue and a 40-room Gothic castle on the Hudson, travelled in a private railroad car, founded his own yachting club, and bought the Empress Josephine's pearls for his wife to wear in the Diamond Horseshoe. He was once rumored to be in the hole for $20,000,000 and answered doubts as to his financial standing by showing stock certificates in his name worth $53,000,000. His daughter Anna made a tragic marriage for a European title, while her sister Helen dressed like a deaconess and was absorbed in good works for which her father supplied the funds. This almost friendless enigma, the hated embodiment of the Horatio Alger legend, walked through Mount Vernon on a hot summer day, listened attentively to Dodge's exposition, recognized the challenge and accepted it on the spot. A rich man's generous impulse—a domestic gesture to please his thoughtful wife and earnest daughter, who doubtless ardently embraced the Mount

Vernon idea—or the inevitable Gould necessity to play God, to frustrate alien enterprise not of his own making, to show the power of his fortune—or was it again the resident Mount Vernon magic, penetrating the hard, embittered misanthrope by its own mysterious means? "Mrs. Gould and the children were delighted with the visit to Mount Vernon," he wrote in reply to the Regent's letter of thanks. It cost him only $2,500 to link his name forever in grace and beauty with the grassy hill where the reservoir now stands, on what is still gratefully known as the Gould Lot.

The next land-acquisition problem was given serious consideration by Dodge when in 1889 he advocated to Council the construction of a permanent rip-rap wall to extend 100 yards either side of the wharf, with a fill behind it of mud dredged from the river channel. The destructive tidal currents on the riverfront caused perpetual anxiety, which he felt could only be solved at some expense and by slow degrees. It would involve drainage of the swampy land known to Washington as Hell Hole, and while there was at first no mention of the connection between it and the deadly malaria which afflicted the whole neighborhood, it had always been considered unhealthy and the night air, when the mosquitoes which bred there were most active, was always suspect.

However, not all of Hell Hole had been included in the original Association purchase, and several acres were owned by their neighbor on the south, Christian Heurich, who refused to sell on the excuse that he intended to build his own wharf and landing there. It was useless to drain only part of the swamp. Dodge called on Mr. Heurich and made a "joking" reference to Gould's generosity at the other side of the estate, with the implication that Heurich was in a position to do as well. Again, something worked. Heurich talked it over with his wife, and in 1893 they donated the remaining 4 acres of swamp land to Mount Vernon.

Work had already begun on the rip-rap wall, which could now, as funds became available, be extended across the whole Mount Vernon riverfront, preventing erosion and storm damage to the wharf. Mrs. Hearst that year made her second appearance at Council, two years having elapsed since her first. She had gone abroad after the death of her husband in Washington and sold their house there, expecting to live in California henceforth.

In those days it was customary for each State to read a Report to Council in person, and for California Mrs. Hearst expressed her regret that illness and absence had prevented her attention to work for the Association, but hoped "with the approval of the Regent and Vice-Regents to have the marsh land thoroughly drained and thereby improve the health of the Mount Vernon residents as well as increase the value and utility of the above-mentioned land."

Council must have gasped—and then accepted with thanks. Perhaps no one realized at that time the extent of her undertaking.

This extraordinary woman cannot be casually passed over. Modest to shyness, and seldom speaking in Council, which she rarely attended, deceptively fragile in appearance, Phoebe Apperson Hearst, widowed mistress of her husband's fortune, gave to Mount Vernon freely, without contribution from her State, over $20,000, not including relics sent as gifts, extra checks for $50 or $100 in the years when she could not attend, to be used as needed, and a generous annual "Christmas present" to be divided among the employees.

She had been a Missouri school-teacher, eighteen years old, small, clever, and very pretty, when George Hearst returned home from the Gold Rush—he had struck silver in the Comstock Lode—intending to enrich his mother's last years with his new wealth. He was a strapping Forty-niner, twice Phoebe's age, a very rough diamond whose grammar needed polishing. Her parents thought he wasn't good enough for her, but Phoebe knew her own mind and after his mother died they were married. To spare his bride the dangerous, wearisome journey across the plains, he took her by train to New York, by boat to Panama, and thence by boat to San Francisco, where their only child, William Randolph, was born. Before long George struck gold and copper—the Anaconda Mine—and they built a house on fashionable Nob Hill, and bought ranch land above the sea.

From the first Phoebe used her husband's money well, establishing kindergartens for what would now be called under-privileged children, financing budding careers in education and the arts, which were encouraged in a sort of salon for young intellectuals, and sending her son East to St. Paul's School and Harvard. George bought the *San Francisco Examiner*, which he later turned over to "Willie." When he was elected to the Senate in 1887 they moved to Washington and took a house in New Hampshire Avenue, where the Leland Stanfords became their close friends. Senator Hearst was soon known affectionately around the Washington bars as "Uncle George," and took up horse-racing, while his wife and son spent much time abroad. She encouraged the boy to appreciate and buy the priceless antiquities and *objets d'art* which later grew into a famous collection.

Phoebe was only forty-eight when George Hearst died late in 1891 and left his entire estate to her, confident that she could administer it and provide suitably for their son, who was then a sophisticated and wilful twenty-four. She built the beautiful "Hacienda" at Pleasanton, California, where several Vice-Regents, including Mrs. Pringle, visited her, and she endowed the Mining and Engineering Building at the University of California as a memorial to her husband. She gave away millions, not extravagantly, but with forethought. And she never lost touch with Mount Vernon, though in nearly thirty years as Vice-Regent she attended Council less than a dozen times.

Her arrival in 1893 was memorable because she lent her yacht, the *Vamoose*, to the Regent on the occasion of the visit to Mount Vernon of the Infanta Eulalie, aunt to the infant King Alphonso XIII of Spain. As it was only a few days before Council was to convene, many of the Vice-Regents had already gathered in Washington, and the reception committee of Vice-Regents travelled down the river on the swift *Vamoose* ahead of the regular Mount Vernon boat, which had been chartered by the State Department to convey the Infanta's party, and was furnished with a military band and a bower of flowers in her honor.

The Banquet Hall was closed to visitors that day, and a refreshment table was spread there at one side. The Vice-Regents were grouped around the impressive Mrs. Townsend to receive the royal guest, who arrived "leaning upon the arm of the Secretary of State, her official attendant in Washington," Mrs. Hudson recorded as Secretary. "A sweet-faced, Titian-haired, graceful young Princess, she was presented by the Secretary of State to the Regent, who presented the ladies to the Infanta. The Regent offered a superb bunch of roses which was accepted in pretty, broken English; more at ease in French or Spanish, the Infanta expressed her pleasure in being able to visit the home of Washington and thanked the ladies for their courteous reception. Perhaps her most characteristic attraction is the royal repose of her manner, gracious and charming. She is certainly a pretty woman. Her coloring is lovely. She was well-gowned. What more can one ask of a Princess?" wrote Mrs. Hudson, then sixty-nine, and well-travelled abroad. Mrs. Hearst was one of several Vice-Regents who were able to put the Infanta at her ease in French, having learned the language thoroughly during her sojourns in Europe. And when the Infanta had departed in the chartered boat, Mrs. Hearst invited all the Vice-Regents for a late afternoon trip on the river in the *Vamoose*.

Dodge noted in his book, though not in his Diary, that he had had some difficulty convincing the U.S. Naval officer in charge that it was not necessary to bring ashore a strong party of Marines to guard Her Highness while she was the guest of Mount Vernon, and mentioned that the Naval gentleman thought the venerable wharf-bus unsuitable for a lady of such distinction.

The final redemption of Hell Hole and its conversion into a piece of meadow land was not accomplished until 1912. Meanwhile the guilt of the malaria-carrying mosquitoes was discovered, though in 1898 Dodge commented to Council: "It is true that our familiar enemy, malaria, was more in evidence than usual, but we have learned to expect that as a matter of course." During the years of work on the riverfront he was more often out and daily exposed to the mosquitoes, and his own attacks of malaria appreciably increased in the mid-1890's. He found that a sea-trip by slow boat to Boston afforded the best relief, and his assistant Mr. Young, also a victim of "chills," used boat trips as a remedy. Both Dodge and Archer went as far as California for their vacations in 1916.

It was really thanks to Mrs. Hearst's liberality in financing the extension, year after year, of the sea-wall, replacing the old rip-rap wall by solid masonry to the extent of 2,150 feet, 6 feet high above the mean low tide, and 3 feet thick at the bottom, while at the same time the swamp land was drained and filled and planted, that the Mount Vernon "sickness" was finally conquered as soon as it was, and the employees were freed from what was once the inevitable penalty of devoted service. In 1912, as part of the general sanitation program and malaria precautions, further attention was given to the screening of doors and windows in the employees' homes, for it was noted that the drainage of Mount Vernon's swamp did not prevent wind-borne mosquitoes from arriving from other marshes along the rivershore, and 1913's cool wet summer was distinguished by "unprecedented swarms" resulting in an increase of disability among the Mount Vernon employees. Efforts to raise any sort of crop in Hell Hole met with defeat, though it grew a little food, mainly potatoes, in the war-gardens. It was sown to grass in 1947, and is made to produce turf for re-sodding the lawn in the much-punished Exihibition Area.

ii

It is difficult for the present-day visitor, arriving by the broad and beautiful highway which runs along the river to a sweeping terminus outside the handsome north gate at Mount Vernon to visualize the untidy appearance of that approach up to so relatively a recent time as to be within the memory of the present Resident Director. The transformation was largely due to the increasing use of the motor-car and motor-bus for transportation, gradually supplanting the long-dreaded railway from Alexandria, which arrived in 1892—the railway having supplanted, as was feared at the time, the leisurely little steamer from Washington City which was for so many years the only comfortable way to reach Mount Vernon.

"My flesh creeps at the thought of a depot behind the servants' houses, and a whistle daily disturbing the sanctity of the Tomb," Miss Cunningham had written to Miss Tracy in May, 1866, from her War-time exile in South Carolina. Miss Tracy "saw a lawyer" and that threat was somehow averted until 1892. The new steamer *Charles Macalester* had just been added and was making two trips a day, when Council was confronted with a *fait accompli* by the railroad, and only the point of entrance remained to be determined. A delegation from the railroad company was received during Council, which must have been an uncomfortable experience for the intruders, encountering that group of ruffled femininity; legal advice was taken by the Association, stipulations were laid down and agreed to—and the railroad, in the shape of electric cars without engines, was in. A bleak-looking stone depot went up beside the tracks, and turnstiles were installed at the new "Texas" or North Gate, which was erected by Mrs. Maxey with contributions from her State. It was soon discovered that on days when severe weather kept the boat in her Washington dock "the cars" still ran and receipts did not drop, though Dodge reported with regret that the railway had brought in a new "unruly" type of people, "just for an outing." Two modes of transportation in opposition, the boat and the railroad, caused some difficulty in clearing the grounds at closing time, when the bell which hung in the Summer House was rung at 4 P.M. Extra guards became necessary, and a sentry-box was installed at the Tomb for the man on constant duty there in all weathers.

By 1897 it was admitted that the bulk of travel was by rail. The following year the boat company failed, and the mail service too was transferred to the railroad. The boat company was soon re-organized and run by the receivers, and there is still a summer boat from Washington for those who prefer the more picturesque approach.

In August, 1904, Dodge noted in his Diary without excitement or animus that "a touring automobile from Omaha brought 5 visitors this afternoon. The first auto that ever came to the Mansion door." A few years later two more cars, travelling together, made the bumpy trip from Washington, and one of their drivers wrote an indignant article describing the approach road as "literally a disgrace to the country." He had taken, and published, photographs to prove it, having driven his open four-seated car right up to the west front. His article reported that the "custodian" required them to walk through the turnstile at the gate and pay their money, and then walk back to take the cars through. "And we must keep them very quiet," his account ran, "and not make any noise, nor must we go on the grass, and so we had to do without the picture we wanted most, of the autos in front of the porch where George Washington used to sit and watch the river flowing by; but we got some photographs of the other side of the Mansion, and they are sufficient evidence that we really made the trip—20 miles and return—in 6 hours. It is a rough trip, a trip hard on car and man, but a motor achievement."

The reception does not sound much like Dodge, and it is possible that he was away, as the Diary seems not to mention a second visitation. In 1911, doubtless as a result of further motor incursions, Mrs. Ball offered a resolution, seconded by Mrs. Hudson, that no automobiles should be allowed within the gates.

There was an effort by the DAR in 1912 urging a roadway from Washington City to Mount Vernon, and a request from Mrs. Taft to bring a party of guests by motor-car had to be cancelled "in view of the bad roads." Additional road signs were placed along the route, and Mount Vernon teams and labor were loaned by Dodge to assist in repairing the approach roads just before the arrival of the Wilson party in 1913.

A long-projected highway from Washington to Richmond, now known as U.S. 1, was completed about 1916, passing only 2 miles from Mount Vernon at the place called Gum Spring. An unpaved road ran from there to the North Gate, where the present concrete drive brings motor-cars and buses with a flourish right to the ticket-window. The Service Entrance—an iron gate in the high brick wall on the other side of the concession building—now admits the employees' cars and those of the Vice-Regents and their guests to the official parking area.

The Landon gift in 1926, resembling Gould's, was designed to enlarge the northeast boundary, outside which Gibbs's restaurant, a parking lot, and "other unsightly buildings" for which the Association was often blamed, had long disfigured the approach to the main gate. Mr. and Mrs. Landon visited Mount Vernon with their agent, and Dodge "called their attention" to the threatened erection of a resort hotel and similar undesirable projects on the wooded ridge in full sight of the Mansion on the northwest, adjoining the Gould Lot—with the happy effect of deciding the donors to include the ridge with the "lunchroom corner," amounting to some 22 acres.

Exasperating delays in clearing the Landon tract occurred

throughout 1928 and 1929 because of the proposed Memorial Highway to be built by the Federal Government as its main contribution to the Washington Bicentennial observance scheduled for 1932, to accommodate the anticipated increase in motor traffic. By 1926 Dodge had reported that "water travel to Mount Vernon has long ceased to be the attraction it once was. The hurry and rush of the present day demands quicker mobility, as evidenced by the throng of automobiles crowding the roads of approach."

The electric railway from Alexandria, once a dreaded innovation, was "permanently discontinued" in 1930, when the right of way was purchased by the Government. The highway planners made an extensive survey of the welter of tracks and unorganized parking provision, surrounded by a tangle of untended vegetation, which was in sharp contrast to the orderly estate so carefully preserved within the brick walls marking the Association boundary—beyond which it had no authority to undertake a clean-up. The solution of the growing traffic problem involved first of all adequate parking, loading, and turn-around space for public and private motor vehicles. The present leafy parking lot for private cars, and the colorful planting between it and the gate—with seedlings from inside the grounds—the well-planned concession building which replaced the Gibbs restaurant shack, and the absence of billboards or advertising signs are all the result of action by the National Park Service.

In 1931 Mrs. Landon's sudden death brought a bequest by her will of 157 more acres of woodland adjoining the northwest boundary. This unexpected acquisition raised the estate area to more than double the original purchase in 1858, and with pardonable pride Dodge mentioned in his Report that he "had had to do, more or less," with each of the additional donations, amounting to 216 acres. The wooded Landon tract was to be bisected by the Memorial Highway, and would further protect the approach from filling stations, refreshment stands, souvenir shops, and such disfigurements.

It was at this time that the additional brick wall bordering the parking plaza on the east was built at the Association's expense, extending westward of the Service Gate some 2,300 feet in all. The following year the boundary wall was lengthened to the west gate, 3,400 feet, the ground at its foot was graded and sown, and ivy was planted at intervals. At Dodge's request the telephone company removed its disfiguring poles, providing underground cables for its service. The boundary wall now measures some 6,400 feet, and its cost if attempted today would be astronomical.

The car carrying President and Mrs. Hoover to Mount Vernon for the ceremonies which would officially open the Bicentennial observance was supposed to be the first to drive along the new Memorial Highway on February 22d, 1932, a formality which caused a mammoth traffic jam for people who hoped to reach Mount Vernon in time to hear the President's speech, which was to be broadcast by radio from the piazza. Thirty-one of the thirty-eight Vice-Regents then on the roster were present as hostesses to the Hoovers, and admission for the public was free for the day. Tea was served in the Administration Building to the Vice-Regents' invited guests.

The high hopes for an unprecedented attendance and consequent prosperity in the Bicentennial year were frustrated by the financial disaster called the Depression which enveloped the whole country during the early 1930's. Travel and spending of family funds on holidays were diminished to such an extent that the gate receipts at Mount Vernon were so reduced by a lack of visitors—the attendance dropped nearly 200,000 from 1930 —that even in those hard times the Regent reluctantly authorized a general cut in employees' salaries up to 10 per cent, "which was accepted as perfectly just by all concerned." The Treasurer weighed in with a stern recommendation "to consider all possible economies in appropriations for the coming year, owing to the curtailment of income and impairment of capital," and a possible future reduction in the payroll was contemplated. Council ruled it inadvisable to buy any more relics at that time, and only drainage and termite-proofing activities were to continue under the direction of Professors Williams and Killam. Mr. Wall, then the Assistant Superintendent, was in charge of day labor, which was then paid the standard 40¢ an hour for an 8-hour day.

Preparations for the Bicentennial at Mount Vernon had included an extensive refurbishing of the Mansion, which of course was not wasted in the end. The Committee, headed by Mrs. Maxey and the Regent, had met at Mount Vernon in the autumn of 1930, and again in 1931, to inspect samples of old brocades as well as reproductions of old patterns and wall-papers. A beautiful blue brocade procured by Miss Virginia Leigh Porcher (South Carolina) was chosen for the West Parlor, always known to Washington as "Blue," and the curtains and bedspread for Washington's Bedroom were reproduced by the Baltimore School of Needlework from those in the Museum said to have been worked by Martha. The interesting discovery was made that the original materials had undoubtedly been im-ported from England and were still obtainable there, but not in this country. The Council of 1931 went through the Mansion room by room, noting changes to be made, and approving work recently done. Red damask was chosen for the Family Dining-room, antique red *toile* for the Lafayette Room, and there was a general put-and-take of furniture everywhere.

No sooner had the north entrance been saved than anxiety about the westward vista began, as the question of the much-punned-against Erk corner opposite the old West Gate was raised. This was the original entrance to Mount Vernon in Washington's time, where there was a little gate-house and a well for the use of the lodge-keeper, nearly a mile distant from the west front, but visible in a vista cut through the trees. An old short-cut road used by Washington can still be traced in the south woodland. The Erk transaction dragged on for years, while land values in the area mounted steadily, and sub-divisions multiplied. The Erk tract—3 acres—was eventually secured, to-gether with 3 acres on the opposite corner known as the Moul-ton or Stewart property, in 1955. Thus, as Miss Cunningham so earnestly enjoined in her Farewell Address, Mount Vernon has been preserved from change and encroachment, until only the Maryland shore view, which is equally essential, remains to be ransomed.

Mount Vernon has been lately threatened with a new dese-cration, too big for it to handle alone—the Maryland shore op-posite the east lawn has been in danger of becoming a modern skyline, in which the chimneys of a garbage-disposal plant and high-rise apartment houses would disfigure the green serenity of the countryside on which Washington's eyes could rest at the end of his busy days, and which now brings exclamations of spontaneous delight from traffic-harassed modern visitors. The house has escaped ruin by decay and by fire, it has been spared the overlook by resort hotels and commercial picnic grounds, and the threat of a criminal penitentiary and asylum at its very gates was averted in 1912. It is to be devoutly hoped that at this late date a means can still be found to preserve forever the timeless beauty of the eastward view. A bill has been passed and signed by the President. The necessary appropriation by Congress is still pending.

iii

Although Mrs. Robert Campbell of Missouri died only two years after her appointment as Vice-Regent and attended Council only once, in 1880, her three sons asked permission a few years later to restore and stock, as a memorial to their mother, the deer-park on the wooded hillside between the Mansion and the river, which Washington had fenced as a paddock for tame deer in 1786. She may have expressed to them a wish to see it re-established, notwithstanding that Washington within ten years had found his deer an expensive nuisance and turned them all loose, after a buck had wounded a slave woman known as Dolshy, who required Dr. Craik's attendance. But as the Messrs. Campbell were so tactful as to send their check for the estimated cost of fencing and shelter in advance, the work was accomplished and reported at the Council of 1888. The 7-acre park was enclosed by a high iron fence for 750 feet, and a wooden stockade ran another 1,637 feet, with gates, pens, and a shelter house, which must all have been very "unsightly" from the piazza. Spring water and what was thought to be ample foliage for food were available. The deer were carefully chosen, a buck from Tennessee, and six does, with three more to come.

By 1890 the herd had increased to seventeen, and their browsing had depleted the natural food supply to such an extent that extra feed of hay, corn, turnips, potatoes, and honey-locust pods, of which they were very fond, was required daily. This threatened to become expensive, and Dodge was worried about the inevitable increase. That year his Report to Council remarked briefly that the "tame" Tennessee buck had become vicious and dangerous and must be disposed of. Doubtless his hearers were already aware that in the preceding February he had entered the paddock, not for the first time, wearing an overcoat, hat, and gloves, to pick up some litter thrown in by the visitors, and had turned just in time to face the charge of the antlered buck. Instinctively he caught the horns in his hands, one of which was pierced clean through by the sharp prong, but managed that way to protect his body from the first attack, which knocked him to the ground against the wall. He held on, until Young and some of the other men could reach him, but his thighs and legs were found to be lacerated through his clothing—an attacking deer slashes with its sharp front hooves—and he had a badly injured knee-cap; injuries which kept him in bed at home for three weeks, leaving Young and Whelan in charge at Mount Vernon.

Two bucks were sold to a Long Island deer-park, and two others had killed each other in a fight. The park was enlarged in 1910 to provide more space for natural forage, and the herd was reduced to twelve. Some "escaped," and four white-tailed deer, buck and does, were brought in from Michigan in 1925. By 1931 there were fifteen, and the browsing was again exhausted. Finally in 1934 it was decided on Washington's own example to abandon the deer-park feature "for a while." The remaining animals were given away to the Shenandoah National Park, and are said to be the forebears of a current over-population along the Skyline Drive.

All traces of the fencing and depredation by browsing on the grassy slope in front of the Mansion have disappeared. The lawns, encouraged by frequent seeding and a sprinkler system installed in 1953, are now in the busy season divided into thirds, with barriers of inconspicuous chain between thin iron stakes, and by rotating the sections over a 6-day period the turf is enabled to recover almost unnoticed from the wear and tear which the freedom accorded to visitors entails. Watering is done at night, by an underground irrigation system with surface nozzles for large-volume sprinklers which operate in a wide circular pattern. These can be moved from one valve to another without interruption of the whole operation. More than a half-mile of water-pipe has been laid, with branches around the east and west lawn and the Tomb approach and through each Garden. Recent drought years have indicated a necessity to augment this water supply still further.

iv

The acquisition of a sun-dial for the west front courtyard was first moved in 1884, as it was understood that Washington had had one there when he laid out the grounds. The original seems to have been sold by one of the later Washingtons to an unknown in New York City and was thought to be unobtainable. Mrs. Abby Wheaton Chace, first Vice-Regent for Rhode Island, therefore undertook to have a substitute made, and raised the money by donation in her State for a granite pedestal and a bronze dial-plate. Lossing's 1859 book on Mount Vernon was consulted as to its exact location, and in excavating for the new shaft what appeared to be the wooden stump of the original pedestal was found.

Washington's Diary of 1785 recorded the setting out of the turned locust wood posts connected by chains which surround the circular grass plot where his sun-dial stood. The posts were still there in 1857, though the sun-dial had gone. In 1917 new posts and chains were installed at Miss Failing's expense, and Mrs. Chace's bronze dial-plate was remounted on a turned locust post, while the search for the original plate went on.

Some of the posts decayed and they were all restored in 1938, the chains hand-made and the posts turned at a nearby mill. At a dramatic evening session of Council in the Banquet Room, Miss Jennings (Connecticut), dressed in white, placed a "queer-shaped" box on the table and opened it to reveal the original sun-dial plate, "a treasure she had tried for years to obtain." Everyone was touched by this surprise gesture, and according to Wyoming's Mrs. Lucy Ramsay Taliaferro's account some years later, "there was hardly a dry eye in the room." This was Miss Jenning's last appearance at Council, her twenty-second, and she was not able to be present the following year when Council assembled in the west forecourt to watch Professor Morley Williams, who was briefly Director of Research and Restoration during Mrs. Richards's regency, align the gnomon of the dial

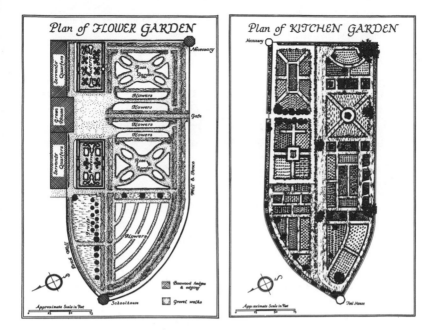

THE KITCHEN GARDEN PLANTING LIST

Anise
Artichokes, French
Asparagus
Balm, Lemon
Basil, Sanctum
Basil, Sweet
Beans, Bush
Beans, Bush Lima
Beans, Pole Lima
Beets
Broccoli
Cabbage
Caraway
Carrots
Catnip
Cauliflower
Chives
Cucumbers
Eggplant
Germander
Horseradish
Hyssop
Kale
Lavender
Lavender Cotton
Lettuce, Head
Lettuce, Loose leaf
Lovage

Marjoram, Sweet
Nasturtiums
Okra
Onions
Oregano
Parsley
Parsnips
Peas
Pennyroyal
Peppers, Sweet or Bird
Peppers, Red
Potatoes, Irish
Potatoes, Sweet
Radish
Rhubarb
Rosemary
Rue
Rutabaga
Sage
Salsify
Spinach
Squash, Summer
Swiss chard
Tarragon
Thyme, English
Thyme, French
Thyme, Golden
Thyme, Silver

Tomatoes
Turnips
Winter Savory
FRUITS:
  Apples
  Apricots
  Cherry, Morello
  Currants
  Figs
  Grapes
  Nectarines
  Peaches
  Pears
  Plum, Damson
  Quince
  Strawberries
ESPALIER FRUITS
  Wall trees:
    Apples
    Apricots
    Cherry, Morello
    Nectarines
    Peaches
    Pears
  Hedges:
    Apples
    Pears

with the north star. A telegram from Miss Jennings was read out, expressing her joy at the establishment of her gift.

She was followed as Vice-Regent for Connecticut by her niece Mrs. Annie Burr Auchincloss Lewis, wife of Wilmarth Lewis who edited the Horace Walpole Correspondence published by the Yale Press. Mrs. Lewis received from Mrs. Towner's hands in 1942 the badge her aunt had worn more than twenty years.

v

In the dark days of the 1860's Miss Cunningham despaired of "ever seeing my first grand plans carried out in reference to adorning the place, with a first-rate horticulturist to attend to certain kinds of improvements. All I expect now," she wrote grimly to Miss Tracy, "is to be able to secure a fund sufficient at interest to maintain a superintendent and the requisite number of laborers to guard and keep all in order."

She has her first-rate horticulturist today, in Robert Fisher, who arrived in 1946 straight from the Army, an able and valuable man commanding a crew of six gardeners and twelve grounds-men. And with the improvement in public transportation since Miss Cunningham's day, the paid annual admissions far exceed the modest amount kept "at interest," for the maintenance of the place. But the original dream was hers, however tragically deferred, without which Mount Vernon today might be nothing but another cellar-hole with crumbling chimneys falling into it, behind a sign-post and a parking lot.

Even in Miss Tracy's time, while the War was still on, there was a desire on the part of visitors for plants or flowers, any living thing, to take away with them from Washington's home. During the years the boat was stopped because of Federal fears that it would be used by Southern spies, the little war-time garrison of three at Mount Vernon found their small salaries in arrears and the admission fees dropped to less than a dozen a week, so that they had hardly enough cash on hand to provide their food and necessities. Miss Tracy in this emergency drew on her own small resources to buy flower seeds, which she planted and tended herself, to supply souvenirs to the small parties of soldiers and other venturesome visitors who found their way to

Mount Vernon overland. "I was determined I would not live here without flowers," she wrote the Regent. "We had some roses, some of my own, and some Mr. Herbert had bought for the place. I expended about $8, not more, in seeds and plants for my own comfort. We planted, transplanted, and trimmed the plants ourselves. We had just got things in fine condition when came a rush of visits from the soldiers. They were crazy for flowers. We had no gardener. So Mary and I gathered the flowers, made bouquets, and sold them." And a few months later she wrote: "I see no help for it, no one is going to raise or give us any money, and we must do our best to save and make; notwithstanding the imperfections of our greenhouse and the terrible winter on plants, we have saved a number of cuttings and plants ourselves, and I have spent hours every day it was possible to wade out there. I hope we may make something by it when the sun shines, we have not seen his majesty since last Sunday."

When the War ended Miss Cunningham assumed charge of the place with a gardener called Craig, and Miss Tracy and Mr. Herbert departed, their exhausting and perilous duty well done. Craig was a competent man, but the climate—which is to say the malaria—drove him away to preserve his family's health by taking a job in the Valley. There was then a gap of nearly ten years without any reliable help, until the devoted Whelan arrived in 1881. He lived till 1926, with various assistants under his direction as his health failed, notably Garfield Duvall, who received his forty-year watch from the Regent's hand in 1952. Duvall's brother Jesse, a mason, still works in the grounds.

The Minutes for 1939 record that when Council assembled for the afternoon session on May 11, "A bunch of the Regent's roses was on the table, and the Regent spoke of the tradition that Council could not be opened until these roses were in bloom." It was apparently Whelan who established the charming tradition of the yellow roses "sacred to the Regent," and he always presented greenhouse roses as a farewell gift to the Vice-Regents at the end of Council. In 1948 the Annual Council date was changed from May to October, when the yellow roses at Mount Vernon had finished blooming, but Ohio (Mrs. Bolton) at that time a member of ten years' standing, still maintains the pretty courtesy of sending the Regent a box of yellow roses from a

Washington florist each year at the autumn meeting.

Whelan made an educated attempt to restore to the Flower Garden the old-fashioned blooms known to Washington— hibiscus (the Syrian rose of Sharon), hollyhocks, sweet Williams, snapdragons, balsam, the old-fashioned lily *candidum*, and heliotrope, which the exiled former Queen of Spain on her 1937 visit recognized with delight as the herb known to her English childhood as "cherry pie." It always grieved Whelan that Council met too late, even in May, to enjoy the spring display of tulips, which in 1920 he noted as particularly fine. The Garden Club seemed to him and to Dodge always to have chosen the worst possible time for its visit, a perpetual lament of all gardeners who always find their most cherished exhibits just "gone by" when they most desire to make an impression. In 1930 the Garden and Greenhouse Committee said the box and privet-hedges and the flower-beds had never looked so trim and beautiful. "The sales of flowers have increased greatly," ran their Report, "and the income from the proceeds has gone a good way towards defraying the expenses of this department, which contributes so much to the beauty and interest at Mount Vernon. The conditions for flower growing at Mount Vernon are at all times exceptional, owing to a lack of free circulation of air consequent upon the brick walls, the overshadowing trees, and the tall box hedges. For this reason we may never be able to raise flowers that will take premiums at horticultural shows, but for picturesqueness of general effect, in the grouping of roses, irises, peonies and other plants, and in the beauty of the box hedges we may well challenge comparison with any garden in the country."

The true York and Lancaster striped rose, feared to be extinct, was heard from in 1906 in a letter from Germantown, Pennsylvania, to Miss Comegys. "Miss Baines, the proprietor of the nursery, brought it over from England herself, and it was vouched for as such in the English nursery. She tells me that it is distinctly striped, but can hardly be called red and white, but deep pink and pale pink. I want to have the privilege of sending one to Mount Vernon at the proper time to transplant. . . ." Two healthy plants were received. In 1907 and 1911 Mrs. Hudson secured from a friend in Fishkill several more plants raised from historic roots which were said to have bloomed when Washington was there, and more plants were received from Delaware in 1939. This unique little rose, four plants of which were sent to the writer from the Far West many years ago, still flourishes in a rather overgrown Vermont garden, and is truly striped irregularly pink on deeper pink, symbolizing the union, the story goes, of the white York rose and the Lancaster red, by the marriage in 1486 which founded the Tudor line of English royalty.

In 1916 it was noted that "roses of approved antique varieties" (not named) were planted to replace more modern strains which were removed to the cutting garden, and imported bulbs were set out. Laurel was brought in from the woods, as Washington had done, and lilacs, hollies, and sweet-brier roses were transplanted into the spaces bordering the Bowling Green which he called "shrubberies." The roses and jasmine once climbing on the restored Quarters had been smothered by the ivy, as Whelan had prophesied they would be.

Washington himself did not note down in any detail the varieties of flowers in that part of the gardens, which were doubtless left to Martha and the gardener, though he often lists the flowering shrubs and trees which he caused to be transplanted from the surrounding woods, or which were presented to him by admiring friends, who knew his love of botanical rarities and oddities. The magnolia and the palmetto royal brought back from South Carolina by his nephew George Augustine in 1785, and the foreign seeds and cuttings were carefully set out and labelled in the little Botanical Garden behind the Spinning House. The blue larkspur or delphinium did make a sufficient impression on his love of color and form to be recorded, almost the only purely ornamental herbaceous plant to be so recognized. It was sent in 1787 by the Reverend William Gordon, who during a visit at Mount Vernon in the 1780's became an informal and privileged member of the household, while writing a highly unsuccessful history of the Revolution.

The parterres in front of the Greenhouse had been established before Benjamin Latrobe's sojourn at Mount Vernon in 1796, and were one of the few things which did not arouse his wholehearted admiration. "On one side of this lawn is a plain kitchen garden," he wrote, "on the other side a neat flower garden laid out in squares, and boxed with great precision. Along the north

wall of this garden is a plain greenhouse. For the first time since
I left Germany I saw here a parterre clipped and trimmed with
infinite care into the form of a richly flourished fleur de lis, the
expiring groans, I hope, of our grandfathers' pedantry." The
parterres were perhaps the work of the Dutch gardener Ehler,
and could have been copied from some book on European
horticulture, in which publications Washington's library was
rich. It doubtless represented to him the last word in formal
elegance, though to young Latrobe's eyes it was already out-
moded.

It has been twice replanted in the same design and is kept
clipped low, having been reset in 1948 with sweet alyssum,
verbena, portulacas, and African marigolds to enliven the dis-
ciplined green pattern, which does not, so far as anyone at
Mount Vernon today is aware, have any mysterious Masonic
significance, as has sometimes been alleged. In 1953 it was again
altered slightly for the sake of symmetry, and in the same year
the Minutes recorded with astonishment that the pink hyacinths
all turned out to be blue!—but the daffodils were of a tremendous size. In 1960 the attractive new Gardens booklet went on
sale, complete with planting lists for both the Flower and Vegetable Gardens, and diagrams which show the position of the
fourteen trees which are believed to survive from Washington's
plantings in the 1780's, including the hemlock brought to Mount
Vernon by General Benjamin Lincoln from Massachusetts—
he who at Yorktown in '81 had preserved protocol by deputiz-
ing for the Commander-in-chief to receive from Cornwallis's
deputy the sword of the defeated British general, and with
superb spur-of-the-moment tact returning it at once—and the
weeping boxwood tree presented by the gay and ill-fated Light-
horse Harry Lee of Stratford.

The boxwood hedges in the gardens, many of the plants believed to have been rooted by Washington—the green arch over
the entrance to the Kitchen Garden probably dating to 1790—
have been much cherished, coddled, and doctored through the
years. In the Minutes for 1911 it is recorded: ". . . the care
bestowed on the preservation of the Boxwood Hedges by the
head gardener, which are a special feature of this old colonial
garden, is admirable. In the winter, during heavy snow-storms,

the garden force is kept busy day and night brushing the accumulations of snow from the hedges so as to avoid breaking the boxwood."

In 1912 Dodge wrote: "We were most particular, during every snowfall, to prevent such accumulation of weight as might cause damage to the Boxwood, and our guards frequently had to take turns at night in brushing the snow from these venerable relics of Washington's planting." One reads it again, in some surprise. Up all night with the boxwood? The tall, wide hedges which line the garden paths are cut square and level across the top, but —? Again in 1914: "Our men, by working at night oftentimes, kept the boxwood free from damage." Sleet storms were dreaded, because ice was harder to remove. In 1942, in the middle of another war, there was a freak March snowstorm: "In all, over a foot of wet heavy snow fell—several times more than had fallen all winter. The night watchman cleaned the boxwood hedges once and then called for assistance. All the available men were soon engaged in the effort, largely successful, to prevent breakage of the hedge"; and in 1958, "the two Embrey boys and the outside foreman had to keep brushing the snow off the boxwood from three in the afternoon until midnight." A half-skeptical query last year to Mr. Fisher brought a matter-of-fact reply in the affirmative. In this mechanized age Mount Vernon really does turn out all night to remove snow gently, by hand, from its boxwood. Once it was covered in with scaffolding and burlap—but this defaces the gardens on sunny winter days and was ruled out. All the year round it is constantly cleaned and pruned of its tiny dry twigs, and tenderly trimmed level on top and straight up the sides. In 1921 the retirement was sadly noted of old William Harrison, who since 1892 had performed the trimming of the boxwood hedges "with such pride and precision" until he got too feeble to wield the shears, and Garfield Duvall, who had begun as an outstanding day laborer, rose to a steady job as Assistant Gardener, for another forty years.

In 1936 they hired a boxwood expert, or specialist, a Mr. Hodgin, to give advice and prescribe, and he visited the hedges periodically, as though with a doctor's little black bag, over the next twenty years, while various feedings and preservative measures were faithfully followed under his direction. In 1961 the American Boxwood Society was organized by a Dr. Smith, who had spent his life growing and studying just boxwood, and felt that most of its problems were "man-made," due to either neglect or too much attention. Mount Vernon's Mr. Fisher was present at the Society's first meeting, and there is recently a general conclusion that—except for snow—boxwood is better left alone to suck the nourishment out of the surrounding soil in its own selfish way, to the detriment of nearby plants, which must be fed.

Little potted boxwood and ivy cuttings are popular items in the Sales Room, and flourish on many a window-sill in the visitors' homes in every State in the Union.

The pampering of hypochondriac plant life at Mount Vernon included the oleander and the lemon and orange trees, whose tendency to scale-pest was thwarted by careful scrubbing of the leaves with Ivory soap and applications of antiseptic. The elderly fig-bushes were persuaded to bear again by being tucked up each autumn under a coverlet of straw and leaves. Everything is fed with periodic doses of manure, suckers are pruned out, shrubs and trees broken by bad weather are tenderly trimmed and grafted.

The dreaded Japanese beetles were slow to make their appearance at Mount Vernon, which remained an oasis from the plague until they were discovered in the rose garden in 1938. They were not unexpected, and immediate steps were taken to destroy as many as possible and the soil was treated to kill the larvae. It was remarked too that fortunately boxwood and evergreens were more or less immune. Mount Vernon soil was naturally hostile to burrowing larvae, and the sanctuary provided to a large bird population within the walls added a natural means of destruction, but the sale of rooted plants was brought for a while under rigid quarantine regulations.

Another interesting case of delicate health in the vegetable world was the famous Sago Palm, which was originally owned by Washington and was "given away" by Martha after his death, to some one who carried it to New York, where it was purchased by the great horticulturist Henry Winthrop Sargent for the greenhouse at his famous place Wodenethe on the Hudson. The Sargent genealogy, which includes John Singer, the

painter, has more great-nephews than can be successfully dia-
grammed, but somehow stemming from the Henry Winthrop
line occurs a Charles Sprague Sargent, who became director of
the Arnold Arboretum at Harvard and professor of Arboriculture at that University in 1879.

It was through Professor Sargent's interest that the Sago Palm
returned to Mount Vernon in 1918. "I went up the other day to
see it," he wrote the Regent, "and found it to be a very fine
plant in excellent condition. The story about it seems to be
straight enough. It has been in the possession of the Sargent
family certainly for seventy years, and before that it was owned
by only one person and he, the story goes, obtained it direct
from Mount Vernon. The size of the plant indicates that it was
no doubt alive in Washington's time." The Sago was established
in the Palm House, and at once its new home was found to be
too small. It nevertheless developed a new crown, but the next
year seemed to fall ill, and then was found to be fruiting, after
which it recovered to become the center of attention for visitors,
as it had presumably in its youth beheld Washington himself.
Soon it drooped again, and was variously dosed and operated
upon and re-potted, and then was exposed to direct sunlight in
1931, which caused it to put out new shoots. Three years later
it simply rotted away, but scions of a contemporary plant at
Tudor Place in Georgetown were presented by Mr. Armistead
Peter in 1941—himself a descendant of Martha's granddaughter
Martha Custis Peter, to whom one of three original plants was
presented by Washington, another going to Gouverneur Morris at Morrisania in New York, and the third to Mount Vernon.

In the exasperating fashion of people so well acquainted with
their subject that they take no thought of ignoramuses to come,
the Minutes wrote the obituary of Mount Vernon's Sago Palm
in 1941, "its history being too well known to need repeating,
and its untimely end following the lowering of the Greenhouse
ceiling still regretted." Perhaps if it had lived to see the present
Greenhouse it might still survive. The tubbed plant from Tudor
Place is still there, where tubbed oleanders, lantana, and orange
and lemon trees flourish, being brought outside each summer to
stand along the gravelled paths near the parterres until cold
weather drives them in again.

In accordance with the Mount Vernon policy of always going to the top, Mrs. Townsend as Regent had written to Professor Sargent at Harvard inviting him to visit Mount Vernon and prescribe for their cherished trees, and he made a tour of inspection there with the Gardens, Grounds, and Trees Committee in 1901. This remarkable man would have been a consultant after Washington's own heart, as the planning and planting of the grounds seem always to have been of more interest to the General than the Mansion itself. But Sargent's stipulation that he must have a "free hand" before he undertook the much needed work on the old trees and overgrown grounds gave the headstrong ladies pause, and Dodge was instructed to engage a less eminent tree man, who worked under his direction by a book Sargent had left with him. It was not until more than ten years later, when Miss Comegys was Regent, that the distinguished Harvard horticulturist was finally induced to take charge of Mount Vernon's arboreal invalids and treasures. During those intervening years considerable correspondence had taken place, and some long-range advice had been given, even with reference to the cherished boxwood plants, about which he was consulted, perhaps badgered, by Mrs. Brown of Rhode Island, who appears to have been related to his wife. He replied with some asperity:

"Dear Mrs. Brown:—

Certainly Box-trees sometimes grow in limestone soil, but if the plants at Mount Vernon are doing well, why fool with them at all? I have little confidence in the experts of the Department of Agriculture and it is always a good plan to leave well enough alone, especially in the case of old plants and old people.

Faithfully yours,
C. S. SARGENT"

Again the following year Mrs. Brown invoked the lightning, and it struck again: "Of course it is many years since I was at Mount Vernon," he wrote. "Certainly then the trees were in bad condition and the Japanese *Retinosporas* and other plants discovered long after Washington's day seemed to me to strike a very inharmonious note. You certainly wouldn't hang a modern chromo on the walls of Washington's room because some important person gave it to you, and there doesn't seem to be much difference between a chromo on the wall and a purple modern tree in the garden."

When at the Council of 1915 Miss Comegys was able to announce that she had secured Sargent's services to take charge of the grounds at Mount Vernon she read into the Minutes a somewhat more gallant reply: "You speak about compensation, a retainer, etc.," he had written. "Please dismiss any such subject from your mind. I consider it a great privilege and honor to be allowed to do anything in my power to restore the grounds of Mount Vernon to the condition in which they were when Washington was alive. This pleasure is the only compensation I want." He had returned to Mount Vernon in September of 1914, when Miss Comegys as Regent made a special trip there to hear his opinions and authorize Dodge to carry out whatever of his recommendations she approved of. The weather was good, and they spent the entire day out-doors, selecting and condemning for removal many trees and shrubs which obviously could not have been known to Washington. Many new plantings were also required as replacements, and proper treatment for the "wounded trees" was prescribed. A list which was then compiled by Sargent after a study of Washington's records and Diaries, of which the Association had secured typescript copies from the Library of Congress, included 1,000 dogwoods, 117 redbuds "at wide intervals among them," 1 linden by the colonnade between the Mansion and the Office, and 6 magnolias back of the Spinning House and Quarters.

It was partly due to Sargent's use of the Diaries that the Association's interest was aroused in their publication—the typescript copy ran to 1,800 pages—and they finally appeared in four handsome volumes in 1926 edited by Dr. Fitzpatrick, a very fortunate choice after two less-qualified men had withdrawn.

Miss Comegys was duly impressed after her first tour of the grounds with Sargent and Dodge, and reported enthusiastically to her colleagues: "We have been most fortunate in having made no mistakes in restoring the architectual features of Mount Vernon as designed by Washington," she said. "In order that we may be able to claim that the perfect colonial atmosphere pervades the out-of-doors which characterized Mount Vernon in

Washington's lifetime, I consider it important that we should obtain the services of the most distinguished arboriculturist in our country, that no mistakes shall be made on the lawns and in the gardens, in an endeavor to achieve the result here, so far as is possible, that Washington must have had in his mind's eye when the careful planting was done according to his orders. This can only be accomplished by one who has made a study of the subject."

But there is evidence that Sargent still encountered some interference or restraint, and he was never backward about expressing his exasperation to the Regent, with whom he seems to have early established a sound understanding and rapport. "Of course it is a very difficult matter to keep Mount Vernon trees in good condition if the removal of every worthless tree has to be passed on by a Committee of the Council, the members of which cannot be expected to have technical knowledge about trees and their requirements and prospects of long life. Some expert has got to be trusted in such matters," he reminded her in the autumn of 1917. "So far as the trees are concerned, the most important thing is the removal of the wreck of the Ash tree on the right hand side of the garden gate, which I have recommended for years, and the planting in its place of a young Ash tree and Holly. I hope to live long enough to see this Ash tree removed, but I confess to some discouragement. This raises the whole question of the importance of providing trees to take the place of those planted by Washington. It is not probable that any one of his trees, with the exception perhaps of the Hollies, will be alive at the end of another century, and perhaps not at the end of another fifty years, and it would seem the part of wisdom to plant now as far as it is possible to do so young trees of the same kinds to take the place of the original trees."

Washington's own deep love for his trees is evident in a letter he wrote to Chastellux, one of the volunteer French officers who accompanied him, via Mount Vernon, to Yorktown in 1781, and proposed another visit three years later before his return to France: "I repeat to you the assurance of my friendship and of the pleasure I should feel in seeing you in the shade of those trees which my hands have planted, and which by their rapid growth at once indicate a knowledge of my declining years and their disposition to spread their mantles over me before I go hence to return no more. For this, their gratitude, I shall nurture them while I may."

Sargent was never, of course, a full-time resident member of the Mount Vernon Staff, as was Archer and Sargent's successor Harold Abbott. But he paid frequent visits to Mount Vernon in all weathers, and wrote many informal letters to Miss Comegys recommending treatment for specific trees which had become his favorite patients. In 1917 he submitted a detailed Report on the trees at Mount Vernon, which was printed as a booklet—and the Minutes for that year reproduced his numbered diagram showing the position of each tree, an invaluable record for future maintenance and replacements, with a sub-headed paragraph for each type of tree and individuals in that group. "By request of Professor Sargent I measured and plotted on a map all the trees surrounding the Mansion and Bowling Green," says Dodge's Report, he having done the tedious job for the autocratic expert.

Thereafter the trees could be referred to by the Regent as "Ash No. 63 (on our map of trees) and the Coffee Bean No. 84, which are near the garden gate and are injuring Hemlock No. 83. The Hemlock was planted by Washington." Again, Mr. Wall was able to report as late as 1933, "One of the aged elms (#107) next the Office is decidedly on the wane, in spite of the enrichment and watering bestowed." Each loss was a personal grief, as though the trees were faithful servitors, which indeed as to Washington they have become to the Association.

Sargent revised his booklet in 1926, taking account of the newly published Diaries of Washington, and the recent storm and lightning damage, but by 1936 it had again to be ruled obsolete. In the preface to the 1926 edition he wrote:

"It appears desirable to place on record the size and condition of trees planted by Washington near his house at Mount Vernon, and of those now standing which have been planted or have sprung up naturally in the neighborhood of the Mansion since Washington's death in 1799.

"Washington's early interest in trees is shown by his grafting fruit trees and planting the seeds of the Mediterranean Pine in

1760, and those of the Walnut three years later, but the largest
trees, which border the Bowling Green, were probably planted
from 1783 to 1785, for it was in these years following the end
of the Revolutionary War and preceding his election to the
presidency that Washington was most actively engaged in the
improvement of Mount Vernon, and it was at this time that the
Bowling Green and the adjoining gardens were laid out.

"A few of the trees planted by Washington, in spite of the
poor soil at Mount Vernon, have grown to a large size. Among
the Live Oaks and Pecans planted in Louisiana after Washington's time there are larger trees than any now at Mount Vernon,
and some of the Elm trees planted in front of New England
farm houses after the middle of the eighteenth century have
thicker trunks and broader heads of foliage. Larger planted trees
exist in Europe, and in Japan many Cryptomeria trees, some of
them planted six or seven centuries ago, surpass in size and
grandeur all other planted trees; but no trees planted by man
have the human interest of the Mount Vernon trees. They belong to the nation and are one of its precious possessions. No
care should be spared to preserve them, and as they pass away
they should be replaced with trees of the same kinds, that Mount
Vernon may be kept for all time as near as possible in the condition in which Washington left it.

"On June 8, 1924, Mount Vernon was visited by a severe
cyclone which destroyed twenty-seven trees and seriously injured several others. Of the trees planted by Washington or in
his time, seven were destroyed by this storm and five others have
died in recent years, so that there are now left only forty-five
trees planted by him."

And he listed them, by number.

Today there survive only fourteen—ashes, buckeyes, hollies,
boxwoods, a hemlock, and a coffee-bean.

The Professor did not confine himself to arboriculture alone,
and he made many unrelated suggestions in his extensive correspondence with Miss Comegys—such as the removal of iron
rails at the Kitchen entrance, where Washington would have
had none, and the elimination of the substitute sun-dial which
he said bore no resemblance to Washington's, adding that more-

over there was some prospect of acquiring the latter—which came to pass in the 1930's, though the posts and chains around the margin of the green circle where it stands were before then renewed at his suggestion. These were shown in a little picture on the title page of a facsimile edition of Washington's Army Accounts, annotated by Dr. Fitzpatrick, which Sargent presented to the Association Library in 1917. He objected to the way rubbish accumulated around the lodge-keeper's dwelling at the West Gate, which had been allowed to run down perceptibly. He pointed out that Washington could not possibly have had the hybrid grape-vines now available for vineyards, and advised against the expense of adding grape-culture to the Association program, as well as vetoing a project to re-establish an orchard, since extra guards would be needed to protect the fruit from the visitors as it ripened. He did the grafts from the dying pear-trees planted by Washington in the Flower Garden, and nursed them along in the Arboretum till they were large enough to be planted where Washington had first placed them. They were flourishing by 1918. He recommended that the wire fence boundary should be replaced by a high brick wall—which was begun in 1929 and finished in 1933, to its present footage of 6,400 feet.

Nothing escaped him. "From my point of view the Flower Garden looks more hopeless than ever," he wrote in 1917, "and it is impossible to include it in the plan for restoring Mount Vernon to the condition in which Washington left it, until the Committee which has the garden in charge feels more strongly the Washington spirit than it does now, and is willing to give up the flowers which Washington could not possibly have had but which are supposed to please the public." That Committee included his connection Mrs. Brown, and Miss Townsend, Mrs. Richards (as Vice-Regent for Maine), Mrs. Maxey, Mrs. Leary, and Mrs. Denham—a formidable group to chastise. The aging Whelan was still the gardener. Sargent went on to demolish the Mary Washington Rose myth, as having no basis in the Diaries, and named the so-called Martha Washington Rose as a noisette hybrid which was not created till after she had died.

A bad knee cartilage had begun to interfere with his travels as early as 1920—he was seventy-seven—although he made con-

Numbers in heavy face type indicate trees probably planted during Washington's lifetime. Numbers in italics indicate trees possibly planted during Washington's lifetime. Other numbers indicate trees planted since Washington's death.

Apple—No. 71.
Ash—Nos. 26, *29*, 38, 43, **47, 50, 58**, 67, 87, 94, *96*, 102, **110.**
Beech—Nos. **90, 99.**
Black Walnut—Nos. 114, 135.
Box—Nos. **66, 77, 80.**
Buckeye—Nos. **24, 28, 32,** 59, **79,** 85, **92.**
Butternut—No. 100.
Cedar of Lebanon—No. 123.
Chestnut Oak—No. 124-1.
Cherry—No. 137-1.
Coffee Bean—Nos. **70, 76,** 84, **88, 89,** *120.*
Dogwood—Nos. *22, 23.*
American Elm—Nos. 1, 8-1, 36, **44,** 56, **103,** *106,* *107,* **109,** 111, 132, 134-1.
European Elm—No. 8-1.
English Walnut—Nos. 68, 93.
Hemlock—Nos. 2, 7, 8, **31,** 31-1, 31-2, 37-1, 40-1, 40-2, 40-3, *52,* **55, 83.**
Holly—Nos. **11, 13, 18-1,** 27, **34, 40,** 49, 60, **64,** 86, **91, 127, 128.**
Honey Locust—Nos. *30, 45,* **70,** *101.*
Horse-chestnut—Nos. *46,* 116, 117.
Linden—Nos. 25, 48, **50,** 54, 114, 115.
Magnolia—No. **97.**
Mulberry—No. 20.
Nettle-tree—No. 134-1.
Pear—Nos. *10, 72.*
Pecan—Nos. **118,** 120, **129.**
Redbud—Nos. 35, 52, 61, *121.*
Red Cedar—Nos. 3, 4, *5,* 16, 17, 18, 19, *53,* 134.
Red Maple—No. **33.**
Red Oak—Nos. 13, 14, 15, 122.
Sassafras—Nos. 21, 137.
Sorbus—No. **37.**
Sugar Maple—No. **69.**
White Oak—Nos. 6, 126, 130, 131, 136, 137.
White Pine—Nos. 28, 81, 112.
Yellow Poplar or Tulip-tree—Nos. **57, 62, 65.**

Arnold Arboretum, May, 1917.

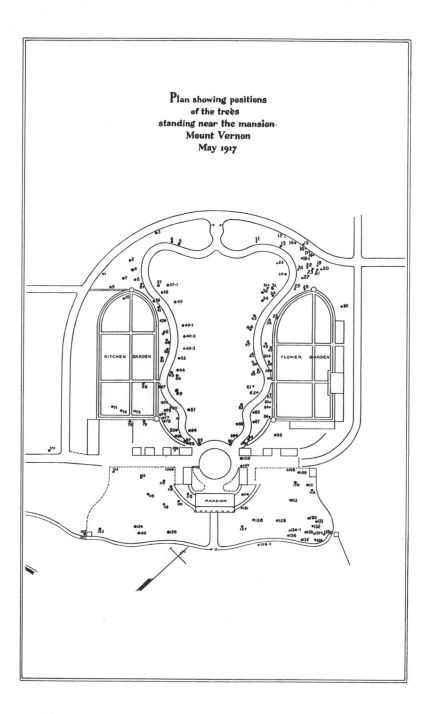

Plan showing positions
of the trees
standing near the mansion.
Mount Vernon
May 1917

scientious annual trips to Mount Vernon, and his friendly and outspoken correspondence with Miss Comegys was maintained —a sort of elderly and decorous conspiracy of two against such stuffy back-numbers as Dodge and the Council. In 1922 he visited her at her home, The Green, at Dover, and called it a "beautiful and restful spot."

He was at Mount Vernon in November, 1922—"It would have been much pleasanter if you could have been there at the same time, so that we could have inspected the grounds together and discussed various matters," he wrote her—and approved the location of the proposed reservoir and the plans for the fireproof house for what he called "Mount Vernon treasures," himself rejecting the term *relics*—and advised more dogwoods —500, at $1 each. He complained to Miss Comegys of the planting near the Tomb—"It is a great regret that having devoted ten or twelve years of my best thoughts and attention to Mount Vernon, I have been unable to secure the confidence of the Council to the extent of letting me carry out my planting plans," he remarked with his caustic frankness. "The trouble is that these plans necessitate the removal of three or four trees of no interest and value, which have sprung up naturally years after Washington's death. You and I cannot live long enough to see such a planting as I propose at anything like its best, but in a hundred years from now thoughtful visitors to Mount Vernon would ask the name of the Regent under whose administration the trees were planted. I wish the Council had more imagination and power to look into the future. The thing which I feel sure about in this matter is that if Washington were here himself he would be on my side."

It is probable. But Washington's courage under fire was never tested by the united front of some thirty opinionated middleaged ladies determined to act for his own good.

When Mrs. Brown wrote to Sargent lamenting the loss of many prized historic trees in the 1924 cyclone, she got the impatient reply of a testy old man: "The destruction of the trees is unfortunate, but a hundred years or so will repair the damage," he snapped. He was by then too much disabled to get to Mount Vernon himself, and sent in his place a Mr. Van der Voet, to give an expert opinion on what should be done for the wounded and broken trees. He hoped, in a tart aside to the Regent, that Dodge would not be jealous of the newcomer, implying that such was his habit. The Regent was not well enough to go to Mount Vernon then herself, to meet Van der Voet, or invite him to Dover, and Dodge was too occupied to give him more than about ten minutes' attention. Sargent wrote Mrs. Brown that Van der Voet reported "a phenomenal ignorance about trees" on the part of everyone engaged in their care at Mount Vernon.

After Sargent's death in 1927 Harold Abbott, another Harvard man, was appointed with the title of Landscape Architect, and made regular Reports to Council, which must have seemed rather dull after Whelan's informal charm and Sargent's quick acerbity, but provided a conscientious account of the work going on under his supervision. He drew a detailed scale map of the Flower Garden, showing the location of every planting, and at once set out 23 species of "old-fashioned roses," listing the Marie Van Houtte as the best old yellow tea. He was successful in persuading the scarlet honeysuckle to clothe the pillars and arches of the colonnades as directed by Washington from Philadelphia in 1787. He made minor alterations in the Greenhouse —the old one, which Sargent had complained bitterly about ever since 1916, on the grounds that Washington could never have had anything like the one constructed piecemeal by the Association since 1869, and in the belief that the sale of plants would gradually be given up. The latter conviction fortunately was wrong. Abbott filled the existing Greenhouse building with bloom and decorative foliage plants in time for the General's birthday in 1935.

Nowadays the birthday plant is a special pure white cyclamen raised to be in blossom on that date. Pots of this superb plant are always on display in February, and it never fails. Carried to Vermont by the writer as a treasured gift, the birthday cyclamen has remained healthy and beautiful for several years, putting out cycles of large blossoms with rest periods between when the crown is still full of tiny leaf buds—but it always knows when February 22d is coming round. Though treated as an annual at Mount Vernon, this plant promises to reach a considerable age in its northern home, presumably because it enjoys the fresh, undoctored spring water which it receives from the tap each day.

In 1936 interesting old varieties of plants with charming names—king's spear, crane's bill, jupiter's beard, and the chinquapin rose—were noticed at Wakefield, which had been visited by Council on their way back from an afternoon at Stratford, then recently opened by the Robert E. Lee Foundation. The rose was sent to Mount Vernon.

One lingers over the Superintendent's and Garden Committee's Reports in the Minutes year by year, as one would linger in the gravelled paths at sundown, breathing the fragrance of flowers long gone and dreaming of color past recall—finding imprisoned in the stiff, tightly bound pages the joy of "resplendant" bloom, the minor disappointments, the unflagging hopes, and the unceasing vigilant toil which are the true gardener's reward. Here is Dodge in 1923:

"By direction of the Chairman of the Garden Committee [Mrs. Brown] the tulip bulbs of the year before were taken up to make room for fresh stock she had ordered from Holland. The latter arrived on October 26th and were immediately planted in the parterres, as we were instructed to do.

"As advised by the soil experts of the U.S. Department of Agriculture some years ago, we changed the soil of certain rose beds in the Flower Garden, substituting rich meadow earth for garden soil exhausted by the ravenous Box hedges. The effect of this improvement is apparent.

"Well rotted cow manure was used to enrich the beds most needing that stimulant. There has been much thinning out of such plants as Iris and Peonies, which have a tendency to become root-bound.

"Dwarf roses were procured to replace some that did not succeed; and seeds of many old-fashioned flowers were sown with the view of establishing 'succession of bloom' more effectually in the future planting.

"The visit of the Garden Club of America, October 24th, was at a period when the floral attractiveness of the Mount Vernon garden is always at lowest ebb. To offset this we supplied color by potted Chrysanthemums.

"The rich green of Washington's wonderful boxwood hedges, and the pleasing way in which they are arranged, elicit expressions of admiration by all who come. The protection of these hedges claims our solicitude at all times, especially on the approach of winter when ice storms and heavy snowfall imperils them. Happening to have on hand some old wire fencing, salvaged from the former stockade of the Deer Park, we stretched it along each side of the hedges, wiring it *through* the hedge at intervals so as to bind together the fragile branches—not too closely—but sufficient to support them against whatever over-weighting might occur. The efficacy of this method was tested successfully by the ice-storm in March which did much damage elsewhere, while our beloved boxwood escaped injury entirely.

"There was a disturbing episode last autumn, shortly after the imported Tulip bulbs were planted, when it was discovered that a *rat* had—over-night—dug up and carried off a large proportion of them. After an exciting hunt we not only 'ran the pillaging rascal to earth' but were fortunate enough to locate his 'cache' and recover practically all his loot. Luckily the stolen bulbs were not seriously harmed, so we planted them again.

"To meet the popular demand for rooted plants of Box and Ivy from the Mount Vernon garden we propagate thousands of cuttings yearly and sell them profitably.

"In the Kitchen Garden the usual work was carried on throughout the year to keep it in the attractive order of production insisted upon always by General and Mrs. Washington. As a substantial aid to plant-growth a system of sub-irrigation has been found effectual in overcoming the depleting draft from the roots of the boxwood and nearby trees. To this end 300 feet of porous tile have been laid, and the result plainly shows its benefit to the adjoining vegetable beds.

"The venerable Fig bushes too—by their increase of yield—endorse this kind of treatment.

"Mrs. Brown sent us some 'sods' of old-fashioned chrysanthemums from her home, and Mr. Archer procured other old varieties from the neighborhood, all of which are being cared for temporarily in the Kitchen Garden, pending the Committee's decision how to use them."

Mrs. Brown, whose husband, John Carter Brown, was of the family for whom the University was named, all her life loved gardens, and during the almost thirty years of her vice-regency was most active in that department, contributing from her own Rhode Island garden hardy plants of phlox, iris, asters, and chrysanthemums. The improved condition of the Mount Vernon flowers during her chairmanship was attributed partly to the extra visits she made in March and November between Councils to oversee the planting—visits which the gardening staff must have held in dread, as her Reports show that the Kitchen Garden also came under her critical eye—as in June 1925:

"The asparagus bed is in need of attention. The space between the ridges should be levelled up, making the bed an even height —the spaces to be filled with loam and compost—equal quantities.

"A Hollyhock to be planted by the steps to match the other one.

"The whole Garden needs fertilizing.

"The box branches near the gate to be tied back—they droop too much.

"More assistance should be given this Garden, which is quite a large one."

Whelan had by now begun to fail, and the Kitchen Garden obviously wanted jacking up. Following this Report Mrs. Brown appeared at Mount Vernon again in October to inspect progress, and in November was called upon to represent the Regent (Miss Comegys) during the visit of Prince and Princess Asaka of Japan, who were escorted by the Coolidges and Secretary of War Kellogg. Mrs. Brown reported that the little ladies in the Japanese party were the prettiest she ever saw.

When in 1931, at the age of eighty-three, she felt unable to be of further use as Vice-Regent, she wrote a letter of resignation, which the Regent (then Mrs. Richards) read in Council, and her devoted colleagues returned a unanimous refusal to accept it. Two days later Mrs. Richards read them Mrs. Brown's reply, which was in the form of a night-letter: "I am going to bed very happy tonight knowing I am still a Vice-Regent of Mount Vernon. As I sponsored the motion that two years absence would require a resignation I felt I must resign." Again the tactful honorary membership was invoked, but she never returned to Council.

Sometimes it almost seems that the vice-regency is a guarantee of longevity, so many have reached their eighties still on the active list. Even in the most casual day-visitors the tranquillity and peace of the place in its enchanted sleeping-beauty remoteness from the stress and fears of today's grim world inspire a desire to return another day, and as the years run out for those who really "belong" it must be a strong and sustaining emotion —the determination, the necessity, to see Mount Vernon once more—once more—till one of them pushed her luck too far and died there, in her bedroom, the day after Council adjourned.

One realizes with surprise that Dodge actually lived at Mount Vernon longer than Washington did, arriving there to begin his duties in 1885, and being still at work in his office up to within a few days of his death at eighty-five in 1937—52 years. Washington acquired the place from Lawrence's widow in 1754, and died at sixty-seven in 1799—45 years. Dodge's successor, a man still of no great age, has already chalked up nearly 40 years, and along with a few employees, most of whom have worn very well indeed, remembers with affection Dodge's amusing ways and his undiminishing authority; but of the active Vice-Regents at present only three can have even a brief personal recollection of him. There was a proposal in the 1930's that each Vice-Regent should write a sketch of her predecessor, to be placed in the album beside her photograph. Unfortunately this suggestion has not been faithfully carried out, nor are all the photographs supplied, which will become an even more grievous lack as time goes on, and the legends perish with the human memories which hold them.

The Dodge legends are now told with kindling eyes and reminiscent smiles—how he was always being recognized by countless people to whom he was a well-known figure, but whom he had no slightest cause to remember—how when arrayed in formal dress to receive distinguished visitors it was his habit to revolve slowly before a jury assembled from the Staff who were charged to remove any last-minute threads, lint, or dust from his immaculate attire—how in the mornings he would post himself inside a window to check the arrival of employees and take note of tardiness, which had to be accounted for—how he would take the Sunday and holiday duty himself, to release other members of the Staff.

His Diary, so faithfully kept in the early years, is nevertheless sometimes brief to the vanishing point, unless eked out with his Letter-books, and is more and more minutely written in pencil in small note-books, with the last lines of each page squeezed up to make room for more, and the new year beginning in the middle pages to avoid wasting the rest of the book by dividing them yearly. The original stiff cover gave way to limp paper covers with an end-opening, awkward to write in and awkward to read, the pencil was hard, and the paper of poor quality. It was a record kept only for his own use, as an aid to making up his Reports. But his was not a personality to be easily submerged, if only as expressed in the vigorous comment of "Hot! *Hot!!* HOT!!!" or "SNOW!" or even "ZERO!!" Like Washington, he was much preoccupied with the weather, even when it was proceeding normally, and events such as the "terrific storm" of June, 1914, and the "violent gale" of 1924, which destroyed historic trees and kept the men working for days to "clear the havoc" were given more space.

It may be possible, with a few random samples, to convey something of the rare flavor of this remarkable record, which compressed into its inadequate space a nevertheless vivid image of the daily life at Mount Vernon during what might be called the Second Empire of the Association. For in spite of himself, as in Washington's case, the intrinsic color and vitality of the man escaped into the brief, depersonalized memoranda. Notes on the weather and attendance predominate.

"Only 1 visitor today. Every attention shown him." Dec. 14, 1885.

"Not a single pilgrim today." Dec. 6, 1886.

"Made an early start this morning for distant farms. Found near Broad Run, Fauquier County, a pair of horses suited to my purpose. Bought them for $300. (pair) and ordered them delivered to Alexandria next Tuesday. Drove back to Marshall and took freight train to Alexandria; walked thence to Mount Vernon, arrived here at 11:15 P.M. Found work had been carried forward as ordered. Young remained here in charge." July 30, 1887.

"It being very malarious and damp in our quarters here now, I shall give as frequent chances as possible to employees who wish to absent themselves at night." Aug. 16, 1887.

"Today [Monday] being observed as Christmas holiday quite a bunch of visitors came—53 in all. Young and I came down, but I returned to Washington 2 o'clock to be present at my children's Christmas tree. Mount Vernon servants all given holiday from work." Dec. 26, 1887.

"Young and I came down this morning with 19 visitors. Harding working but other men taking a holiday (by permission.) Young and I drove out after dinner and killed a few partridges. Whelan sick again this evening with chill." Dec. 27, 1887.

"Cloudy and cold. Our two teams, and a team hired from Mr. Gibbs, hauling good ice from creek. I gave personal attention to packing the ice in old house. Took roses to town but could not sell them. Stems too short." Jan. 25, 1888.

"Sent wagons to creek for ice and directed men to stop cutting there and start at our wharf. This afternoon I worked with the men cutting ice at wharf. Tonight I paid off extra men, and wrote up accounts for January." Jan. 31, 1888.

"Snow about 3″ deep. Men clearing walks. Only 55 visitors by boat, 123 by [electric] cars." Feb. 22, 1894.

"Great day! Hot as blazes. Governor and wife, and 100 colonial Dames of Md. and D.C. Collation served around 12:30." June 12, 1894.

"Effects of recent tornado sickening." Oct. 7, 1896.

"Stout's foot crippled yesterday while at stable work. Young and I milked cows this morning. Thomas getting out sheathing to repair Watch Room. (Gardener's House.)" Sept. 5, 1898.

"Closing our fiscal year. Greatest travel in the history of the Association. 87,171 visitors during the year." Apr. 30, 1901.

"Took Jasper to town to be measured for uniform to be used by him. Neitzey spreading manure, Vickers ditto, Rouse repairing chimney breast in Laundry." Dec. 17, 1901. Old Jasper claimed descent from one of Washington's Negroes. His appointment to the proud post of Tomb guard ended with his death two years later.

Christmas, 1903, begins with the statement: "Nothing but routine work today. Few visitors, as weather is poor. My family here for dinner. One of the farm horses—Martha—taken sick and died about midnight." All this was routine. The rest of the entry follows: "John Brown, permitted to go away in the afternoon, returned drunk. Became so abusive and disorderly I was forced to tie him for a time. Found a loaded pistol on him. Sent for the magistrate, and his father. Watched him all night." Christmas night, that would be, with Dodge's family there. The following day John Brown was paid off and discharged, tried before a local magistrate, and fined for carrying concealed weapons. The whole thing occupies a dozen crowded lines.

"Cold blizzard raging. Braxton only laborer here. Neitzey, Permar, and Vickers cleaning walks. Young and Whelan went home this afternoon. 88 idiots here in spite of weather." Jan. 24, 1908.

"None of the laborers here today. Off for Christmas. A strange black horse found swimming near our wharf was jammed in ice but rescued by McCally and J. Rouse." Dec. 24, 1915.

"Flock after flock of canvas-back ducks on northward flight passed over us; all the early morning they flew by." Feb. 3, 1921.

"N.E. storm. 'Nothin' doin'.' O. J. Thomas laid up with rheumatism. Rouse Sr. detailed as gate-keeper *ad interim*. Regular men on regular stunts." Mar. 15, 1922. The word, under a glass, is not *stints*. Dodge was feeling gay.

Preparations for Council then show the same organized panic which is likely to prevail today as the date draws near, and which has long been known to the Staff as Council-itis. In May of 1916: "Regular men putting up Council table and moving required chairs, etc. Rouse and J. Rouse put up cots and put in screens. Neitzey whitewashed fence. W. Neitzey motor-mowed. Rogers trimmed grass around trees and helped Thomas with trunks. Mount Vernon ladies arrived 6:30." In May of 1924: "Everything 'on the jump' for Council. Rouse and Dickson helping 'set' Council table, filling inkstands, sharpening pencils, etc. Vice-Regents arriving by trolley, auto, and boat. Rouse extending table to seat more. All not here yet. Rain began tonight."

The older men recall that it was sometimes necessary to take down the stair-rails in order to man-handle the Vice-Regents' wardrobe trunks to the second-floor bedrooms in the Spinning House and Quarters—and having been put back up for the use of the ladies during the week, the rails would of course have to come down again for the departure of the trunks.

In the middle of the 1892 GAR Reunion of some 150,000 in Washington, which was expected to overflow on to Mount Vernon precautions were taken for the protection of the Mansion against unaccustomed crowds, and Dodge wrote: "Weather opened cloudy and rain commenced to fall about 10 o'clock. Boats arrived as early as 9 o'clock, and continued to come and go until 6 p.m. There were over *10,000* visitors here today. The electric cars made several trips this afternoon, bringing about 200. The tramping crowds of wet people soon made a hog-mire of Mount Vernon."

On the following day: "Raining all this morning and part of the afternoon. Boats brought nearly 7,000 and the railroad 500. The house and surrounding grounds and gardens are in a disgraceful condition."

On Sunday, with the GAR convention still going on: "Young and I kept busy all day turning back people who applied for entrance to Mount Vernon."

On another Sunday during 1893 with an inaugural (second Cleveland term) in Washington: "Swarms of people tried to get into Mount Vernon. All extra men busy keeping them from climbing the guard fence."

Most of the time Mount Vernon was for Dodge, as it still is today, another world, a microcosm into which the echoes and repercussions of international anxieties sometimes penetrate with an effect of delayed-action shock. In the writer's own experience some one passing through the Reference Library brought without excitement but with only a kind of detached compassion the startling news of Dag Hammarskjöld's death in 1961. So it was that in April, 1898, at the end of an entry which detailed the hunt for more springs, Thomas putting up brackets for portiéres in the Michigan Room, easing windows in the East Quarters, and making a tester for the bed in the Connecticut Room—preparations for Council—there came to Dodge a sudden recollection to be set out in capitals and underlined: "SPANISH WAR DECLARED! Now will you be good!!" Mc-Kinley's death in 1901 of an assassin's bullet received the week previous, was noted without comment, after the churning, mowing, and the week-end absence of Whelan and Neitzey. August 4th, 1914, passed in the normal routine without forebodings—Neitzey cleaned the chemical extinguishers discharged yesterday in a drill, and then refilled by Neitzey and Rouse—Duvall and McCally cultivated corn in #7 field—4 extra men filled in the ditch of the fire-main and graded ground where the old carnation-house had stood. And the world outside caught fire. On the April day in 1917 when the German Ambassador in Washington was handed his passports, Mount Vernon was working on her wharf road again, Permar did the milking as usual, and it rained. A few of the men, notably Duvall, joined up and went to war, and eventually returned.

The 1918 flu epidemic wrought havoc among the employees, and one day Rouse, Miller, Murray, McCally, and Monroe Thomas were all sick abed. Illness usually deserved mention, and there was a good deal of it. Archer was repeatedly laid up in his Washington hotel for days at a time, and Young was often on sick leave. Dodge himself went down with malaria periodically, and having dislocated a shoulder during a vacation at the King Ranch in Texas when his saddle girth gave way, returned to duty while still in a cast. When Dodge was away Young took over the Diary, and even Archer filled in, with much less readable pages but the same careful accounting for time and occupation, so that a change in the handwriting is often the only indication that things were not exactly as usual. After Archer's death in 1924, it was one of the duties of Edward Kent, who followed him, to keep up the record, and Dodge would annotate along the margins and at the bottom of the pages, his sharp-pointed, minuscule hand-writing outstanding.

His daughter Anna notes with some indignation the impersonal character of the record, so that family events such as her own brilliant military wedding in Washington in 1899, and the birth of her son, Dodge's first grandchild, the following year, were omitted in favor of such entries as: "3 laborers here.

Dodson and Holland spading rose-beds, Stout mowing lawns. Sold calf this morning, $10."

An afterthought on January 19, 1904, records that "Mr. Young goes away today. Wedding tomorrow." The following day Rouse was tightening hinges on doors in the Mansion, Permar and Neitzey were burning brush in the vista, Anderson and Archer were "monkeying with the river pump," Vickers attended to the stock, Holland cleaned up the yard, and Young, who had worked beside Dodge for seventeen years, got married and was allowed ten days for his wedding trip.

In 1915 he jotted down: "Wedding tonight (at Mrs. Mc-Cally's) Maggie Neitzey and Jimmie Rouse." Mrs. McCally was the housekeeper, and the Neitzeys and the Rouses were neighbors inside the gates. There was a week-end. On Monday J. Rouse, with Duvall and Thomas, was hauling rubbish at Mount Vernon. The Rouse entries alone are a fascinating study of versatility and industry. Up until 1913, Rouse meant W.L.

"Rouse making calf-pen in stable." March 8, 1904.

"Rouse working in Delaware Room and other Mansion repairs," Dec. 11, 1906.

"Rouse repairing door to Washington's Room, where piece was cut out." Feb. 12, 1909.

"Rouse packing box of cherry bounce to be sent to Regent." Dec. 29, 1911. Mount Vernon's cherry bounce had been famous since the 1870's, or before, and Dodge must have inherited the recipe.

"Rouse making basket for discarded drinking-cups." Oct. 30, 1911.

"Rouse fishing for visitor's lost eyeglasses in well." Aug. 26, 1912.

Early in 1913, while engaged in putting metal noses on the steps of the main staircase in the Mansion, Rouse fell ill. For weeks the daily entries began laconically—"Rouse still sick." On March 12th James Rouse, his son, came in his place, and at once went to work on the window-screens for the Quarters where the Vice-Regents' bedrooms were. This was the wizard Jimmie, who only two years later would marry the girl who must have been his playmate since childhood. Thereafter, when his father had recovered, it was "Rouse" and "J. Rouse," who was soon putting up electric lines and running the light-plant. Nowadays it would be H. for Harry, the third Rouse, born to Jimmie and Maggie in 1919, and heir to his father's skills.

Thus, in December, 1917, it followed that "Rouse and son packed ice and helped getting ashes from the boiler room," and "Rouse and son and J. Neitzey hauled brush along road to wharf, piling it in Hell Hole for burning," and in January, 1918, "Rouse, Jr., and Neitzey cleaning walks of snow, Rouse Sr. calking chimney and doors of Office to keep out cold. Therm. 6° above." On Nov. 16, 1923, "Rouse put up walnut hand-rail on stairway to General Washington's Room" and on Nov. 20th, "Rouse re-seating chairs with hair-cloth," and sometimes just "Rouse, odd jobs."

Neitzey didn't stand around. He spent Oct. 28, 1912, "re-covering boats and decoys set adrift by boys of the Industrial School excursion here today," and in 1914 "dragged out log in boat channel with motor boat." This was all Joseph. When he died in 1922, another junior, Wilfred, was within the week at work plastering the Spinning House, and repairing the old horse-carriage.

The list of distinguished visitors and the variety of unlikely societies and organizations who brought wreaths to the Tomb becomes overwhelming, except as evidence of the amazing universal appeal of the pilgrimage. Dodge received them all in formal attire, with punctilious courtesy, but he was not always impressed. "A batch of Japanese naval officers here." May 10, 1907. Orientals, in particular, have always shown an appreciation of Mount Vernon.

In 1919 the grounds were closed to the public while Belgian royalty placed a wreath at the Tomb. Mrs. Heiberg, who was presented as Dodge's married daughter, recollects that when the Visitors' Book was brought out for King Albert to sign, he inquired why some pages had been clipped together. Never at a loss, Dodge explained that they had come loose and were in need of repair. Tactfully concealed within the closed pages were the signatures of Prince Henry of Prussia and his suite, set down in 1902.

The Sunday closing rule was revoked by telephone by Miss Comegys in 1922 to permit Lord and Lady Astor (the famous

Nancy, herself a Virginian), accompanied by a representative of the State Department, to visit Mount Vernon.

On a June day of the same year there occurred the curious juxtaposition of several hundred nuns representing educational convents of the U.S. and Canada, wearing their various pictur-esque habits, and a crowd of Confederate Veterans from their Reunion at Richmond—in uniform.

In October, 1923, not in Dodge's handwriting, it is recorded: "Lloyd-George an Englishman, here today and placed a wreath."

A delegation of Puerto Rican and Philippine officials led by Governor Towner of Puerto Rico, whose wife was the Vice-Regent for Iowa, placed a wreath in February, 1924.

"M. Jean Patou of Paris, a leading designer of women's clothes," in October, and a Russian Grand Duchess in December finished that year in style.

It is regrettable that this first-hand record of Dodge's fabulous days at Mount Vernon was allowed to lapse in 1926, ten years before his death. Perhaps the best of his enthusiasm was spent, or perhaps the telephone and typewriter are again to blame. His annual Reports continued to be voluminous, alert, and enter-taining. His successor's Reports compare very favorably with those of the man who trained him, but he disclaims any supple-mentary record of every-day affairs—another loss to posterity, as his more formal product reveals a notable grace of phrase.

vi

Crossing the Bowling Green and passing under the old box-wood arch, the visitors descend a few steps to the Kitchen Garden, which lies in two terraces on a lower level, surrounded by brick walls against which espalier fruit trees grow, with tidy beds of herbs and small plants laid out around two cisterns or "dipping wells," always a feature of this design. It is the older of Washington's two Gardens, having been laid out in 1760, with the vegetables separate, and espalier fruits and hedges. Wash-ington's gardeners were usually European and sometimes un-satisfactory, being unaccustomed to the sort of assistance the "family" of slaves provided.

For a time the Vegetable or Kitchen Garden had been allowed to deteriorate while the Flower Garden was encouraged to provide saleable bouquets and plants. It was somewhat renovated in the '80's, when small fruits were planted and the ancient fig-bushes were persuaded to bear again. The box bushes were trimmed, the asparagus bed was reset, and vegetables for the Council table were grown. By 1912 there was enough excess produce to be canned by the cook for use at Council time, and during the first War some was sold. The surplus is now frozen for winter use at the Staff table.

The versatile Archer did much to restore the original appearance following old prints and descriptions, before his death in 1924, and twelve years later the Kitchen Garden was entirely replanted according to research done by Harold Abbott and Professor Williams of the Harvard School of Landscape Architecture. In evolving the new design, books from Washington's library, his accounts, and letters of instruction to his gardeners and managers were carefully studied. All of the plants now to be seen there were familiar in the 18th century, and are planted in amounts proportionate to Washington's household. The cisterns were installed to "soften" the water by exposure to the air, as water freshly taken from wells was "by no means proper for any sort of plants."

The two little structures in the far corners of the Gardens arouse curiosity. Originally intended as seed or tool houses for the use of the gardeners, the one in the upper or Flower Garden became known as the School-house, and has been furnished as such, with children's books and desks, on the supposition that the Custis children, or more likely the later Washington children in the 1800's, had done their lessons there. The other has always been used for the storing of gardening paraphernalia.

A picturesque bee-house was constructed in the opposite corner of the Kitchen Garden in 1949—a reproduction based on what might have been used in Washington's time, adapted to meet the requirements of modern Virginia law.

Described by its Committee in the '30's as "an enchanting place," with its brimming cisterns, herb-bordered paths, fruit-trees trained against the brick walls, box and herbs scenting the air, and the singing of birds, it was pronounced in 1949 "approaching perfection." In the 1950's the drought became serious, and a sprinkling system was installed, the sprinklers being con-

nected with a main pipe brought in from the Bowling Green
and when turned on in the late summer light creating a delightful effect of spontaneous fountains everywhere. Lines of plastic
sprinkler-hose laid under the boxwood hedges were discovered
by thirsty rabbits, who chewed holes in them to provide a
private leporine water supply. Suspended pipes were devised
with small nozzles to syringe the interior foliage with water
that then drips down to the roots, a dual operation which also
controls the red spider infestation.

"The Kitchen Garden," the Committee noted in 1961, "receives much praise, no matter what the season, for it is always
interesting to visitors, perhaps because a truly beautiful vegetable
garden is a rarity. Few people realize what attractive garden
material vegetables can be, and still be eatable, and what charming borders result from using herbs. The wall trees and espalier
hedges flourished. All of the beds were productive throughout
the season. There were enough spring peas to freeze for Council; asparagus was beautiful, but was limited to about two serv-
ings at the table in the spring; the lettuce, beets, carrots, spinach,
cauliflower, cabbage, and broccoli that we are being served at
Council were processed for our use. The figs, strawberries,
currants and honey are a great treat. The General's Greenhouse
too furnishes fruit. The Seville oranges, which make such delicious marmalade, were used with shaddocks for decoration on
the dessert-table in the Family Dining-room during the holidays
and were used again in the Mansion at Easter. The large oleander was re-tubbed, as were the Sago Palms. The new tubs
were lined with sheet-lead to preserve the wood, and to ensure
isolation of the soil from the treated wood. The old tubs and containers were mended when an oak tree was found for hoops."

Plant sales now amount to over $12,000 annually. Miss Tracy
was happy to earn $250 with her little bouquets, just a hundred
years ago.

It is gratifying to know that at last by its own efforts and
economies and forethought the Mount Vernon Ladies' Association is solvent and beholden to nobody—sometimes just *barely*,
but occasionally able to afford such necessary outlay as the new
lodging erected in 1950–1952 for the Vice-Regents at Council
time; the periodic purchase of a valuable painting or piece of

furniture which adds to the authenticity and beauty of Mount
Vernon; or the acquisition of a plot of land to protect the
boundaries of the estate or the view.

It used to be that the colored guard at the Tomb—that
coveted post of prestige and importance—would make the
quiet suggestion: "Hats off to de Gineral," with what one
visitor called "a magical effect. All hats were lifted and an expression of reverence came upon the faces of the men who
stood there."

In this hatless generation when in reverse the women sometimes do not trouble to cover their heads in church, reverence
for the Tomb must be shown in deportment only. The condition of the Tomb is at last excellent, though the constant necessity in the early years to preserve it against decay and the
morbid tendency of visitors to possess themselves of a sprig of
myrtle or a leaf of any foliage in the vicinity, as part of the
ruthless pillage of the whole estate for small souvenirs, is a constant refrain in the annals of the Association.

But while the resting place of a great man's mortal remains
is infinitely to be cherished and revered, the Tomb is not what
Mount Vernon means today, or should not be. We visit tombs
because usually that is all we have left—the last abode. But
Mount Vernon is the life, as well as the death, and the Mansion
and its surroundings are therefore the triumphant, touching
thing, the immortality made visible—because in the house, or on
the piazza with its still splendid outlook towards the green Maryland shore, he lives.

Bibliography and Acknowledgments

Most of the research background for this book was contained in the files of the Association and is drawn from the printed Minutes which are sequestered in the Library, along with Dodge's Diaries and Letter-books, and the correspondence of the Vice-Regents. I am also indebted to the first-hand recollections of Mrs. Elvin Heiberg, as well as the verbal information derived from conference with the Resident Director and the senior employees, and some correspondence with the senior Vice-Regents and the present Regent. I must also make my usual genuflection in the direction of the New York Society Library, whose capacity to supply miscellaneous information at a moment's notice is never called upon in vain.

A list of the published books consulted follows:

BONFILS, W. B., *The Life and Personality of Phoebe Apperson Hearst*, San Francisco, John Henry Nash, 1927.

DODGE, HARRISON HOWELL, *Mount Vernon*, Philadelphia, Lippincott, 1932.

HARRISON, CONSTANCE CAREY, *Recollections Grave and Gay*, New York, Scribner's, 1911.

HERBERT, LEILA, *The First American*, New York, Harper, 1900.

JOHNSON, GERALD, and C. C. Wall, *Story of a Shrine*, New York, Random House, 1953.

LOSSING, BENSON, *Mount Vernon and Its Associations*, New York, Townsend & Co., 1859.

———, *Mary and Martha*, Harper & Brothers, New York, 1886.

MOORE, CHARLES, *The Family Life of George Washington*, Boston, Houghton Mifflin, 1926.

PRINGLE, ELIZABETH ALLSTON ("Patience Pennington"), *A Woman Rice-planter*, Cambridge, Mass., Harvard University Press, 1961 (reprint).

————, *Chronicles of Chicora Wood,* Scribner's, 1922.

WASHINGTON, GEORGE, *The Collected Writings of George Washington,* prepared under the direction of the U.S. George Washington Bicentennial Commission and published by authority of Congress, J. C. Fitzpatrick, editor, U.S. Government Printing Office, 39 vols. with index, 1931–1944.

————, *The Diaries of George Washington, 1748–1799,* J. C. Fitzpatrick, editor, Houghton Mifflin, 1925.

WILSTACH, PAUL, *Mount Vernon,* New York, Doubleday, 1916.

The Regents and Vice-Regents of the Mount Vernon Ladies' Association of the Union Since Its Organization

Regents

Miss Ann Pamela Cunningham, 1853–1874; resigned 1874; died May 1, 1875
Mrs. J. Scott Laughton (formerly Madame Berghmans), 1874–died 1891
Mrs. Howard Townsend, 1891–1909; died April, 1912
Miss Harriet Clayton Comegys, 1909–1927; resigned May, 1927; died July, 1927
Mrs. Alice Haliburton Richards, 1927–died 1936
Mrs. Horace Mann Towner, 1937–died 1942
Mrs. Lucien M. Hanks, 1943–1948; died December, 1959
Mrs. Albert Harkness (formerly Mrs. Thomas Ives Hare Powel), 1948–1958
Mrs. Francis F. Beirne, 1958; re-elected 1963

Vice-Regents

ALABAMA
  Mrs. Henry S. LeVert, 1858–1877
  Mrs. Hilary Herbert, 1882–died 1884
  Miss Leila Herbert, 1894–died 1897
  Mrs. Robert D. Johnston, 1900–died 1934
  Mrs. Morris Williams Bush, 1946–resigned 1959
  Mrs. Preston H. Haskell, Jr., 1963

ARIZONA
  Mrs. Arthur Newton Pack, 1962

ARKANSAS
  Mrs. Robert Ward Johnson, 1858–died 1866
  Mrs. C. L. Scott, 1872–resigned 1878
  Mrs. Celsus Price Perrie, 1919–resigned 1922
  Mrs. J. Fairfax Loughborough, 1932–died 1962

CALIFORNIA
  Mrs. William Blanding, 1859–resigned 1884
  Mrs. George Hearst, 1889–resigned 1918; died 1919
  Mrs. Charles S. Wheeler, 1920–resigned 1940
  Mrs. Lockwood de Forest, 1956

COLORADO
  Mrs. Nathaniel P. Hill, 1889–died 1908
  Mrs. Horton Pope, 1919–resigned 1947

CONNECTICUT
  Mrs. Samuel G. Goodrich, 1858–resigned 1864; died 1868
  Mrs. Susan E. Johnson Hudson, 1870–died 1913
  Miss Annie Burr Jennings, 1915–died 1939
  Mrs. Wilmarth S. Lewis, 1942–died 1959
  Mrs. Clifton McCausland Bockstoce, 1965

DELAWARE
  Mrs. Joseph P. Comegys, 1858–died 1888
  Miss Harriet Clayton Comegys, 1888–1927; elected Regent, 1909
  Mrs. Antoine Lentilhon Foster, 1911–died 1934
  Mrs. Thomas F. Bayard, 1937–resigned 1958
  Mrs. C. Lalor Burdick, 1961

DISTRICT OF COLUMBIA
  Mrs. George W. Riggs, Acting Vice-Regent 1858; appointed 1867–resigned
    1868; died 1871
  Mrs. William H. Emory, 1870–1871
  Mrs. Joseph K. Barnes, 1873–died 1912
  Miss Jane A. Riggs, 1912–died 1930
  Miss Helen Louise Sargent, 1931–died 1948
  Miss Constance Ellen Tyler, 1952–died 1963
  Mrs. Randall H. Hagner, Jr., 1965

FLORIDA
  Madame Achille Murat, 1858–died 1867
  Mrs. David Levy Yulee, 1868–died 1884
  Mrs. James M. Baker, 1888–died 1901
  Mrs. Thomas Palmer Denham, 1913–resigned 1948; died 1950
  Mrs. LeRoy Collins, 1961

GEORGIA
  Mrs. William J. Eve, 1858–died 1889
  Mrs. Joseph John Wilder, 1891–died 1914
  Mrs. Jefferson Randolph Anderson, 1919–resigned 1949; died 1956
  Mrs. Barnwell Cubbedge, 1958

ILLINOIS
  Mrs. William Barry, 1859–died 1883
  Mrs. Levi Z. Leiter, 1885–died 1913
  Mrs. George A. Carpenter, 1916–resigned 1947; died 1948
  Mrs. Henry Porter Isham, 1949

INDIANA
  Mrs. Graham Newell Fitch, 1859–died 1880
  Mrs. Charles Denby, 1901–died 1906
  Mrs. Benjamin D. Walcott, 1914–resigned 1932; died 1933
  Mrs. Benjamin D. Hitz, 1936

IOWA
  Mrs. VerPlanck Van Antwerp, 1858–died 1870
  Mrs. John F. Dillon, 1872–resigned 1873; died 1898

Mrs. Horace Mann Towner, 1913–1942, elected Regent 1937
Mrs. Douglas Nelson Gibson, 1955

KANSAS
Mrs. Milan Lester Ward, 1876–died 1910
Mrs. John V. Abrahams, 1916–resigned 1921
Mrs. John Reynolds Shelton, 1923–resigned 1930
Mrs. Earl K. Lord, 1930–died 1956

KENTUCKY
Mrs. Alexander Jeffrey, 1858–resigned 1885; died 1894
Mrs. George W. Woodward, 1885–resigned 1889; reappointed 1891–died 1897
Mrs. William F. Barret, 1901–died 1920
Miss Mary Mason Scott, 1923–died 1934
Mrs. Mason Barret, 1938–resigned 1953; died 1955
Mrs. Walter N. Haldeman, 1960

LOUISIANA
Mrs. Isaac E. Morse, 1858–resigned 1872; died 1893
Mrs. David Urquhart, 1873–resigned 1876
Mrs. Tobias G. Richardson, 1880–died 1910
Miss Annie Ragan King, 1912–died 1933
Miss Sarah Duncan Butler, 1936–resigned 1960
Mrs. Frank G. Strachan, 1963

MAINE
Mrs. Josiah S. Little, 1858–resigned 1866; died 1893
Mrs. Lorenzo M. Sweat, 1866–died 1908
Mrs. Alice Haliburton Richards, 1911–1936; elected Regent 1927
Mrs. Harold Lee Berry, 1930

MARYLAND
Miss Emily L. Harper, 1866–died 1891
Mrs. George R. Goldsborough, 1893–resigned 1904; died 1906
Mrs. Henry W. Rogers, 1905–died 1931
Mrs. DeCourcy W. Thom, 1935–resigned 1946; died 1963
Mrs. Francis F. Beirne, 1948, elected Regent 1958

MASSACHUSETTS
Mrs. Horatio Greenough, 1858–resigned 1865; died 1891
Miss Alice M. Longfellow, 1879–died 1928
Mrs. Nathaniel Thayer, 1930–died 1934
Mrs. John Templeman Coolidge, 1940–resigned 1948; died 1964
Mrs. Samuel Cabot, 1949

MICHIGAN
Mrs. Elon Farnesworth, 1858–resigned 1877; died 1879
Mrs. Joshua Henry Rathbone, 1885–resigned 1918; died 1923
Mrs. Edward H. Parker, 1923–died 1924
Mrs. Benjamin S. Warren, 1925–resigned 1958
Mrs. Alexander L. Wiener, 1964

MINNESOTA
  Mrs. Henry H. Sibley, 1859–died 1869
  Mrs. Charles Eugene Flandrau, 1889–died 1911
  Mrs. Charles Eliot Furness, 1914–died 1935
  Miss Anna E. Ramsey Furness, 1940–died 1964

MISSISSIPPI
  Mrs. William McWillie, 1858–1873
  Mrs. William Balfour, 1873–resigned 1885
  Mrs. Kate Walthall Freeman, 1885–1888
  Mrs. Benjamin Sherrod Ricks, 1907–resigned 1914
  Miss Mary Govan Billips, 1916–resigned 1963

MISSOURI
  Mrs. Robert R. Walton, 1858–resigned 1858; died 1867
  Mrs. Wilson Price Hunt, 1860–died 1878
  Mrs. Robert Campbell, 1879–died 1882
  Mrs. Benjamin Graham, 1893–died 1915
  Mrs. Charles Nagel, 1916–resigned 1943; died 1951
  Mrs. Marvin E. Holderness, 1948–resigned 1959
  Mrs. Robert Neill, Jr., 1964

NEBRASKA
  Mrs. Robert H. Clarkson, 1894–resigned 1900; died 1902
  Mrs. Charles F. Manderson, 1900–died 1916
  Mrs. Alexander C. Troup, 1923–died 1950

NEVADA
  Mrs. M. E. Hickman, 1866–resigned 1874
  Mrs. John P. Jones, 1875–resigned 1876

NEW HAMPSHIRE
  Mrs. Salma Hale, 1858–resigned 1861; died 1865
  Mrs. Onslow Stearns, 1866–resigned 1873
  Mrs. Abby Godwin Winder, 1890–died 1906
  Miss Harriet L. Huntress, 1914–died 1922
  Mrs. Gordon Woodbury, 1929–resigned 1949
  Mrs. John Lawrence Sullivan, 1952

NEW JERSEY
  Miss Phoebe A. Ogden, 1858–died 1865
  Mrs. Nathaniel Norris Halsted, 1868–died 1891
  Mrs. Francis S. Conover, 1893–died 1914
  Mrs. William Hall Bradford, 1915–resigned 1939
  Mrs. Thomas Turner Cooke, 1946

NEW YORK
  Miss Mary M. Hamilton (later Mrs. George Lee Schuyler), 1858–resigned
    1866; died 1877
  Mrs. James Brooks, 1867–resigned 1876
  Mrs. Howard Townsend, 1876, elected Regent 1891; resigned 1909; died 1912
  Mrs. Philip Schuyler, 1893–resigned 1894

Miss Amy Townsend, 1894–died 1920
Mrs. Henry Gold Danforth, 1922–resigned 1948; died 1961
Mrs. Thomas Stilwell Lamont, 1952

NORTH CAROLINA
Mrs. P. K. Dickinson, 1858–resigned 1859; died 1881
Mrs. William Richmond Walker, 1859–died 1908
Mrs. Alexander Boyd Andrews, 1909–died 1915
Mrs. William Ewen Shipp, 1919–died 1936
Mrs. John Witherspoon Labouisse, 1944

OHIO
Mrs. George H. Pendleton, 1858–resigned 1863; died 1886
Mrs. Emily R. McIlvaine Hewson, 1866–resigned 1873
Mrs. Samuel J. Broadwell, 1875–died 1890
Miss Mary Lloyd Pendleton, 1893–resigned 1897
Mrs. James E. Campbell, 1897–resigned 1902
Mrs. Lewis W. Irwin, 1907–died 1916
Mrs. Charles J. Livingood, 1919–resigned 1935; died 1936
Mrs. Chester C. Bolton, 1938

OKLAHOMA
Mrs. Russell Story Tarr, 1947

OREGON
Miss Mary F. Failing, 1907–died 1947

PENNSYLVANIA
Miss Lily Lytle Macalester (Madame Berghmans, later Mrs. J. Scott Laughton, Second Regent), 1859–died 1891; elected Regent, 1874
Mrs. J. Dundas Lippincott, 1893–died 1894
Mrs. Charles Custis Harrison, 1896–died 1922
Mrs. William R. Mercer, 1924–resigned 1928
Mrs. Benjamin Franklin Pepper, 1929–resigned 1948; died 1955
Mrs. Henry Norris Platt, 1948

RHODE ISLAND
Mrs. George I. Chace, 1858–died 1893
Mrs. William Ames, 1894–died 1904
Mrs. John Carter Brown, 1907, Honorary Vice Regent 1935; died 1936
Mrs. Albert Harkness (formerly Mrs. Thomas Ives Hare Powel), 1936, Regent 1948–1958

SOUTH CAROLINA
Mrs. James Chesnut, 1860–died 1864
Mrs. Francis Wilkinson Pickens, 1866–died 1899
Mrs. John Julius Pringle, 1901–died 1921
Miss Virginia Leigh Porcher, 1924–died 1940
Mrs. Benjamin Allston Moore, 1948

TENNESSEE
Mrs. Francis B. Fogg, 1858–died 1872
Mrs. Aaron V. Brown, 1874–died 1889

Miss Mary Polk Yeatman (later Mrs. Thomas Shapard Webb), 1893–died 1917

Mrs. Horace Van Deventer, 1920–died 1956

Mrs. Marvin E. Holderness, 1959

TEXAS

Miss Ella Hutchins, 1866–resigned 1872

Miss Mary E. Maverick, 1873–resigned 1873

Mrs. Thomas S. Maxey, 1896, Honorary Vice Regent 1937; died 1938

Mrs. John Mirza Bennett, 1940–died 1963

VERMONT

Mrs. Hampden Cutts, 1859–resigned 1878

Mrs. J. Gregory Smith, 1878–resigned 1884

Mrs. Cornelius Low King, 1885–died 1896

Miss Mary Evarts, 1911–resigned 1923; reappointed 1924–died 1928

Mrs. Horace Brown, 1930–resigned 1940; died 1943

Mrs. James Dennis, 1946–died 1946

Mrs. A. John Holden, 1961

VIRGINIA

Mrs. William F. Ritchie, 1858–resigned 1866; died 1870

Mrs. Thomas Francis Mason, 1872–died 1873

Mrs. Charles B. Ball, 1874–died 1918

Mrs. William Ruffin Cox, 1921–died 1925

Mrs. Fairfax Harrison, 1927–died 1943

Mrs. Edward Clifford Anderson, 1947–resigned 1960

Mrs. John H. Guy, Jr., 1963

WASHINGTON

Mrs. John Leary, 1907–died 1935

Mrs. Stanley D. Lyle, 1944–died 1955

WEST VIRGINIA

Mrs. Lewis William Washington, 1870–died 1898

Mrs. Eugene Van Rensselaer, 1900–died 1923

Miss Constance Lee Peterkin, 1924–resigned 1946; died 1948

Mrs. Augustine Jaquelin Todd, 1955

WISCONSIN

Mrs. Alexander Mitchell, 1858–died 1902

Mrs. Lucien M. Hanks, 1914, elected Regent 1943–1948; resigned 1956; died 1959

Mrs. John Cunningham Lobb, 1960–resigned 1962

WYOMING

Mrs. Thomas F. Taliaferro, Jr., 1936–resigned 1950; died 1953

Index